PERSONAL INJURY TITLES FROM WILEY LAW PUBLICATIONS

ANATOMY AND PHYSIOLOGY FOR LAWYERS
Mikel A. Rothenberg

ARBITRATING PERSONAL INJURY CLAIMS
John Farrell Fay

AUTOMOTIVE ENGINEERING AND LITIGATION (VOLUMES 1–5)
George A. Peters and Barbara J. Peters

AUTOMOTIVE ENGINEERING AND LITIGATION (VOLUME 6): THE INTERNATIONAL DIRECTORY OF EXPERTS AND CONSULTANTS IN AUTOMOTIVE ENGINEERING 1993
George A. Peters and Barbara J. Peters

CALIFORNIA WORKERS' COMPENSATION CITATOR
C. Duke Marsh

EVALUATING AND SETTLING PERSONAL INJURY CLAIMS
George M. Gold, Editor

EVALUATING TMJ INJURIES
Reda A. Abdel-Fattah

EVALUATING TMJ INJURIES: RATING PERMANENT IMPAIRMENT
Reda A. Abdel-Fattah

FIRE LITIGATION SOURCEBOOK (SECOND EDITION)
Alexander J. Patton

FIREARMS LITIGATION
Windle Turley and James E. Rooks, Jr.

LITIGATING HEAD TRAUMA CASES
Arthur C. Roberts

LITIGATING SPINAL CORD INJURIES: LAW, MEDICINE, AND ECONOMICS
Mark R. Kosieradzki

LITIGATING STRESS CASES IN WORKERS' COMPENSATION
Steven Babitsky and James Mangraviti

LITIGATING TMJ CASES
A. Clark Cone and Michael J. McHale

ORTHOPEDIC DISABILITY AND EXPERT TESTIMONY (FOURTH EDITION)
Harold F. Goodman

MODERN TORT LIABILITY: RECOVERY IN THE '90S
Terrence F. Kiely

PERSONAL INJURY DAMAGES LAW AND PRACTICE
Edward C. Martin

PERSONAL INJURY TRIAL HANDBOOK
John A. Tarantino and David J. Oliveira

PSYCHIATRIC CLAIMS IN WORKERS' COMPENSATION AND CIVIL LITIGATION
Herbert Lasky

PSYCHOLOGICAL EXPERTS IN DIVORCE, PERSONAL INJURY AND OTHER CIVIL ACTIONS (SECOND EDITION)
Marc J. Ackerman and Andrew W. Kane

THE RIGHT TO DIE
Alan Meisel

THERMOGRAPHY AND PERSONAL INJURY LITIGATION
Samuel D. Hodge, Jr.

TRIAL ATTORNEY'S GUIDE TO INJURY COVERAGE AND BAD FAITH
Paul J. Skok

UNDERSTANDING THE AMA GUIDES IN WORKERS' COMPENSATION
Steven Babitsky and Harry Dean Sewall

WHAT YOU NEED TO KNOW TO SETTLE WITH INSURANCE COMPANIES
Thomas H. Veitch

LITIGATING SPINAL CORD INJURIES
LAW, MEDICINE, AND ECONOMICS

SUBSCRIPTION NOTICE

This Wiley product is updated on a periodic basis with supplements to reflect important changes in the subject matter. If you purchased this product directly from John Wiley & Sons, Inc., we have already recorded your subscription for this update service.

If, however, you purchased this product from a bookstore and wish to receive (1) the current update at no additional charge, and (2) future updates and revised or related volumes billed separately with a 30-day examination review, please send your name, company name (if applicable), address and the title of the product to:

Supplement Department
John Wiley & Sons, Inc.
One Wiley Drive
Somerset, NJ 08875
1-800-225-5945

For customers outside the United States, please contact the Wiley office nearest you.

Professional and Reference Division
John Wiley & Sons Canada, Ltd.
22 Worcester Road
Rexdale, Ontario M9W 1L1
CANADA
(416) 675-3580
1-800-567-4797
Fax: (416) 675-6599

John Wiley & Sons, Ltd.
Baffins Lane
Chichester
West Sussex, PO19 1UD
UNITED KINGDOM
Phone: (44) (243) 779777

Jacaranda Wiley Ltd.
PRT Division
P.O. Box 174
North Ryde, NSW 2113
Phone: (02) 805-1100
AUSTRALIA
Fax: (02) 805-1597

John Wiley & Sons (SEA) Pte. Ltd.
2 Clementi Loop
#02-01 Jin Xing Distripark
SINGAPORE 0512
Phone: 4632400
Fax: 4634604

LITIGATING SPINAL CORD INJURIES
LAW, MEDICINE, AND ECONOMICS

MARK R. KOSIERADZKI

Sieben, Grose, Von Holtum, McCoy & Carey, Ltd.
Minneapolis, Minnesota

Wiley Law Publications
JOHN WILEY & SONS, INC.
New York · Chichester · Brisbane · Toronto · Singapore

This text is printed on acid-free paper.

Library of Congress Cataloging-in-Publication Data

ISBN 0-471-11433-2

Printed in the United States of America

10 9 8 7 6 5 4 3 2 1

Dedicated to Those Courageous People who have been Paralyzed as a Result of the Negligence of Others

PREFACE

The first time I undertook the enormous responsibility of representing a paralyzed person, I went to the library to learn whatever I could in order to represent my client. I was astounded to find that no books had been published on the representation of clients who were paralyzed. What was even more shocking was the absence of any compilation of medical literature that would help me understand the injury, treatment, and medical complications involving such patients. As a result, I was forced to seek out countless articles and treatises in an attempt to represent my client. Over the years I have gathered more and more information not only involving spinal cord lesions cases but also other cases involving catastrophic injuries.

Litigating Spinal Cord Injuries: Law, Medicine, and Economics attempts to organize the information necessary for the trial of a spinal cord injury case. The structure of the book starts with the focus on anatomy, the mechanism of injury, treatment, medical complications, and life care plan. Once the injury and care are understood, the focus shifts to the associated economic principles inherent in such litigation.

Spinal cord injury cases, as in all cases involving catastrophic injury, require a thorough understanding of the economic principles associated with the development of the future claim of medical expenses and wage loss. Wage loss claims require the integration of spinal cord victim demographics, vocational options, and the economic principles associated with the principle of present cash value as it relates to our economy. However, medical economics require a totally different analysis. Inasmuch as medical inflation far exceeds that of the general economy, a different economic model must be utilized. Understanding the principles of medical economics reveals that a significant larger sum of money is necessary to provide the appropriate medical care to such patients than is often expected. In analyzing the principles of discount and medical economics we reveal the fallacies associated with the use of annuities in the evaluation of the present cash value of any particular claim.

It is the hope of all the authors, that the information we have provided will facilitate heightened representation of catastrophically injured persons resulting in fair and equitable resolution of claims that can then increase the quality of life these courageous people.

Minneapolis, Minnesota
September 1995

MARK R. KOSIERADZKI

ACKNOWLEDGMENTS

This book is a result of the years of research and experience arising from the representation of catastrophically injured people. Many have helped make this compilation possible. Certainly this book would not have been complete without the materials contributed by John Wolfe, J.D., D.C., Clay M. Kelly, M.D., Karen Schmitz, P.T., Michael Jovoronok, J.D., Joan Fox, M.D., Michael Pietrzak, M.D., Jack Dahlberg, M.A., C.I.R.S., Phillip Haber, Ph.D., David Stofferahn, J.D., Steve Laird, J.D., John Leighton, J.D., Donald House, Ph.D., Greg Jones, J.D., William Harper, J.D., and Michael J. DeVivo, Dr.P.H.

I also wish to express my appreciation to the staff of my office, Judi Jackson, Jane Werman, Shari Adams, and Lisa Nafranowicz for their work in developing the manuscripts and coordinating the authors while working with my law practice.

A special thanks is owed to Bill Schmitz, my law clerk and colleague, for his efforts in organizing, researching, and editing much of the medical material contained in the manuscripts. His work was invaluable in the final completion of the project.

And finally, I would like to thank all of the families who have entrusted their cases to me over the last 15 years in allowing me to come to understand what it means to be injured.

M.R.K.

ABOUT THE EDITOR

Mark R. Kosieradzki is a nationally recognized attorney representing injured people. He is certified as a civil trial advocate by the National Board of Trial Advocacy and as a civil trial specialist by the Civil Litigation section of the Minnesota Bar Association. He is the past president of the Minnesota Trial Lawyers and a member of the Association of the Trial Lawyers of America Board of Governors. He has been a member of the faculty of the National College of Advocacy since 1989 and is the author of numerous publications in the area of trial practice.

ABOUT THE CONTRIBUTORS

Mary A. Albury-Noyes, CMI, is a medical illustrator for her business, Medical Art Services, Inc., in Burnsville, Minnesota. She received her training at the Minneapolis College of Art and Design and her medical training at the University of Minnesota Medical School. Ms. Albury-Noyes has contributed to numerous medical and medicological textbooks.

John E. Dahlberg, M.A., is owner and president of Dahlberg & Associates, Rehabilitation Consultants in Denver, Colorado. His company specializes in case management and analysis of future life costs of catastrophic injuries, especially spinal cord injuries, adult head injuries, and young children with brain damage or cerebral palsy. Mr. Dahlberg has the additional personal insight of having lived with a spinal cord injury as a result of a snowskiing accident in 1968.

Michael J. DeVivo is an associate professor in the Department of Rehabilitation Medicine at the University of Alabama at Birmingham, Alabama and co-director of the National Spinal Cord Injury Statistical Center. He received an undergraduate degree in biology from Johns Hopkins University and received MPH, MBA, and DrPH degrees from the University of Alabama at Birmingham. Dr. DeVivo has written on the epidemiology and treatment outcomes of spinal cord injury and provides expert testimony in the life expectancy and long-term outcomes of persons with spinal cord injury.

Joan M. K. Fox, M.D. is a board certified associate consultant in pulmonary and critical care at Park-Nicollet Medical Center and a clinical assistant professor of medicine (pulmonary and critical care) at the University of Minnesota. Dr. Fox received her Bachelor of Science, Bacteriology degree from Iowa State University and received her Doctor of Medicine degree from the University of Minnesota. She is an active lecturer and author. Dr. Fox belongs to the American Thoracic Society, Minnesota Thoracic Society, and American Sleep Disorder Association.

Phillip B. Haber, M.S., Psy. D., is a psychologist and certified rehabilitation counselor at Metropolitan Rehabilitation Services, Inc., Minneapolis, Minnesota. He directs a comprehensive rehabilitation center providing vocational and psychological/rehabilitation services to severely impaired individuals. As a rehabilitation psychologist, Dr. Haber has served as a trial consultant and expert witness as a rehabilitation psychologist.

William D. Harper has a law office in Woodbury, Minnesota. Mr. Harper is certified as a civil trial specialist by the National Board of Trial Advocacy and served as the Dean of the Academy of Certified Trial Lawyers of Minnesota.

Donald R. House is president of RRC, Inc., in Bryan, Texas. Dr. House received his Ph. D. degree in Economics from Texas A&M University.

Michael Javoronok is a practicing attorney in Gering, Nebraska. He received a B.A. degree from the University of Pennsylvania and a J.D. degree from the Creighton University Law School. He is a member of the American Trial Lawyers Association. Mr. Javoronok lectures on personal injury and products liability litigation, use of experts as witnesses, use of the *A.M.A. Guides,* discovery techniques, and opening statements.

Gregory G. Jones is a partner in the law firm of Russell, Turner, Laird & Jones, LLP, in the Irving, Texas office, where he specializes in personal injury, wrongful denial of insurance claims, and wrongful death cases. He received B.A. and J.D. degrees from Southern Methodist University. Mr. Jones is a member of the Texas bar and he is chairman of the Motor Vehicle Collision, Highway and Premises Liability Section of ATLA. He is a frequent lecturer at continuing legal education seminars.

Clay M. Kelly, M.D., is a board certified staff physiatrist at the MetroHealth Medical Center in Cleveland, Ohio, and is Senior Instructor at Case Western Reserve University. He received his undergraduate degree from Creighton University and his M.D. degree from Creighton School of Medicine.

Steven C. Laird is a partner in the law firm of Russell, Turner, Laird & Jones, LLP, in the Irving, Texas office. The firm specializes in personal injury, wrongful denial of insurance claims, and wrongful death cases. He received a bachelor of business administration degree from Texas Tech University, a masters degree from Texas Christian University, and a J.D. degree from South Texas College of Law. He is board certified in personal injury trial law and civil trial law by the Texas Board of Legal Specialization. He is a frequent lecturer at State Bar of Texas's continuing legal education seminars, ATLA seminars, and Texas Trial Lawyers Association.

John Elliott Leighton is a partner in the law firm of Leesfield, Leighton, Rubio & Hillencamp in Miami, Florida, where he limits his practice to negligence, product liability, and professional malpractice, with special emphasis on inadequate security and defective children's and consumer products.

He received B.A. and J.D. degrees from the University of Florida. Mr. Leighton is an active lecturer and author.

Michael P. Pietrzak, M.D., is a board certified emergency medicine physician. He is currently the Chief of Clinical Medicine at Air Education and Training Command in the Air Force as well as consultant to the Surgeon General for Emergency Medicine. His academic presentations of cervical spine management have been presented at several conferences domestically and overseas.

Karen Tomec Schmitz, R.P.T., currently works at the Institute for Athletic Medicine in Minneapolis, Minnesota. She received her B.S. degree in exercise science from the University of Southern California and completed her graduate work in physical therapy at Northwestern University School of Medicine.

David A. Stofferahn is associated with the law firm of Sieben, Grose, Von Holtum, McCoy & Carey in Minneapolis, Minnesota, where he represents employees in workers' compensation cases. He received an undergraduate and J.D. degree from the University of Minnesota. Mr. Stofferahn is a member of the Minnesota Trial Lawyers Association. He is a frequent lecturer at continuing legal education seminars in his area of practice.

John B. Wolfe, Jr., D.C., is a trial attorney at Sieben, Grose, Von Holtum, McCoy & Carey, Ltd., in Minneapolis, Minnesota, and is also a licensed chiropractor and an adjunct faculty member at Northwestern College of Chiropractic, teaching courses in jurisprudence and ethics. He received an undergraduate degree at Creighton University, a chiropractic degree at Northwestern College of Chiropractic, and a J.D. degree from William Mitchell College of Law.

SUMMARY CONTENTS

DETAILED CONTENTS

CHAPTER 1

BASIC ANATOMY OF THE SPINE AND SPINAL CORD

John B. Wolfe, Jr.

§ 1.1 Axial Skeleton

An understanding of the basic anatomy of the spine and spinal cord is essential to later discussions of the mechanisms and consequences of spinal cord injury.

The axial skeleton consists of the spinal column and the structures immediately adjacent to it: the occiput (the base of the skull), which rests atop the first cervical vertebra, the pelvis, which articulates with the sacrum at the base of the spine, and the ribs.

The spinal column consists of 24 movable vertebrae: seven cervical vertebrae make up the neck, 12 thoracic vertebrae make up the midback, and five lumbar vertebrae make up the low back. The sacrum is the triangular shaped bone that articulates with the pelvis and forms the base of the spine. The sacrum consists of five fused sacral vertebrae, while the coccyx, the small tapering bone that projects from the bottom of the sacrum, consists of four fused coccygeal vertebrae. Thus, the spine is often said to consist of 33 vertebrae.

Except for the first and second cervical vertebrae (the atlas and axis), each of the 24 movable vertebrae consist of the same anatomical elements: a vertebral body, which functions to support weight and between which the intervertebral discs are located, and a vertebral arch, which is attached to the vertebral body and encloses the vertebral canal through which the spinal cord travels. The vertebral arch consists of two pedicles and two laminae. From each vertebral arch arise several processes: two transverse processes, one spinous process, and four articular processes. Most of the muscles that control movement of the back attach to the transverse and spinous processes. The articular processes form joints with the articular processes of the vertebra above and below and control the movement between the vertebra.

While each of the vertebra (except the atlas and axis) consist of these same components, their size and configuration varies significantly depending on location within the spine. For example, in the cervical spine, the vertebral bodies are much smaller than in the lumbar spine, where the entire weight of the upper body is borne. In addition, the size of the vertebral canal is different at different levels in the spine, corresponding to the size of the spinal cord at various levels within the spine. Finally, the shape and orientation of the articular processes and the spinous and transverse processes also varies according to the particular movements common to an area of the spine. (See **Figure 1–1.**)

When stacked on top of each other, with an intervertebral disc between the bodies, the vertebrae do indeed form a column. The posterior arches form the spinal canal. (See **Figure 1–2.**)

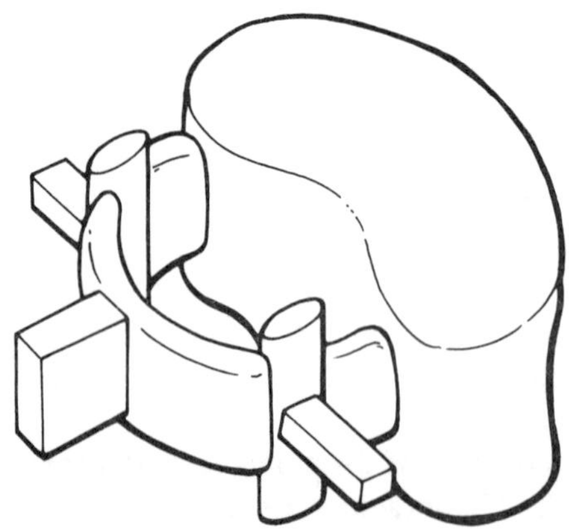

Figure 1–1. Processes of the spine.

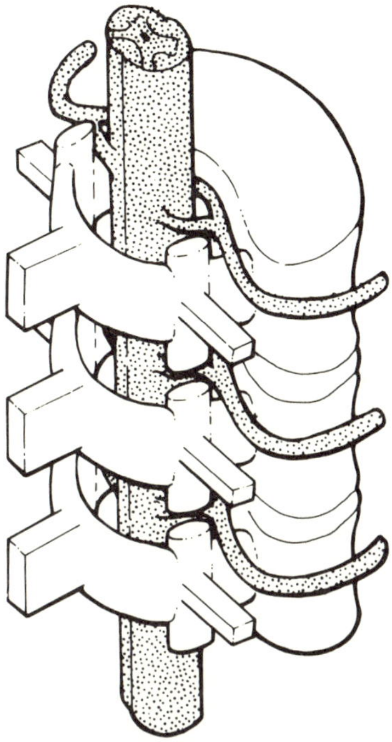

Figure 1–2. Spinal canal.

The spinal cord travels within the canal, and the spinal nerves exit the canal through the intervertebral foramina. Each foramen (opening) is framed above and below by the pedicles, on the front by the vertebral bodies and intervertebral disc, and on the rear by the articular processes.

§ 1.2 Upper Cervical Spine

As noted, the first two cervical vertebrae (the atlas and the axis) are anatomically very different from the other vertebrae.

The atlas has no vertebral body or spinous process. Rather, it is simply a ring with two lateral masses and two transverse processes. Each transverse process has a transverse foramen through which the vertebral artery passes. The base of the skull, or occiput, sits on top of the superior articular processes of the atlas. The foramen magnum (large opening) in the base of the skull sits directly atop the large opening in the middle of the atlas. The spinal cord, which attaches to the base of the brain, exits the skull through the foramen magnum, and enters the spinal canal through the atlas.

The next cervical vertebra, the axis, is also atypical. Projecting upward from its very small vertebral body is the odontoid process, or dens (Latin for tooth like or tooth). The dens projects upward through the ring of the atlas. A strong transverse ligament holds the atlas in place on the dens. This configuration allows a great deal of rotation of the atlas on top of the axis. This anatomical arrangement also makes this region susceptible of injury, and since the spinal cord travels through this region, it is susceptible of injury at this level as well.

§ 1.3 Lower Cervical Spine

Anatomically, the remainder of the cervical vertebrae are similar to each other in structure. Each has the parts of a typical vertebra. As with atlas and axis, the transverse processes both have a transverse foramen through which the vertebral artery passes. There are no transverse foramina in the remainder of the spine.

The facet joints in the cervical spine are at an approximate 45 degree angle. This allows the increased degree of flexion and extension, rotation, and lateral bending required for neck motion.

§ 1.4 Thoracic Spine

The thoracic spine differs significantly from the cervical and lumbar spine in that the ribs articulate with the thoracic vertebrae. The rib attachments diminish the movement of the thoracic spine. The orientation of the facets changes from the upper thoracic spine toward the thoracolumbar junction. In the upper thoracic spine, the orientation of the facets is similar to that of the cervical spine. In the area of the thoracolumbar junction, the orientation of the facets changes to become similar to that of the lumbar spine. That is, in the lower thoracic spine, the plane of the facets is more nearly sagittal, or parallel to the plane that divides the body into right and left halves.

§ 1.5 Lumbar Spine and Sacrum

The facets in the lumbar region are configured along the sagittal plane. This configuration makes flexion and extension the primary motion in the lumbar spine.

The sacrum, or base of the spine is also atypical. The *sacrum* is a large triangular shaped bone that forms as a result of the fusion of five sacral vertebrae. The sacrum supports the entire vertebral column and forms the rearmost portion of the pelvis. Although the sacrum is atypical in shape, it still forms a canal through which the lowermost spinal nerves travel. These lowest nerves exit through paired foramina on both the front and back surface of the sacrum.

§ 1.6 Ligamentous Anatomy

The vertebrae are held together, and their movement is restricted by numerous ligaments. The anterior longitudinal ligament lies along the anterior aspect of the vertebral bodies from C to the sacrum. The posterior longitudinal ligament lies along the posterior aspects of these same segments and is within the spinal canal. In the posterior arch, the ligamentum flavum (or yellow ligament) lies along the anterior aspect of the posterior arch. The supraspinous ligament attaches to the tips of the spinous processes, and the interspinous ligament fills the space between the spinous processes, attached to the supraspinous ligament in the rear and the ligament and flavum in front. The intertransverse ligament attaches to the transverse processes.

In addition, there are capsular ligaments which form capsules around the facet joints.

All of these ligaments function to limit flexion (forward bending) and extension (backward bending) during normal motion. Disruption of these ligaments can cause instability and susceptibility to spinal cord injury.

§ 1.7 Blood Supply to Spinal Cord

The spinal cord receives its major arterial blood supply from one anterior and two posterior spinal arteries. In the area of the cervical cord, the anterior spinal artery is supplied by branches of the vertebral arteries that run through the transverse processes of the cervical vertebrae. In the remainder of the cord, the anterior and posterior spinal arteries receive their blood supply from the spinal branch of radicular arteries that arise from intercostal branches of the aorta. These small arteries enter the canal through the neural foramina, where they connect with the spinal arterial system. The anterior spinal artery supplies the anterior half of the cord, including most of the gray matter of the cord. The posterior spinal arteries supply the posterior aspect of the cord, including the dorsal columns.

§ 1.8 General Design of Nervous System

From an anatomical standpoint, the nervous system consists of two parts: the central nervous system (CNS), comprised of the brain and spinal cord, and the peripheral nervous system (PNS), comprised of the spinal nerves that emanate from the spinal cord and the cranial nerves that emanate from the skull.

Physiologically, the nervous system is also divided into two functional groups. The somatic nervous innervates the body wall, while the autonomic (visceral) nervous system innervates the internal organs and blood vessels.

§ 1.9 Spinal Cord

The spinal cord is a roughly cylindrical structure that extends from the foramen magnum down through the spinal canal to approximately the level of the second lumbar vertebra. The cord is made up of ascending and descending nerve fibers that carry information to and from the brain.

The cord is enlarged in two areas. The first, the cervical enlargement, extends from the C4 cord level to the T1 cord level. This enlargement corresponds to the cord segments that supply innervation to the arms. Similarly, there is a lumbosacral enlargement that extends from the L2 to S3 cord level, corresponding to the cord segments that innervate the legs.

In understanding spinal cord injuries, it is critically important to remember that spinal cord levels do not correspond with vertebral levels.

The illustration shows a cross section of the vertebral column and spinal cord. Note that the cord ends between the L1 and L2 vertebral levels, but that the spinal nerves continue to descend through the canal, and exit through the intervertebral or sacral foramina. (See **Figure 1–3.**)

Note also that the cord tapers as it approaches the L2 vertebral level. This cone-shaped end is called the conus medullaris. From the tip of the conus extends the filum terminale (Latin for terminal thread), that extends all the way to the level of S2 where it anchors the spinal cord to the sacrum.

The cord is enclosed within a three layered sheath. The layers (from outside in) are called the dura mater, arachnoid mater, and pia mater. The dura mater is a tough fibrous membrane that also forms dural sleeves around the nerve roots as they emanate from the cord. The arachnoid mater (Latin for spider-like) is a delicate fibrous tissue that provides space between the dura and the pia. This subarachnoid space is filled with cerebrospinal fluid (CSF). The pia mater lies directly against the cord, and also encloses the blood vessels that supply the cord.

A cross section of the cord itself in **Figure 1–4** shows that it is composed of both gray and white matter, with the gray matter being organized in a butterfly shape. The gray matter consists primarily of nerve cell bodies. In very general terms, the gray matter is where most of the connections occur within the spinal cord. The white matter consists primarily of long nerve fibers that ascend and descend. The ascending tracts carry sensory information from the body to the brain while the descending tracts carry motor information from the brain to the body. Certain of these tracts are discussed at **§ 1.13.**

§ 1.10 Spinal Nerves

There are 31 pairs of spinal nerves that emanate from the spinal cord. While there are seven cervical vertebrae, there are eight pairs of cervical spinal nerves. In the

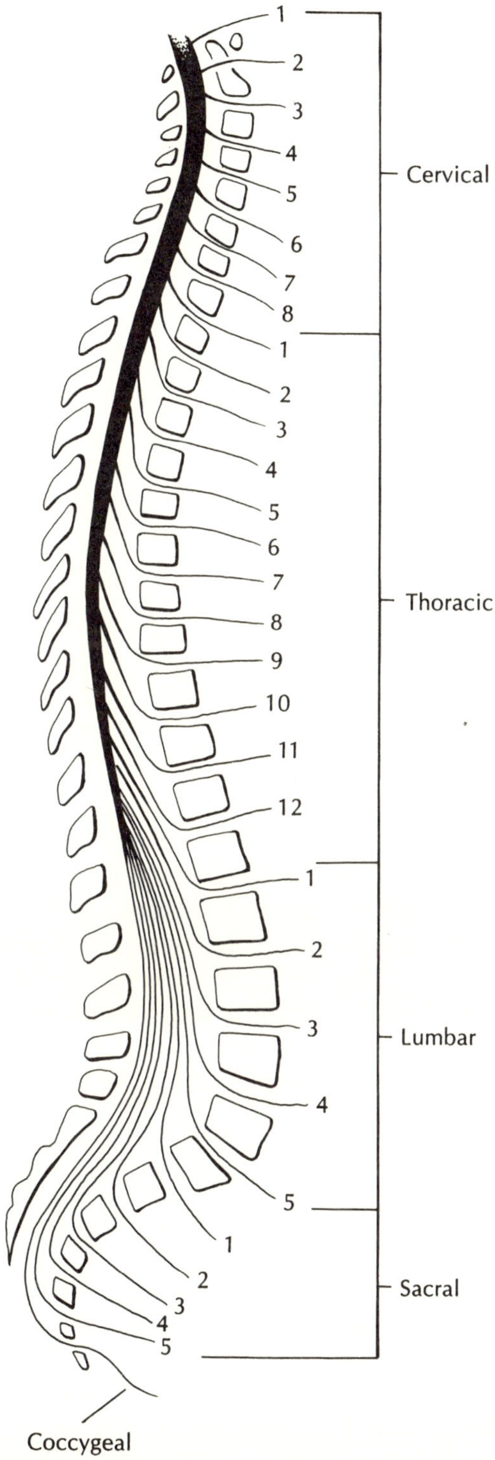

Figure 1–3. Cross section of vertebral column and spinal cord.

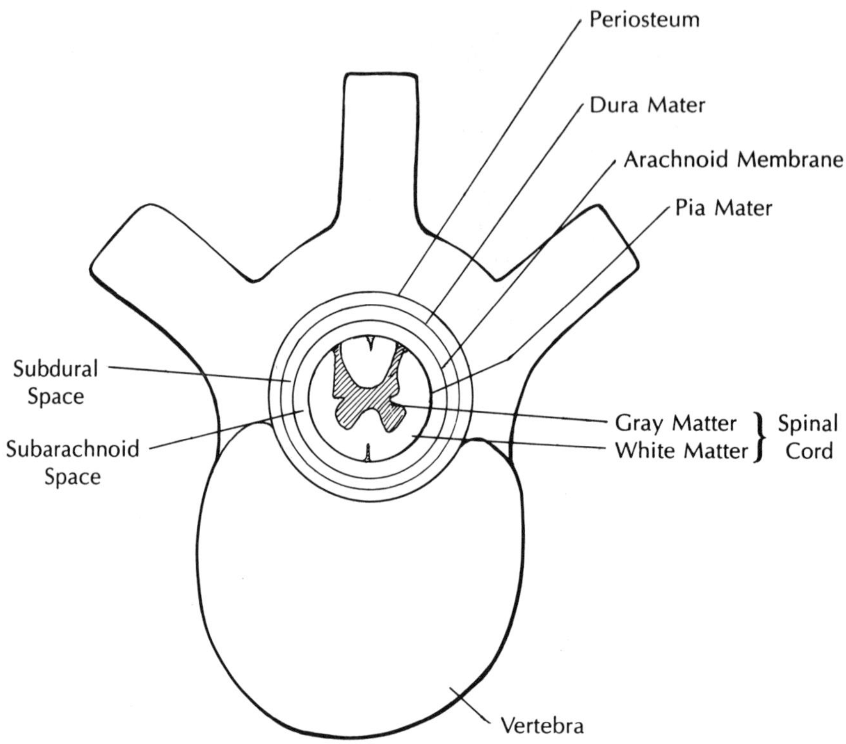

Figure 1–4. Cross section of spinal cord.

cervical spine, the cervical spinal nerves exit above the corresponding cervical vertebra. In the thoracic and lumbar spine, and the sacrum, the spinal nerves exit below the corresponding vertebra. (See **Figure 1–5.**)

Each spinal nerve is formed by the union of a ventral root and a dorsal root. At a particular spinal level, therefore, fibers arising from the anterior aspect of the cord form the ventral root. The ventral root contains almost exclusively motor fibers. The dorsal root attaches to the posterior aspect of the cord and generally carries efferent or sensory information to the cord. The dorsal and ventral roots join to form a spinal nerve.

§ 1.11 Ascending and Descending Pathways

The major ascending pathways carry sensory information to the brain. These include the posterior columns (also called fasciculus cuneatus and fasciculus gracilis), the anterior and lateral spinothalamic tracts, and the spinocerebellar tracts.

The posterior columns transmit the sense of conscious proprioception (the ability to know where a limb is in space, or to sense, for example, whether a joint is flexed or extended), stereognosis (the ability to discern, by sense of touch, the distance between two objects touching the skin), and light touch.

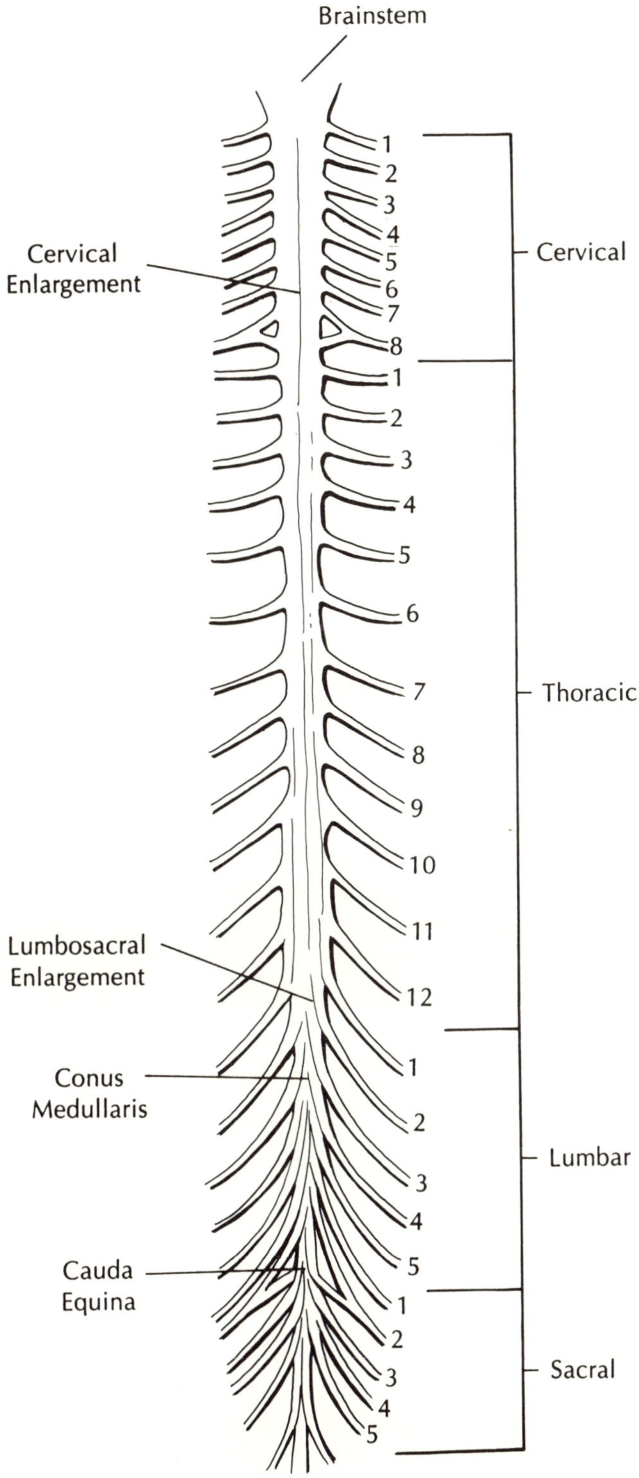

Figure 1–5. Spinal nerves.

The anterior spinothalamic tract transmits light touch and pressure sense. The lateral spinothalamic tract transmits pain and temperature sensation. The spinocerebellar tract transmits unconscious proprioception.

The major descending tracts carry motor information from the brain to the cord. These are the anterior and lateral corticospinal tracts. These major pathways are shown in the diagram below. The descending tracts are on the left. The ascending pathways are on the right. (See **Figure 1–6.**)

It is important to know that the pathways to and from the brain usually crossover from one side to another at some point. The site at that the crossover occurs affords the explanation for asymmetric symptoms. For example, an individual with an incomplete left-sided cord lesion (hemi-section) at the T12 level will have impaired motor function in the left leg, but impaired pain and temperature sensation in the right leg, since the primary pain and temperature pathway crosses over almost immediately upon entering the cord.

Figure 1–7 is a schematic representation of the site at which the major pathways crossover.

§ 1.12 Reflex Arc

Reflexes are subconscious cause and effect loops. In the simplest example, an afferent fiber carries an impulse into the cord, where it synapsis (connects) with an efferent fiber at the same level. The patellar (knee-jerk) reflex is of this type. When the patellar tendon is struck with the reflex hammer, it stretches rapidly and a nerve ending in the tendon sends an impulse through an afferent fiber to the cord. There it connects with an efferent fiber that transmits an impulse to the muscle above the knee causing the muscles to contract and the knee to jerk. (See **Figure 1–8.**)

The organization of the nervous system, however, is so complex that an afferent stimulus may connect with many efferent fibers, as well as connecting

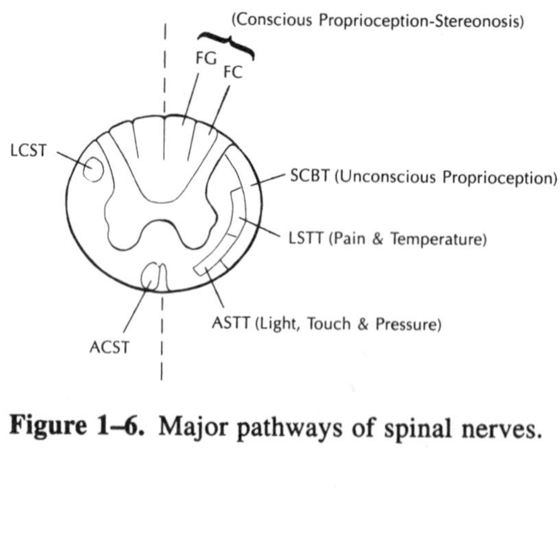

Figure 1–6. Major pathways of spinal nerves.

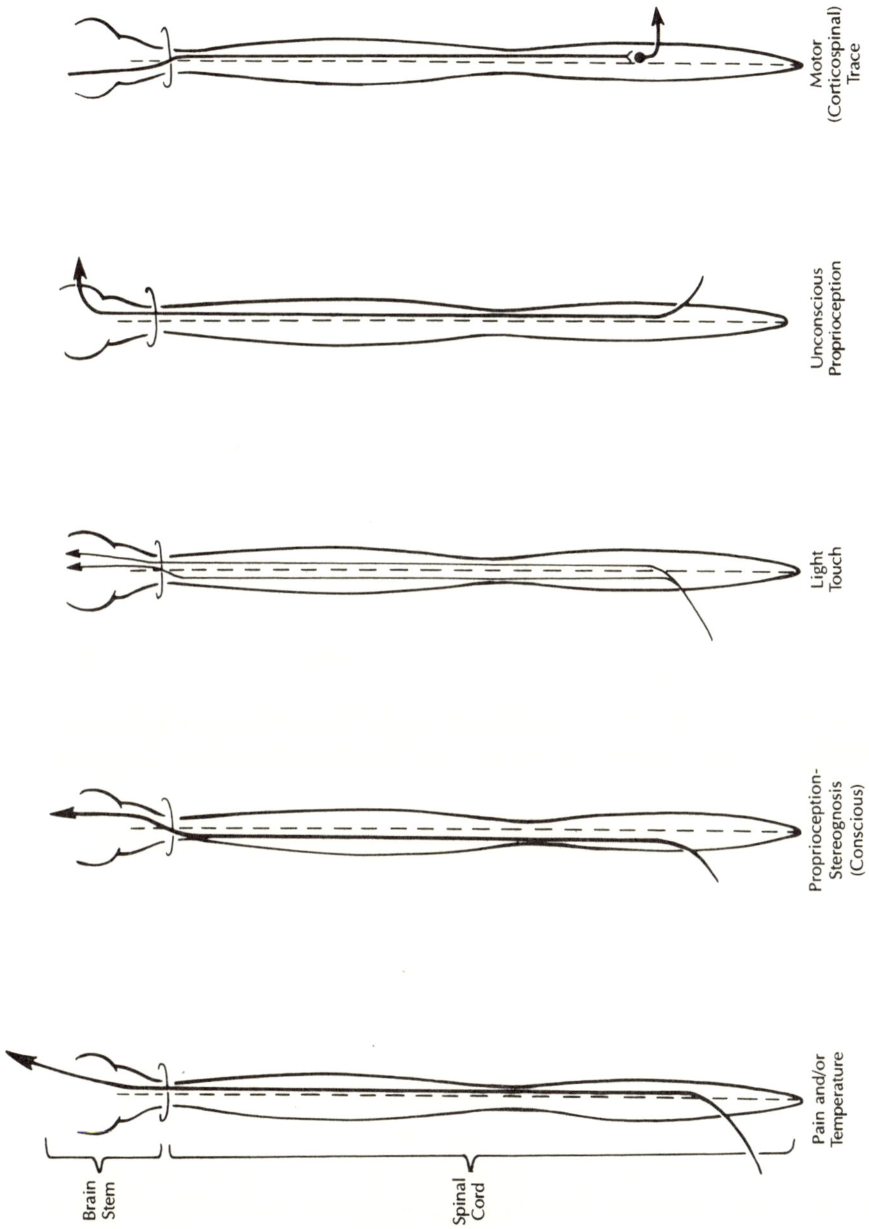

Figure 1–7. Crossover of major pathways in spinal nerve.

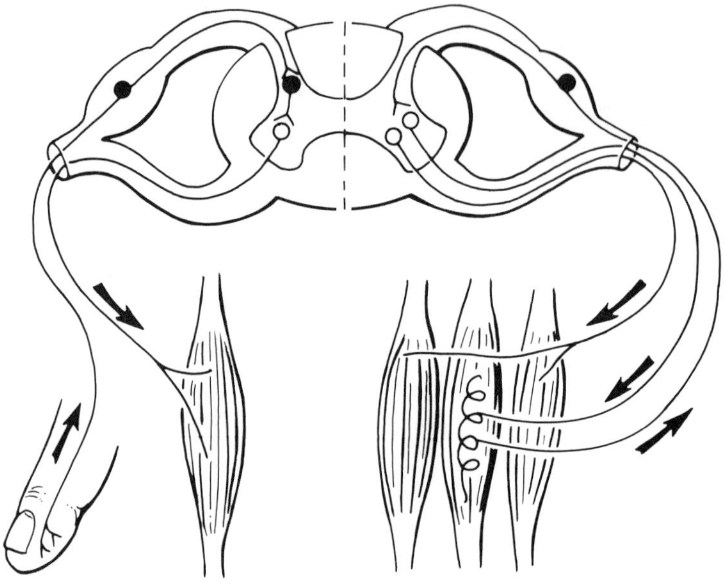

Figure 1–8. Reflexes.

with higher centers in the brain through ascending and descending tracts. Reflexes may be mediated by the higher centers.

An unmediated reflex tends to be exaggerated or self-perpetuating. Thus, if the reflex arc to a muscle or organ is intact but the cord is interrupted at a higher level, the muscle or organ will tend toward spasticity since the reflex activity is unmediated.

If the nerve root or nerve itself (rather than the cord) is severed there is no sensory (afferent) or motor (efferent) activity, the reflex arc is disrupted, and there is flaccidity.

§ 1.13 Cranial Nerves

Not all of the body's nerve supply emanates from the spine. In addition to the nerves emanating from the spine, there are 12 pairs of cranial nerves, which emanate from the cranium, or skull, as their names suggest.

The cranial nerves attach to the base of the brain and pass from the cranium into the face and neck through various openings (called foramina) in the skull. Since these nerves do not exit through the spine, they are not generally involved in spinal cord injury, though the cranial nerves may, of course, be damaged when there is damage to or bleeding within the skull.

Among the functions of the cranial nerves are the transmission of the so called special senses: smell, vision, taste, hearing, and equilibrium. The cranial nerves are generally referred to by roman numerals I through XII. Some of the cranial nerves carry only sensory information toward the brain (afferent), some carry only motor impulses from the brain (efferent), and some carry both. The corresponding names and (very generally) the functions of the cranial nerves are:

I.	Olfactory	smell
II.	Optic	vision
III.	Oculomotor	eye movement and parasympathetic pupil constriction
IV.	Trochlear	eye movement
V.	Trigeminal	sensation (other than taste) from the face and mouth and motor to the muscles used in chewing
VI.	Abducens	eye movement
VII.	Facial	motor to the facial muscles, parasympathetic innervation of tear glands and other minor glands, taste sensation from the front 2/3 of the tongue
VIII.	Vestibulocochlear	hearing and equilibrium
IX.	Glossopharyngeal	taste from the rear third of the tongue, the gag reflex, sensation from the ear and middle ear, swallowing
X.	Vagus	parasympathetic innervation of organs in the chest and abdomen, transmits information from the carotid and aortic bodies, which sense blood pressure, motor to muscles used in speech, swallowing
XI.	Accessory (or spinl accessory)	sternocleidomastoid muscle and trapezius muscles
XII.	Hypoglossal	motor to tongue muscles

Again, while the cranial nerves are not typically involved in spinal cord injury, it is important to know that certain of the cranial nerves (III, VII, IX, and X) contain parasympathetic fibers that may be involved in autonomic dysreflexia (see **Chapter 3**), and it is equally important to remember that much of the parasympathetic innervation of the organs of the chest and abdomen is supplied through the vagus nerve (X).

§ 1.14 Autonomic Nervous System

The autonomic or visceral nervous system controls smooth (involuntary) muscle in the organs, the heart, and various glands. It also regulates homeostasis, the name given to the processes that maintain the body's internal environment.

The autonomic nervous system has two divisions: the sympathetic division and the parasympathetic division.

Sympathetic (Thoracolumbar) Division

This arises from cord segments T1 through L2. From the lateral gray column of the cord, an efferent sympathetic fiber exits the cord through the ventral root. Unlike a somatic efferent fiber, it then travels through a white communicating ramus reaching a sympathetic chain or trunk. These chains or trunks lie next to the vertebral bodies, outside the spinal canal. From this point, the fiber may travel up or down within the sympathetic trunk to connect with fibers at a higher or lower level within the trunk, or pass through the trunk en route to a target organ (usually passing through an additional ganglion or plexus before reaching the target organ). (See **Figure 1–9.**)

Those fibers that will innervate structures within the body wall, such as the tiny muscles that cause hairs to stand erect, the smooth muscles that constrict blood vessels, and the sweat glands, reenter the spinal nerve through a gray communicating ramus and travel to their target area.

Parasympathetic (Craniosacral) Division

This arises from the grey matter of the brain stem and the middle three sacral segments of the spinal cord (S2–S4). Generally, these fibers run uninterrupted from their origin to the organ they supply.

The parasympathetic system innervates organs, not structures in the body wall.

The cranial portion of the parasympathetic system includes cranial nerves III, VII, IX, X. Cranial nerve X, the vagus, is the most important of these in understanding some of the complications of spinal injury. The vagus nerve provides parasympathetic innervation to the heart, lungs, stomach, small intestine and much of the large intestine. Parasympathetic fibers from the sacral segments innervate the sex organs, rectum, and part of the bladder.

Figure 1–10 below show the general scheme of the sympathetic and parasympathetic distribution.

The chart below summarizes some of the functions of the sympathetic and parasympathetic systems on various structures.

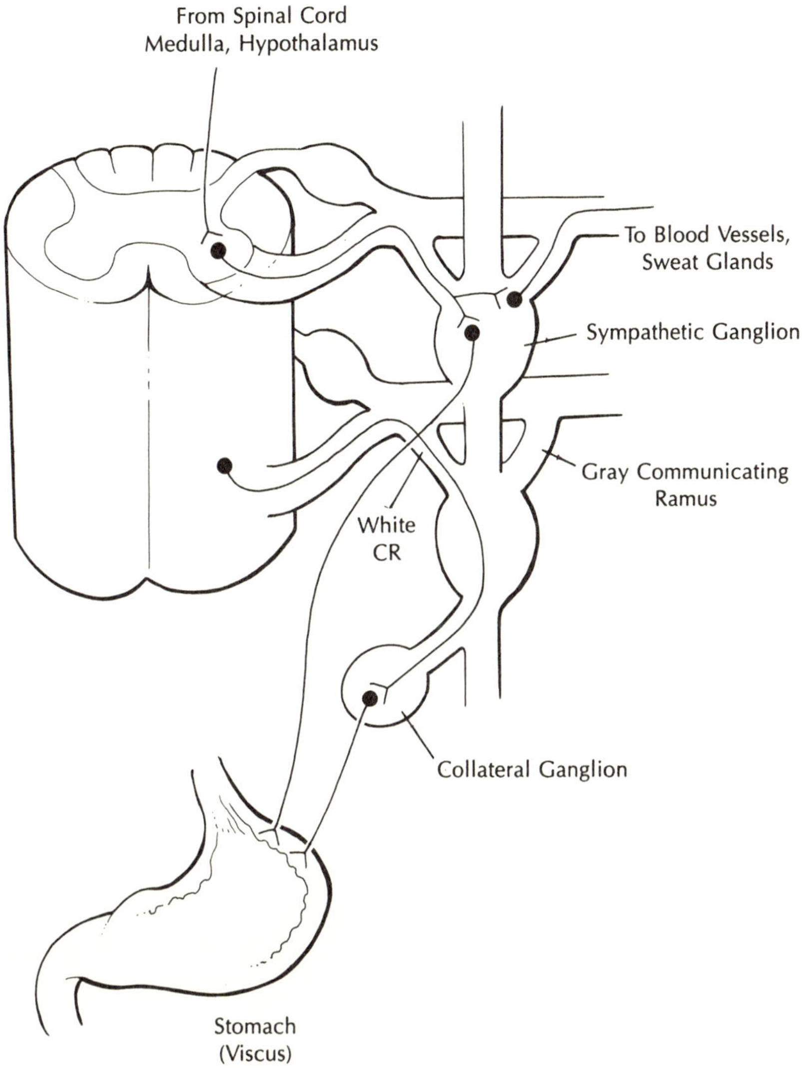

Figure 1–9. Sympathetic division.

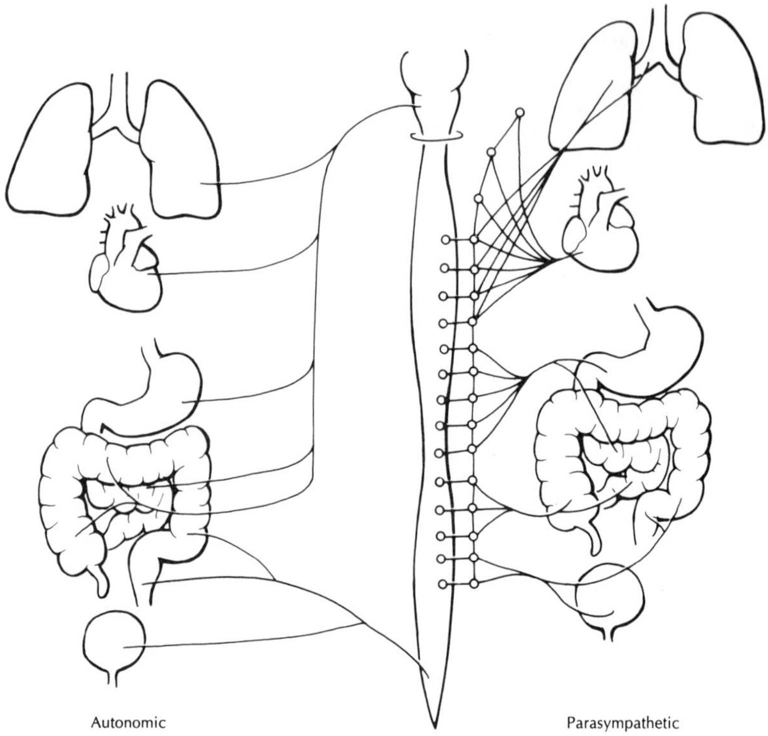

Figure 1–10. Sympathetic and parasympathetic distribution.

Structure	Sympathetic function	Parasympathetic function
Eye	Dilates pupil (mydriasis) No significant effect on ciliary muscle	Contracts pupil (miosis) Contracts ciliary muscle (accommodation)
Sweat glands	Stimulates secretion (cholinergic fibers)	No significant effect
Heart rate	Increases	Decreases
Force of ventricular contraction	Increases	Decreases
Blood vessels	Dilates or constricts cardiac and skeletal muscle vessels Constricts skin and digestive system blood vessels	No significant effect
Lungs	Dilates bronchial tubes	Constricts bronchial tubes Stimulates bronchial gland secretion
Gastrointestinal tract	Inhibits motility and secretion	Stimulates motility and secretion
GI sphincters	Contracts	Relaxes
Adrenal medulla	Stimulates secretion of adrenaline (cholinergic fibers)	No significant effect
Urinary bladder	Unknown	Contracts
Urinary sphincter	Contracts	Relaxes
Sex organs	Ejaculation	Erection

CHAPTER 2

MECHANISMS AND CLASSIFICATION OF SPINAL CORD INJURY

Clay M. Kelly

§ 2.1 Mechanisms Of Injury

The mechanism of injury and level of spinal cord involvement will often produce a characteristic type of injury. Thus spinal cord injuries are classified according to the anatomical description of the involved area and the extent of the involvement. These classifications range from complete transection injuries to lesions identified by the spinal cord level at which they occur and several variations of incomplete injury. Several scales are used to quantify the degree and implications of spinal cord injury.

Direct mechanical trauma, indirect injury, and blood supply disturbance are the three primary and interrelated causes of spinal cord insult.

Direct Mechanical Trauma

This trauma may include:

Penetrating Wounds. A knife, spike, or other sharp object thrust between the bony elements of the posterior arch may sever or partially sever the cord. Bullets and other high velocity projectiles may enter the cord elements.

Dislocation. Disruption or damage to the supporting ligaments of the neck may occur during violent flexion (forward bending), flexion-rotation, extension, or shear. Adjacent vertebrae may become fully or partially dislocated (subluxated). Complete or partial severance of the cord and adjacent nerve roots, disruption of local blood supply, or cord concussion may result. Typically, dislocation occurs at the atlanto-axial complex (C1–2), at C5–6, and near the thoracolumbar junction (T11–12 or T12–L1). The atlanto-axial complex is susceptible due to its inherent mobility: nearly 40 percent of cervical spine rotation occurs here. Absent fracture, flexion is nearly always the mechanism of dislocation at this level. The C5–6 unit is at the apex of the cervical curve, and is particularly susceptible to flexion, flexion-rotation, and extension injuries. The thoracolumbar junction is the transitional area between the relatively immobile thoracic spine and the more mobile lumbar spine. The orientation of the facet joints allows shear-type dislocation, which can happen in auto accidents in which the injured person is wearing a lap belt. Other dislocations or subluxations may occur at any level. In the lower cervical spine, facet dislocations are not uncommon. In severe flexion-rotation injuries, one facet may ride up over another. This type of injury may cause isolated nerve compression, or a Brown-Sequard type syndrome (see § **2.6**).

Bilateral facet dislocations are caused by severe flexion. The lower facets of the cervical vertebral ride up and over those below, causing significant neurological injury, with complete tetraplegia not unusual.

Vertebral Fracture. Fracture of the vertebral body or elements of the posterior arch may occur during violent flexion, flexion-rotation, extension, and axial compression (pressure from the top down through the long axis of the spine), or shear. This injury may cause bone fragments to be thrust into the cord, causing complete or partial transection, disruption of blood supply, or biochemical cord insult resulting from concussive forces. Certain anatomic areas are susceptible to fractures. The atlas typically will be fractured just behind the lateral masses or at the posterior arch. Direct axial compression, as when a victim's head is thrust directly upward into the roof of an automobile, may result in a Jefferson fracture in which the atlas is broken into four pieces. A fracture through the pedicles of the atlas is known as a hangman's fracture. The mechanism is typically severe extension. At the atlanto-axial joint, a fracture of the odontoid process is common following extension injuries. This injury causes instability and subsequent flexion may result in spinal cord insult. In the lower cervical spine a flexion force may cause a compression or crush fracture of the vertebral body rather than ligamentous disruption. The vertebral body will become wedge shaped. With severe force, a comminuted, or tear-drop, fracture may occur, giving rise to the possibility of a retropulsed fragment insult to the cord. A combination of a comminuted fracture with ligamentous disruption results in a fracture-dislocation, which is a very unstable situation. Compression fractures may occur in the thoracic spine. When they are severe they may result in retropulsed bone fragments and spinal cord insult. The thoracolumbar and lumbar spine has facet joints aligned in the sagittal plane. The chance fracture may occur in the hyperflexion injury of a car collision victim wearing a lap belt. A compression fracture from direct axial compression, such as seen in falls from heights, is possible.

Indirect injury

Indirect injury includes injury to the spine or adjacent structure that lead to spinal cord damage.

Epidural hemorrhage. Bleeding within the spinal canal, but external to the dura may cause cord and nerve root compression. This injury is a surgical emergency and can result in progressive paresis.

Subdural hemorrhage. In this condition, bleeding is within the dura. Symptoms are identical to epidural hemorrhage.

Intramedullary bleeding. Bleeding within the substance of the cord (hematomyelia) compresses cord tissue.

Pressure wave. A pressure wave generated by a blow, fall, missile, or other concussive force may cause cord injury ranging from minor concussion to severe hemorrhage.

Blood supply disturbance. Pressure upon, or disruption of the arteries that supply the cord causes ischemic damage (infarction) of the cord.

§ 2.2 Level of Injury

The lowest neurological level at which both motor and sensory function have been normally retained is called the level of injury, or neurological level of injury. Determination of normal motor function requires evaluation of specific muscles. Most muscles, however, receive their innervation from more than one cord level; thus, a muscle strength grade of three (out of five) will be considered normal for the level of primary innervation of that muscle. For example, if the injured person has a C5 neurologic level of injury, then all structures innervated from C1–5 on both sides will demonstrate normal sensation and grade three or better muscle strength. The C6 neurologic level will show abnormal sensation and grade two or lower muscle strength.

§ 2.3 Determination of Level of Injury by Motor Function Level

Certain muscles are generally used to determine neurologic level of injury. These muscles receive primary innervation from identifiable spinal cord levels. The following chart lists the muscles commonly used to determine level of injury.

C4	diaphragm
C5	deltoid and/or biceps
C6	wrist extensors
C7	triceps
C8	flexor digitorum profundus (flexes fingertips)
T1	intrinsic muscles of the hand
T2–L1	use sensory level in combination with abdominal or other specific reflexes
L2	psoas
L3	quadriceps
L4	tibialis anterior
L5	extensor hallucis longus (extends big toe)
S1	gastrocnemius
S2–S5	use sensory level

§ 2.4 Spinal Shock

Immediately following spinal cord injury, there is a period of reflex inhibition, complete flaccid paralysis, and loss of sensation below the level of injury. This is called *spinal shock.* While it typically lasts one to two days, it may last as little as six hours or as long as six months. Following this period, certain reflexes begin to resume. Among the first are reflexes that lie within the sacral segments; including the anal sphincter reflex. Deep tendon reflexes (for example the knee jerk reflex), spasticity, and radicular pain at the site of the lesion may follow.

§ 2.5 Complete versus Incomplete Injury

A complete transection injury occurs when an entire cross sectional area of the cord is damaged such that no viable neural tissue is left intact. If some viable neural tissue crosses the area of injury to distal segments, the lesion is classified as incomplete. Following the period of spinal shock, a return of sensation to the perianal region or sex organs or motor function that flexes the toes indicates that sacral segments have been spared. This is known as *sacral sparing.* The prognosis for recovery of motor, sensory, sexual, and bladder function is greater in patients with incomplete lesions.

§ 2.6 The Syndromes

Lesions, complete or incomplete, are classified by the spinal cord level at which they occur. There are also several syndromes in spinal cord injury that are classified based on the specific area of the cord involved and the resulting pattern of deficit. Patterns showing characteristics of one or more syndrome may be classified as a *mixed syndrome.* **Figure 2–1** illustrates several incomplete lesions.

Brown-Sequard Syndrome. This is a hemi-section of the cord, meaning that one side of the cord has been damaged. This syndrome is uncommon, and typically associated with gunshot or stab wounds. It may also occur in severe lateral bending injuries. Paralysis occurs on the same side of the body as the lesion, as will impairment of light touch and proprioception. Pain and temperature sensation will be impaired on the side of the body opposite the lesion. The prognosis for Brown-Sequard patients is good, as there is usually significant recovery from neurological deficits.

Anterior Cord Syndrome. This usually results from injury to the anterior spinal artery, causing infarction of the anterior aspect of the cord. The lesion may also be caused by fracture-dislocation in which bone or disc fragments are thrust into the anterior aspect of the cord. The syndrome is characterized by loss of motor function and preservation of some sensation. Conscious proprioception and light touch will be spared, as these sensations are transmitted in the posterior columns. If pain and temperature, transmitted in the lateral spinothalamic tract, are spared, the prognosis for recovery is significantly improved. In patients who experience some early motor recovery, the prognosis is better still.

Posterior Cord Syndrome. This is an extremely rare syndrome following spinal trauma (it does occur, however, as a result of advanced syphilis infection). The syndrome is characterized by loss of posterior column function, resulting in lost conscious proprioception and spared pain and temperature sensation as well as motor function.

Central Cord Syndrome. This syndrome most commonly follows a hyperextension injury to the neck. Contusion, edema, and hemorrhage in the central

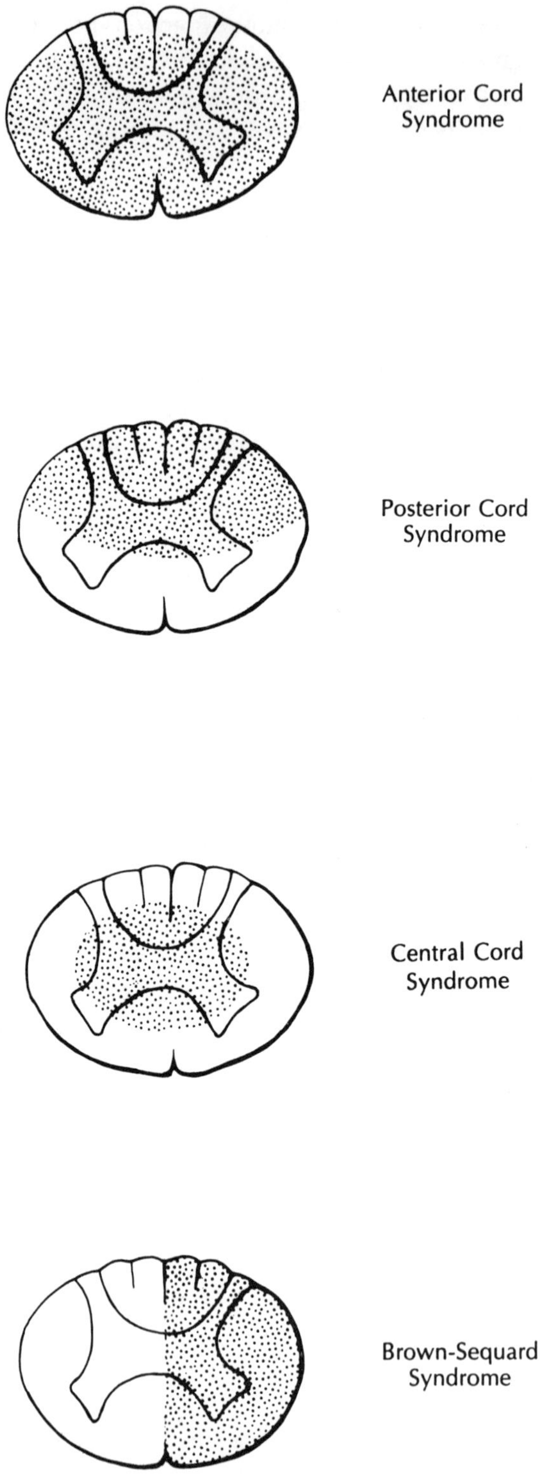

Figure 2–1. Anatomical classification of incomplete lesions.

portion of the cord result in tetraparesis involving the upper extremities to a greater degree than the lower. Pain and temperature sensation may be impaired while other sensation remains intact. The condition typically shows progressive improvement, and most patients regain the ability to walk. Recovery of upper extremity motor function is variable.

Conus Medullaris Syndrome. Fracture-dislocation at the thoracolumbar junction will affect the portion of the spinal cord known as the conus medullaris. Injury at this level will result in damage to both sacral cord segments and lumbar spinal nerve roots. If there is complete destruction of the sacral segments, there is loss of autonomic, bowel, bladder, and sexual function as well as loss of motor function to the muscles that extend the hip, flex the knee, and plantarflex the ankle. The exact clinical picture will vary with the amount of damage to the sacral cord, and the lumbar nerve roots.

Cauda Equina Syndrome. This is an injury below the level of the conus medullaris. At this point, only lumbar and sacral nerve roots travel throughout the spinal canal. The typical syndrome includes loss of all bowel, bladder, and lower extremity reflexive activity, associated dermatomal sensory loss, and flaccid paralysis and atrophy of involved muscles.

§ 2.7 ASIA Impairment Scale Classification of Spinal Cord Injuries

The American Spinal Injury Association (ASIA) system is based on the extent of preservation of function below the level of neurological injury. This is formerly known as the Frankel classification. The ASIA classification is as follows:

A = Complete: No preservation of any motor or sensory function below the level of injury.

B = Incomplete (sensory): Preservation of any demonstrable sensation, *except phantom pain,* below the level of injury.

C = Incomplete (motor nonfunctional): Preservation of voluntary motor function that serves no useful purpose except psychologically. Sensory function may or may not be preserved.

D = Incomplete (motor functional): Preservation of functionally useful motor function.

E = Complete Recovery: Complete return of all motor and sensory function, although some abnormal reflexes may persist.

Of significant importance is the prognosis associated with each of the ASIA grade classifications. The literature suggests the following relationship between

ASIA grade classification upon hospital admission and subsequent ASIA grade upon discharge:

A. Of those classified ASIA grade A at admission, approximately
93.3 percent showed no change at discharge
2.7 percent became grade B
2.2 percent became grade C
1.8 percent became grade D, and
none recovered.

B. In this group, approximately
3.7 percent regressed to grade A
62.7 percent showed no change
13 percent became grade C
19.9 percent progressed to grade D, and
0.7 percent recovered.

C. In this group, approximately
1.1 percent regressed to grade A
0.4 percent regressed to grade B
46.4 percent remained unchanged
51.3 percent improved to grade D, and
0.8 percent recovered.

D. In this group, approximately
0.5 percent regressed to grade A
0.4 percent regressed to grade B
1.2 percent regressed to grade C
93.8 percent did not change, and
4.1 percent recovered.

§ 2.8 Motor Index Score

A commonly used examination in spinal cord injury is the motor index score. This is accomplished through testing of key muscles in ten paired myotomes. (see § **2.3,** the diaphragm is excluded). The strength of each muscle is graded on a six-point scale.

0 = no active movement
1 = minimal palpable or visible contraction
2 = active movement through a full range of motion with gravity eliminated
3 = active movement through full range of motion against gravity
4 = active movement through full range of motion with moderate resistance
5 = normal active movement through full range of motion against full resistance

A normal score is 50 on the right and left sides for a total of 100. This muscle testing should be accomplished as soon as possible postinjury so that future examinations may reflect neurological recovery. In general, the Motor Index Score is considered a research tool, and does not reflect functional outcome well.

§ 2.9 The Functional Independence Measure

The Functional Independence Measure (FIM) is perhaps the most widely employed functional assessment tool in rehabilitation medicine. It allows monitoring of progress, associated with treatment in patients with disability as a standard measure of activities associated with daily living. This measure focuses on six areas of individual functioning: self care, mobility, locomotion, communication, social cognition, and sphincter control. Each focus has two or more activities (for a total of 18) that are rated on a seven-point scale for independence of function.

Independent
7 = complete independence
6 = modified independence—requires an assistive device and/or increased time to perform the activity properly and safely

Dependent
5 = supervision/setup—cueing, coaxing, or setup required
4 = minimal contact assistance—subject expends 75 percent or more of the effort required for the activity, requires no more than touching
3 = moderate assistance—subject expends 50–75 percent of the effort required for the activity, requires more than touching
2 = maximal assistance—subject expends 25–50 percent of the effort required for the activity
1 = total assistance—subject expends 25 percent or less of the effort required for the activity

A completely independent subject scores 126; a completely dependent subject scores 18. Improvement in the FIM score from prior to rehabilitation to following rehabilitation can demonstrate the positive effect of rehabilitation, and ultimately estimate the cost value thereof.

CHAPTER 3

AMERICAN MEDICAL ASSOCIATION (AMA) GUIDELINES

Michael Javoronok

§ 3.1 Background

The AMA *Guides to the Evaluation of Permanent Impairment* (hereinafter *Guides*)[1] has changed considerably since its first publication in 1958 and first complete edition in 1971.

The premise of the *Guides* is that estimates of the severity of human impairment, including spinal cord injury, may be based on accepted medical standards. The present *Guides* is more specific than the original with regard to how to calculate percentages of impairments by required protocols. The AMA itself claims that use of the *Guides* increases objectivity and enables physicians to evaluate and report medical impairment in a standardized manner, so that reports from different observers are more likely to be comparable in content and completeness.

§ 3.2 Standard

In 1988, the American Academy of Orthopaedic Surgeons (AAOS) withdrew from recommended use its *Manual for Orthopaedic Surgeons in Evaluating Permanent Physical Impairment.* Until a new AAOS manual reappears, the AMA *Guides* is the authoritative source. Arguably, if the *Guides* is not used, whatever impairment rating a physician has used is idiosyncratic, therefore not used by other experts and not valid. The AMA strongly discourages the use of any but the most recent edition of the *Guides* as the information in it would not be based on the most current materials.[2] The *Guides* defines:

> *Evaluation of permanent impairment* is acquisition and analysis of information, including clinical evaluation, that is carried out according to Chapters 1 and 2 and the other applicable parts of the *Guides.*[3]

§ 3.3 Protocol

As a practical matter, most doctors will agree that the AMA rating guide is an authoritative text on which experts rely. According to a 1991 AMA survey, 40 of 53 jurisdictions (38 states and two territories) recommended or mandated the use of the *Guides* in workers' compensation cases. The *Guides* defines *impairment* as the loss, loss of use, or derangement of any body part, system, or function. An impairment is permanent when it has become static or well stabilized

[1] American Medical Ass'n, *Guides to the Evaluation of Permanent Impairment* (4th ed. 1993) [hereinafter *Guides*]. Material in this chapter from the *Guides* is reprinted by permission of the American Medical Association.

[2] *Guides* at 5.

[3] *Id.* at 315.

with or without medical treatment and is not likely to remit despite medical treatment. *Disability* is defined as a decrease in, or the loss or absence of the capacity of an individual to meet the personal, social, or occupational demands, or to meet statutory or regulatory requirements.

§ 3.4 Disability, Impairment, and Activities of Daily Living

An impairment gives rise to disability only when a medical condition limits an individual's capacity to meet the demands of life's activities. The *Guides* uses the example that losing the distal phalanx of the little finger of the right hand will impair the functioning of the digit and the hand of both a concert pianist and a bank president; however, the bank president is less likely to be disabled than the pianist; it further explains that a surgeon who loses a hand will be impaired and will be disabled in terms of the ability to operate, but may be fully able to be chief of a hospital medical staff and not disabled for that occupation.[4] Thus, the *Guides* states that when an impairment is associated with an obstacle to useful activity, a handicap may exist. When an impaired individual is not able to accomplish a specific task or activity despite available accommodations, then that individual is both handicapped and disabled. The *Guides* also suggests a functional example of impairment in activities of daily living (Table 3–1)[5] as follows:

Table 3–1

Activities of Daily Living.

Activity	Example
Self-care, personal hygiene	Bathing, grooming, dressing, eating, eliminating
Communication	Hearing, speaking, reading, writing, using keyboard
Physical activity	*Intrinsic*: Standing, sitting, reclining, walking, stooping, squatting, kneeling, reaching, bending, twisting, leaning *Functional*: Carrying, lifting, pushing, pulling, climbing, exercising
Sensory function	Hearing, seeing, tactile feeling, tasting, smelling
Hand functions	Grasping, holding, pinching, percussive movements, sensory discrimination
Travel	Riding, driving, traveling by airplane, train, or car

[4] *Guides* at 2.

[5] *Id.* at 317.

Table 3–1
(continued)

Activity	Example
Sexual function	Participating in desired sexual activity
Sleep	Having a restful sleep pattern
Social and recreational activities	Participating in individual or group activities, sports, hobbies

§ 3.5 The Spine

Since symptoms relating to the back and spine are among the most common for adults, this chapter will focus on that aspect of the *Guides*. One purpose of the *Guides* is to lead to similar results when different clinicians evaluate illnesses and impairments.[6] In previous editions, impairment was based on a loss of a range of motion combined with impairments based on diagnoses or therapeutic approaches or neurologic impairments. The *Guides* now asserts that the prior range of motion system of earlier editions ignored other clinical data and diagnostic information. Physicians complained that prior editions did not adequately deal with the accuracy and repeatability of range of motion measurements. Also, prior editions failed to take into account the effects of aging. Normal will differ through the life span (that is, normal for age 16 will be different from normal for age 70).

§ 3.6 Objective Methods

The *Guides* notes those spine mobility measurements carried out with inclinometers are more difficult to perform than those that suggest using a goniometer. Specifically, the chapter authors cite a recent study that identified seven clinical measurements that distinguished well between the patients with pain and normal patients.[7] Four of these seven measurements were made with inclinometers.

§ 3.7 Two Approaches: DRE and ROM

The present edition suggest two approaches to evaluate impairment: the Injury Model that especially applies to traumatic injuries, and the Range of Motion Model from previous *Guides*. The Injury Model assigns a patient to one of

---

[6] *Guides* at 94.

[7] *Objective Clinical Evaluation of Physical Impairment in Chronic Low Back Spine Pain,* 17 Spine, 617–28 (1992).

eight categories, such as minor injury, radiculopathy, loss of spine structure integrity, or paraplegia based on objective clinical findings. If the patient has a condition listed in Table 70, the evaluator should use that model.[8] If none of the eight categories of the Injury Model apply, then the *Guides* says the examiner should use the Range of Motion Model. If a disagreement about a category of injury exists, then use the Range of Motion Model to provide evidence on the question.[9]

The *Guides* also calls the Injury Model the Diagnosis Related Estimates Model (DRE), especially in the *Spine* section.[10] The Range of Motion Model is also the Functional Model.[11] Each evaluation should include a complete and accurate medical history, a review of all pertinent records, a careful and thorough physical exam, a complete description of the patient's current symptoms and their relationship to daily activities, and relevant laboratory, radiological, and ancillary tests. The condition must not be amenable to further surgery and unlikely to change within the next year.

§ 3.8 Medical History of the Spine

The *Guides* notes that much of the historical part of the evaluation should be based on the patient's own statements, not on second hand information; it is not appropriate to question the patient's integrity. If information does not make sense or is inconsistent, the physician should note this and describe the inconsistency. The medical history should specifically describe how the condition interferes with the activities of daily living.[12] The text requires that the examiner use the patient's own description in the patient's own words as to development, cause, response to treatment, and the study results. The doctor should review the x-rays personally or so state the findings are another's. Similarly, the doctor should note the patient's plans.

§ 3.9 Spine Exam

Because much of the information relating to an evaluation of a spine injury is neurologic in nature, a doctor must have a good grasp of neurologic principles, and the material covered in the *Guides* chapter on the nervous system[13] and in the *Spine* chapter.[14] Thus, guided as above by the patient's

[8] *Guides* at 108.

[9] *Id.* at 94.

[10] *Id.* at 95–106.

[11] *Id.* § 3.3j at 112.

[12] *Guides* at 95.

[13] *Guides* at 139.

[14] *Id.* § 3.1k at 46.

history,[15] the doctor should focus attention on the spine-related physical findings such as motor abilities, reflexes, muscle atrophy, anal tone, and the need for assistive devices. Again, the doctor should note any inconsistencies.

The regions of the spine are difficult to separate where they meet. The *Guides* notes that with the Injury or DRE Model, the respective spine regions and their respective percentages of body as a whole ratings are: cervicothoracic 35 percent, thoracolumbar 20 percent; and lumbosacral 75 percent. For the Range of Motion or Functional Model, the regions and percentages are: cervical 80 percent, thoracic 40 percent, and lumbosacral 90 percent. The text then overlaps the above sections as with the DRE model.

§ 3.10 Differentiators

While using the Injury Model, the doctor may use certain clinical procedures or determinations in placing the patient's impairment in the proper category as follows:

Impairment Category Differentiators

1. guarding: paravertebral muscle guarding or spasm or nonuniform loss of range of motion, dysmetria, is present or has been documented by a physician. Radicular complaints that follow anatomic pathways but cannot be verified by neurologic findings belong with this type of differentiator.
2. loss of reflexes: spine-injury-related loss of arm or leg reflexes is present; this may be verified by differentiator 4. below.
3. decreased circumference, atrophy: spine-injury-related circumferential measurements show loss of girth of 2 cm or more above or below the elbow or knee. The atrophy cannot be explained by non-spine-related problems or contralateral hypertrophy, as might occur with a dominant limb or greatly increased use of a limb. The neurologic impairment may be verified by differentiator 4. below.
4. *electrodiagnostic evidence: unequivocal electrodiagnostic evidence exists of acute nerve root compromise, such as multiple positive sharp waves or fibrillation potentials; or H-wave absence or delay greater than 3 mm/sec; or chronic changes such as polyphasic waves in peripheral muscles.
5. *loss of motion segment integrity: flexion and extension comparison roentgenograms show significant injury-related anterior-to-posterior translation of two adjacent vertebral bodies of 5 mm or more in the lumbar or thoracic spine, or of 3.5 mm or more in the cervical spine; or the roentgenograms show 15° more angular motion in the sagittal plane of L5 and S1 than at L4 and L5, or 11° more angular motion in the sagittal plane of a motion segment above L5 than in the adjacent motion segment.

---

[15] *Id.* Fig. 61 at 96.

6. loss of bowel or bladder control: rectal examination indicates loss of sphincter tone, or there is loss of bladder control requiring the use of an assistive device such as a catheter.
7. *bladder studies: cystometrograms show unequivocal neurologic compromise of the bladder with resulting incontinence.[16]

The * categories contain more objective and important differentiators.

§ 3.11 Range of Motion Model

If the doctor cannot decide to which DRE category the patient belongs, the doctor may use the Range of Motion Model.[17] For that procedure, the doctor combines an impairment based on the patient's diagnosis with a percentage based on the patient's range of motion and any neurologic impairment, if present. The doctor then uses the estimate determined with the Range of Motion Model to determine placement within one of the DRE categories. The DRE category closest to the impairment percentage of the Range of Motion Model is the proper one.

As certain spine fracture patterns may lead to significant impairment and not yield any of the differentiators, these are included in the DRE categories. With more than one structural inclusion, use the higher category of impairment.

§ 3.12 General Approach to Diagnosis

The doctor is directed to start with Table 70[18] as a guide to the proper diagnosis category. The differentiators[19] describe the clinical conditions that correlate with the physiologic dysfunction or structural change to help define the impairment. For example, if the patient has a radiculopathy of the lumbosacral spine, this is a Category III impairment under Table 72.[20]

§ 3.13 Specific Procedures and Directions

The *Guides* suggests the following procedure:

1. Take a careful history from the patient, perform a thorough medical examination, and review all pertinent records.

---

[16] *Guides*, Table 71 at 109.

[17] *Guides*, § 3.3b at 99. *See also id.*, Table 71 at 109.

[18] *Guides* at 108.

[19] *Id.* Table 71 at 109.

[20] *Id.* at 110.

2. Review special studies.
3. Select the region that is primarily involved and identify the patient's most serious objective findings.
4. Consider the permanency of the impairment, referring to the *Guides*, Chapter 1 and the Glossary as needed.
5. If one spine region is primarily involved, determine the spine-related whole-person impairment, using the impairment table referring to that region.
6. If the physician cannot place the patient into an impairment category, or if disagreement exists about which category to use, the physician should use the Range of Motion Model as the differentiator.
7. If there is impairment of the cervicothoracic or thoracolumbar region and, if long-tract signs are present, consider combining another impairment percent from the involved region that reflects the long-tract signs.
8. If more than one spine region is impaired, determine the impairment of the other regions and combine.
9. From history and medical data previously compiled, determine if there was a pre-existing condition and use apportionment.
10. Use the report form on spine impairment and the standard *Guides* Report of Medical Evaluation to describe the evaluation findings and indicate the patient's whole-person impairment.[21]

§ 3.14 Range of Motion Model Approach

The second recommended procedure for evaluation of spine impairment is the Range of Motion Model. The *Guides* suggests that this model should be used only if the Injury Model is not applicable, or if more clinical data are needed, or if the doctor cannot decide which DRE to use.[22] There must exist a medically documented injury or illness with a physiologic residual. A summary of the Range of Motion or Functional Model procedure follows:

1. Select the primarily impaired region.
2. Using Table 75, determine the estimated diagnosis-related impairment percentage for the primarily involved region. This percentage will be combined with those representing the impaired range(s) of motion and neurologic deficit.
3. Test the range of motion and determine any angle of ankylosis or restricted motion.
4. Determine whether the impairment is stable and unlikely to change during coming months.

---

[21] *Id.* § 3.3f at 101.

[22] *Guides* at 112. *See also id.* at 94.

5. Carry out the three steps of measurement: flexion, extension, and movement in the sagittal, coronal, and axial planes.
6. If the measurements do not meet the consistency requirements described in 5 above, perform additional tests up to a maximum of six until the reproducibility criteria are satisfied.
7. Use the maximum angle of a valid set of measurement of the range of motion to determine the impairment percentage from the appropriate table.
8. Determine any impairments due to neurologic deficits.
9. Combine the diagnosis-based and range of motion impairment percentages.
10. Repeat steps 1 through 7 for either of the other regions with significant involvement related to the primary diagnosis.
11. Combine the regional impairments into a single whole-person impairment.
12. Combine the whole-person spine impairment with the whole-person neurologic or nervous system impairment.
13. Record the results.[23]

§ 3.15 General Measurement Principles

Measure impairments only when the condition becomes stable (muscle spasm, pain, fear of injury, or neuromuscular inhibitions may lead to low or inconsistent measurements). Reproducibility of results is an indicator of optimum effort. At least three consecutive measurements and a calculation of the mean of these results are necessary. For an average of less than 50°, three of the measurements must fall within 5° of it; or if the average is greater than 50°, the three measurements must fall within 10°. Take measurements up to six times to obtain the three consecutive readings. If the inconsistency persists, that part of the evaluation is invalid.

The *Guides* mandates procedures[24] for obtaining accurate measurements. *Documentation of Joint Motion* explains the principles necessary for use of an inclinometer to determine range of motion.[25]

Combine the spine impairment as shown on Figure 80,[26] add to the diagnosis from Table 64,[27] and then add this to the loss of strength and sensation from the neurologic system. Regional impairments are combined using the Combined Values Chart.[28] These values represent the chart form of the formula A + B(1 – A)

---

[23] *Id.* at 115–16.

[24] *Guides* at 114–15.

[25] J. Gerhardt, Documentation of Joint Motion (2d ed. rev. 1989).

[26] *Guides* at 135.

[27] *Id.* at 85–86.

[28] *Id. at 322.*

for the combined value of A and B. Repeat the process for multiple values by selecting two at a time and using their combination with the third.

§ 3.16 Intensity and Frequency

The *Guides* suggests the following procedure to grade the intensity and frequency of an individual's signs or symptoms:

> **Intensity** is:
>
> a. *Minimal*: the symptoms or signs are annoying but have not been documented medically to cause appreciable diminution in an individual's capacity to carry out daily activities.
>
> b. *Slight*: the symptoms or signs can be tolerated but would cause some impairment in the performance of an activity that precipitates the symptoms or signs.
>
> c. *Moderate*: the symptoms and signs would cause marked impairment in the performance of an activity that precipitates the symptoms or signs.
>
> d. *Marked*: the symptoms or signs preclude any activity that precipitates the symptoms or signs.
>
> Frequency is:
>
> a. *Intermittent*: the symptoms or signs occur less than 25% of the time the patient is awake.
>
> b. *Occasional*: the symptoms or signs occur between 25% and 50% of the time the patient is awake.
>
> c. *Frequent*: the symptoms and signs occur between 50% and 75% of the time the patient is awake.
>
> d. *Constant*: the symptoms and signs occur between 75% and 100% of the time the patient is awake.[29]

The *Guides* defines the process of assessing and reporting medical impairment with a single set of standards.[30] Thus, if two physicians using the *Guides* have not obtained similar results and reached similar conclusions, a framework exists within which to resolve the discrepancy. The *Guides* suggests, in such an instance, the differences will be in the clinical findings, which are matters of fact, not opinion. Verify the latter by further analysis of the medical records and reports.

For example, when the medical condition has become static or stabilized, the findings should be replicated in repeated examinations. If this is not the case, the stability of the medical condition and the matter of permanent impairment are in question. The *Guides* suggests comparing this practice to the generally occurring practice in disability evaluation, where each physician evaluates,

---

[29] *Guides* at 316. *See also id.* 243–45. Medically documented is defined at *id.* 316.

[30] *Id.* at 7.

examines, and report without protocol, saying, "In such instances, it is impossible to compare reports, because there is no assurance that the physicians have examined the same body parts or systems in the same way."[31] The *Guides* also suggests that without standardization of evaluation and reporting techniques, the person scrutinizing the information would not know which report to believe, which is neither reasonable nor fair and can lead to inappropriate and avoidable confrontations.

Because the protocols are standardized, by consulting the reference tables and reporting procedures of the *Guides*, the reviewer can verify the collection of all necessary information and then check the correctness of the evaluation by comparing it to the tables in the *Guides*. If a disagreement exists on the medical findings, further medical evaluation may be necessary.

§ 3.17 Specific Examples of Spinal Cord Injuries

As a practical matter, the severity of most spinal cord injuries and a general agreement about the diagnosis will preclude the use of the Range of Motion Model. However, the structure of the *Guides*, along with the testimony of the physical or occupational therapist and physiatrist provide a ready framework by using the Activity of Daily Living Chart as revised by what the patient's capabilities exactly are, and providing a numerical rating of what this functional impairment and activity of daily living means.

An example of the injury or diagnosis-related model and how injuries fit into categories for the cervicothoracic spine is as follows:

The *Guides* provides for eight categories to analyze cervicothoracic spine impairment:

1. Category I: Complaints or Symptoms—0% whole-person impairment
2. Category II: Minor Impairment—5% whole-person impairment
3. Category III: Radiculopathy—10% whole-person impairment
4. Category IV: Loss of Motion Segment Integrity or Multilevel Neurologic Compromise—20% whole-person impairment
5. Category V: Severe Upper Extremity Neurologic Compromise—25% whole-person impairment
6. Category VI: Cauda Equina Syndrome Without Bowel or Bladder Signs—40% whole-person impairment
7. Category VII: Cauda Equina Syndrome with Bowel or Bladder Compromise—60% whole-person impairment
8. Category VIII: Paraplegia, Total Loss of Lower-Extremity Function—75% whole-person impairment

---

[31] *Id.*

When long-tract signs are present in the lower extremities or bowel and bladder functions are compromised, then the estimates for impairments of the spine and upper extremities for Categories II through V should be combined by use of the Combined Values Chart,[32] with estimates from cervicothoracic Categories VI through VII for those involvements. If there are injury-related bowel or bladder symptoms without verifiable lower extremity symptoms, the physician should estimate the bowel and bladder impairment according to the criteria in the *Guides* chapters on urinary, reproductive, and digestive systems, and combine the bladder and bowel impairment percentages with an impairment percentage from one of the cervicothoracic impairment Categories of II through V. However, if there is lower extremity neurologic compromise throughout with the involvement of bowel or bladder loss of function, the physician should place the patient in Category V or VI. Cauda equina syndrome or cauda equina compression syndrome results in motor weakness, bowel or bladder dysfunction, incontinence or sexual dysfunction as the result of the underlying compression of the cauda equina or due to an accidental injection of anesthetic directly into the nerve substance, causing similar symptomatology.

The AMA *Guides* provides some examples of how the categories fit. For example, a 28-year-old athlete had a C5 vertebral body fracture with almost 50 percent compression and had radicular pain in the left arm, which was verified as a C6 level radiculopathy by positive sharp waves in three arm muscles. The man underwent a three-level posterior fusion. After his condition became stable, he had no bladder symptoms, but was unable to walk without leg braces. The patient's impairment was in cervicothoracic Category III and also in Category VI because of the lower extremity weakness. The Category III impairment of 15 percent would be *combined* with a 40 percent Category IV impairment representing lower extremity weakness. Thus, the impairment would be a 49 percent whole-person impairment combining the 15 percent with the 40 percent by use of the Combined Values Chart.[33]

A second example describes a 60-year-old woman, after a motor vehicle crash, who had bilateral facet dislocation at the C4 and C5 levels and had loss of C5 and C6 function in the upper extremity, no bowel or bladder symptoms, some remaining motor function of the lower extremities, and an inability to walk. The cervicothoracic Category V impairment of 35 percent is *combined* with 75 percent, which represents the Category VIII long-tract signs, that is, the inability to walk. The impairment is as follows: 84 percent whole-person impairment combining the 35 percent with the 75 percent, again with reference to the Combined Values Chart.

Similarly, the thoracolumbar spine again has eight categories relating to impairment that are listed below. For patients with severe long-tract impairment or paraplegia, impairment estimates for thoracolumbar Categories II through IV should be combined with the impairment estimates for the involvement of the lower extremities. This impairment must be combined with the impairment

---

[32] *Guides* at 322.

[33] *Id.* at 105.

percentage from the most appropriate thoracolumbar impairment category of II through IV.[34] The *Guides* provides that if the thoracolumbar injury-related bowel or bladder symptoms exist without verifiable lower extremity involvement, then estimates for bowel and bladder impairments from the chapters on urinary, reproductive, and adjustive systems should be combined by use of the Combined Values Chart with the impairment percentage from one of the thoracolumbar Categories II through IV. However, if the patient has lower extremity compromise without involvement of the bowel or bladder, the patient should be placed in Category V or VI. The *Guides* provides for eight categories to analyze thoracolumbar spine impairment as follows:

1. Category I: Complaints or Symptoms—0% whole-person impairment
2. Category II: Minor Impairment—5% whole-person impairment
3. Category III: Radiculopathy—15% whole-person impairment
4. Category IV: Loss of Motion Segment Integrity or Multilevel Neurologic Compromise—20% whole-person impairment
5. Category V: Radiculopathy and Loss of Motion Segment Integrity—25% whole-person impairment
6. Category VI: Cauda Equina Syndrome without Bowel or Bladder Impairment—35% whole-person impairment
7. Category VII: Cauda Equina Syndrome with Bowel or Bladder Impairment—55% whole-person impairment
8. Category VIII: Paraplegia—70% whole-person impairment

The *Guides* provides an example of an 18-year-old man who fell from a roof, and suffered a T12 burst fracture. At maximum improvement, the man's signs and symptoms indicated that he had a neurologic impairment of the lower legs, meeting thoracolumbar Category III criteria, and bladder and bowel impairment, meeting thoracolumbar Category VII impairment. The impairment percentage for the radicular signs would be combined with that for the cauda equina syndrome. Thus, he has a 15 percent impairment for thoracolumbar Category III or IIIB as shown on Table 74,[35] combined with a 55 percent thoracolumbar Category VII, Table 74, which charts out at 62 percent from the Combined Values Chart.

Injuries to the spinal cord not related to the above (that is, disorders of nerve impulse transmission controlling motor, sensory, or visceral functions) are estimated according to the effects on daily activities and the results of neurologic examination and testing.[36] These impairments may relate to station and gait (the ability to stand and walk), use of the upper extremities, respiration, urinary bladder function, anorectal function, and sexual function. The AMA *Guides* suggests that documentation of these deficiencies should include, if possible,

---

[34] *Id.* at 111.

[35] *Id.*

[36] *Id.* § 4.9 at 147.

description of the spinal root(s), the portion of the plexus and peripheral nerves that are involved.[37] Thus, the physician would document the extent of the loss of function due to sensory deficit pain or discomfort, muscular strength and control, and alteration of the autonomic nervous system.

Several tables from the *Guides* address the issue of the level of impairment. **Table 3–2** illustrates the maximum upper extremity impairment due to unilateral sensory or motor deficits of individual spinal nerves or to combined deficits (*Guides,* Table 13). **Table 3–3** shows maximum upper extremity impairments due to unilateral sensory or motor deficits of brachial plexus, or to combined deficits (*Guides,* Table 14). **Table 3–4** shows maximum upper extremity impairments due to unilateral sensory or motor deficits or combined deficits of the major peripheral nerves (*Guides,* Table 15). **Table 3–5** shows upper extremity impairments due to entrapment neuropathy (*Guides,* Table 16). **Table 3–6** illustrates impairment of upper extremity due to peripheral vascular disease (*Guides,* Table 17). **Table 3–7** shows impairment values for digits, hand, upper extremity, and the whole person for disorders of specific joints (*Guides,* Table 18). **Table 3–8** shows impairment from joint crepitation (*Guides,* Table 19).

---

[37] *Id.* at 150.

Table 3–2

Maximum Upper Extremity Impairment Due to Unilateral Sensory or Motor Deficits of Individual Spinal Nerves or to Combined Deficits

Maximum % upper extremity impairment*

Spinal nerve	Due to sensory deficit or pain†	Due to motor deficit‡	Due to *combined* motor and sensory deficits
C5	5	30	34
C6	8	35	40
C7	5	35	38
C8	5	45	48
T1	5	20	24

Source: *Guides to the Evaluation of Permanent Impairment,* 4th ed., American Medical Ass'n, ©1993. Reprinted by permission.

* See Table 3 (p. 20) to convert upper extremity impairments to whole-person impairments.

† See Table 11a (p. 48) to grade impairment from loss of function due to sensory deficit or pain.

‡ See Table 12a (p. 49) to grade impairment from loss of function due to motor deficit.

Table 3–3

Maximum Upper Extremity Impairments Due to Unilateral Sensory or Motor Deficits of Brachial Plexus, or to Combined Deficits

Maximum % upper extremity impairment*

	Due to sensory deficit or pain†	Due to motor deficit‡	Due to *combined* motor and sensory deficits
Brachial plexus (C5 through C8, T1)	100	100	100
Upper trunk (C5, C6), Erb-Duchenne	25	75	81
Middle trunk (C7)	5	35	38
Lower trunk (C8, T1) Dejerine-Klumpke	20	70	76

Source: *Guides to the Evaluation of Permanent Impairment,* 4th ed., American Medical Ass'n, ©1993. Reprinted by permission.
* See Table 3 (p. 20) for converting upper extremity impairments to whole-person impairments.
† See Table 11a (p. 48) to grade impairment from loss of function due to sensory deficit or pain.
‡ See Table 12a (p. 49) to grade impairment from loss of function due to motor deficit.

Table 3–4

Maximum Upper Extremity Impairments Due to Unilateral Sensory or Motor Deficits or Combined Deficits of the Major Peripheral Nerves

Nerve	Maximum % upper extremity impairment*		
	Due to sensory deficit or pain†	Due to motor deficit‡	Due to *combined* motor and sensory deficits
Pectorals (Medial and lateral)	0	5	5
Axillary	5	35	38
Dorsal scapular	0	5	5
Long thoracic	0	15	1
Medial antebrachial cutaneous	5	0	5
Medial brachial cutaneous	5	0	5
Median (above midforearm)	38	44	65
Median (anterior interosseous branch)	0	15	15
Median (below midforearm)	38	10	44
Radial palmar digital of thumb	7	0	7
Ulnar palmar digital of thumb	11	0	11
Radial palmar digital of index finger	5	0	5
Ulnar palmar digital of index finger	4	0	4
Radial palmar digital of middle finger	5	0	5
Ulnar palmar digital of middle finger	4	0	4
Radial palmar digital of ring finger	2	0	2
Musculocutaneous	5	25	29
Radial (upper arm with loss of triceps)	5	42	45
Radial (elbow with sparing of triceps)	5	35	38

Table 3–4
(continued)

Nerve	Maximum % upper extremity impairment* Due to sensory deficit or pain†	Due to motor deficit‡	Due to *combined* motor and sensory deficits
Subscapulars (upper and lower)	0	5	5
Suprascapular	5	16	20
Thoracodorsal	0	10	10
Ulnar (above midforearm)	7	46	50
Ulnar (below midforearm)	7	35	40
Ulnar palmar digital of ring finger	2	0	2
Radial palmar digital of little finger	2	0	2
Ulnar palmar digital of little finger	3	0	3

Source: *Guides to the Evaluation of Permanent Impairment,* 4th ed., American Medical Ass'n, ©1993. Reprinted by permission.
* See Table 3 (p. 20) to convert upper extremity impairments to whole-person impairments.
† See Table 11a (p. 48) to grade impairment from loss of function due to sensory deficit or pain.
‡ See Table 12a (p. 49) to grade impairment from loss of function due to motor deficit.

Table 3–5

Upper Extremity Impairment Due to Entrapment Neuropathy

Entrapped nerve	Entrapment site	Degree of severity and % upper extremity impairment Mild	Moderate	Severe
Suprascapular		5	10	20
Axillary		10	20	38
Radial	Upper arm	15	25	45
Posterior interosseous	Forearm	10	20	35
Median	Elbow	15	35	55
Anterior interosseous	Proximal forearm	5	10	15
Median	Wrist	10	20	40
Ulnar	Elbow	10	30	50
Ulnar	Wrist	10	30	40

Source: *Guides to the Evaluation of Permanent Impairment,* 4th ed., American Medical Ass'n, ©1993. Reprinted by permission.

Table 3–6

Impairment of Upper Extremity Due to Peripheral Vascular Disease

Symptoms	Upper Extremity impairment % Class 1 (0%-9%)	Class 2 (10%-39%)	Class 3 (40%-69%)	Class 4 (70%-89%)	Class 5 (90%-100%)
Claudication	None	Intermittent with severe use	Intermittent with moderate use	Intermittent with mild use	
Pain at rest	None	None	None	Intermittent	Severe and constant
Edema	Transient	Persistent and moderate	Marked	Marked	Marked
Elastic support control		Incomplete	Partial	None	None
Signs of vascular damage	Loss of pulses; minimal loss of subcutaneous tissue of fingertips; arterial calcifications on roentgenogram; asymptomatic dilation of veins or arteries not requiring surgery; no decreased activity	Healed painless amputation stump of one digit with persistent vascular disease or healed ulcer	Healed amputation stump of two or more digits with persistent vascular disease or superficial ulceration	Amputation of two or more digits of each extremity, or amputation at or above wrist of one extremity, with persistent widespread or deep ulceration of one extremity	Amputation of all digits or amputation at or above the wrist of each extremity, with persistent vascular disease or widespread or deep ulcerations of both extremities
Raynaud's phenomenon	At less than 0°C (32°F)	At less than 4°C (39°F)	At less than 10°C (50°F)	At less than 15°C (59°F)	At less than 20°C (68°F)
Medication control	Good	Good	Partial	Partial	Poor

Source: *Guides to the Evaluation of Permanent Impairment,* 4th ed., American Medical Ass'n, ©1993. Reprinted by permission.

Table 3–7

Impairment Values for Digits, Hand, Upper Extremity, and the Whole Person for Disorders of Specific Joints

Units and joints	% Impairment of Unit	Hand	Upper extremity	Whole person
Shoulder				
Glenohumeral	—	—	60	36
Acromioclavicular	—	—	25	15
Elbow				
Entire elbow	—	—	70	42
Ulnohumeral	—	—	50	30
Proximal radioulnar	—	—	20	12
Wrist				
Entire wrist	—	—	60	36
Radiocarpal	—	—	40	24
Distal radioulnar	—	—	20	12
Proximal carpal row	—	—	30	18
Entire hand	—	100	90	54
Thumb				
Entire thumb	100	40	36	22
Carpometacarpal	75	30	27	16
Metacarpophalangeal	10	4	4	2
Interphalangeal	15	6	5	3
Index and middle				
Entire finger	100	20	18	11
Metacarpophalangeal	100	20	18	11
Proximal interphalangeal	80	16	14	8
Distal interphalangeal	45	9	8	5
Ring or little				
Entire finger	100	10	9	5
Metacarpophalangeal	100	10	9	5
Proximal interphalangeal	80	8	7	4
Distal interphalangeal	45	4	4	2

Source: *Guides to the Evaluation of Permanent Impairment,* 4th ed., American Medical Ass'n, ©1993. Reprinted by permission.

Table 3–8

Impairment from Joint Crepitation*

Crepitation severity	% Joint impairment†
Mild: inconstant during active range of motion	10
Moderate: constant during active range of motion	20
Severe: constant during passive range of motion	30

Source: *Guides to the Evaluation of Permanent Impairment,* 4th ed., American Medical Ass'n, ©1993. Reprinted by permission.
* Modified from Swanson, AB, Mays, JD, Yamauchi, Y", p. 1011, Fig. 9.
† Multiply by the relative value of the joint (Table 18, p. 58) to determine the joint crepitation impairment percent.

The impairment estimates for each neurologic deficit are determined by combining the motor and sensory impairment by means of the Combined Values Chart.

The *Guides* suggests that conversion of an extremity impairment to a whole-person impairment is made only after all impairments involving that extremity have been combined, and gives the example of those due to loss of motion, vascular disorders, and neurologic deficits. If more than one extremity is involved, each extremity impairment is determined separately, and each converts to a whole-person impairment that is then combined using the Combined Values Chart.

Table 3–9 is a copy of AMA *Guides* Table 20 concerning joint impairment. **Table 3–10** is a copy of AMA *Guides* Table 21 concerning digit impairment.

Table 3–9

Impairment from Synovial Hypertrophy*

Description of joint swelling	% joint impairment†
Mild: visibly apparent	10
Moderate: palpably apparent	20
Severe: greater than 10% increase in size	30

Source: *Guides to the Evaluation of Permanent Impairment,* 4th ed., American Medical Ass'n, ©1993. Reprinted by permission.
* Modified from Swanson, AB, Mays, JD, Yamauchi, Y", p. 1011, Fig. 9.
† Multiply by the relative value for the joint (Table 18, p. 58) to determine the joint impairment.

Table 3–10

Impairment from Digital Ulnar or Radial Deviation*

Deviation	% Digit Impairment†
Mild: less than 10°	10
Moderate: 10° through 30°	20
Severe: Greater than 30°	30

Source: *Guides to the Evaluation of Permanent Impairment,* 4th ed., American Medical Ass'n, ©1993. Reprinted by permission.
* Modified from Swanson, AB, Mays, JD, Yamauchi, Y", p. 1011, Fig. 9.
† Multiply by the relative value of the digit (Table 18, p. 58) to determine the digit impairment.

§ 3.18 Report of Medical Evaluation

The Report of Medical Evaluation[38] in **Figure 3–1** and the history of spine complaint in **Figure 3–2** tie it all together. These provide an excellent framework for the direct examination of the treating physician, surgeon, or physiatrist. Use of this outline, including the current Activities of Daily Living Chart and the previous Activities of Daily Living Chart may help everyone from the medical care provider to the lawyer to the jury, or claims adjuster, to understand the etiology, functional relation, and practical aspects of someone's spinal cord injury in a fashion that may enable them to appreciate the full extent of the injury.

[38] *Guides,* Fig. 61 at 11–12.

Report of Medical Evaluation (Permanent Medical Impairment)

To:

Re:

Case number:

Report date:

Onset of injury or illness:

1. Medical history		Yes	No
a. Medical office records	Reviewed		
	Enclosed		
b. Hospital records	Reviewed		
	Enclosed		
c. From other source (describe)			
d. From patient			

2. Clinical evaluation		Yes	No
a. Physical examination	Reports enclosed		
b. Laboratory tests	Reports enclosed		
c. Special tests and diagnostic procedures	Reports enclosed		
d. Specialist's evaluation	Reports enclosed		

3. Diagnoses
a.
b.
c.
d.

4. Stability of the medical condition	Yes	No
a. The clinical condition is stabilized and not likely to improve with surgical intervention or active medical treatment; medical maintenance care only is warranted.		
b. The degree of impairment is not likely to change substantially within the next year.		
c. The patient is not likely to suffer sudden or subtle incapacitation.		

Figure 3–1. Report of medical evaluation.

Source: *Guides to the Evaluation of Permanent Impairment,* 4th ed., American Medical Ass'n, © 1993. Reprinted by permission.

Report of Medical Evaluation (Permanent Medical Impairment) Page 2

5. Other analyses

a. Explain briefly the impact(s) of the medical condition(s) on the patient's activities of daily living, including occupation (see Chapter 1 and Glossary, p. 315).

List types of daily activities affected:

1.

2.

3.

4.

5.

6.

b. Is there a medical reason to believe the patient is likely to suffer injury, harm, or further medical impairment by engaging in usual activities of living or other activities necessary to meet personal, social, or occupational demands? Explain briefly.

_____Yes No_____

c. Is there a medical reason to believe restrictions, accommodations, or assistive devices are necessary to help the patient carry out usual activities or meet personal, social, and occupational demands? If so, briefly describe them and explain their therapeutic, risk-avoidance, or other kind of value.

_____Yes No_____

6. Impairment evaluation according to *Guides*–Attach a complete report of findings and narrative comments for each body part or system. Each organ system impairment estimate should be expressed in terms of percent impairment of the whole person.

Body part or system	Chapter No.	Table No.	% Impairment of the whole person
a.			
b.			
c.			
d.			

7. Final estimated whole-person impairment: _______________%.

8. _____ This patient has been under my care from _______________ to _______________.

_____ I have not provided care for this patient. I have seen this patient _______ time(s) for the purpose of evaluating medical impairment.

9. I (do) (do not) believe there is inconsistency among the history, physical examination, laboratory finding, and other studies (cross out the nonapplicable verb phrase). If an inconsistency exists, explain it in writing.

_______________________________________, MD
(Signature)

_______________________________________ _______________
(Print name) (Date)

Figure 3–1. *(continued)*

Figure 61. History of Spine Complaint.

Name:____________ Soc. Sec. No.:____________ Date:____________

1. History of impairment or injury

Describe all symptoms, location, frequency of occurrence, duration, quality with particular attention to time and circumstances of onset, course of condition, treatment, treatment response; note presence of pain, numbness, weakness, stiffness:

2. Condition limits the patient or interferes with which daily activities?

List the activities. What activities has the patient reduced or given up? Describe them:

3. Patient's perceptions

a. How long at one time and over an 8-hour period can the patient do the following without serious discomfort? (Express in terms of half-hours or hours and note the unit used.)

Sit____________ Walk____________

Stand____________

b. How many pounds can the patient lift at frequent intervals?____________

Occasionally?____________

4. Present symptoms

a. Starting date of present symptoms____________.

b. How long have symptoms been the same? If they are changing, describe how.

c. Previous back or neck problems or surgeries (give dates):

1.____________

2.____________

3.____________

4.____________

Figure 3–2. History of spine complaint.

Source: *Guides to the Evaluation of Permanent Impairment,* 4th ed., American Medical Ass'n, © 1993. Reprinted by permission.

d. Special tests or procedures:

Type	Date	Results

e. What exercises does the patient usually do to stay physically fit or "in shape?"

Type	Duration	To what heart rate minimum?	Freq./wk.

f. Usual daily activities and postures (check those that apply):

Sit ____________ Walk ____________

Stand ____________ Lift ____________ Max. no. lb. ____________

Other (describe) ____________

____

____

5. Patient's understanding of reason for this impairment evaluation:

____

____

____

____

____

History taken by: ____________
(print name)

Figure 3–2. *(continued)*

CHAPTER 4

OVERVIEW OF SPINAL CORD INJURY EPIDEMIOLOGY AND LONG-TERM OUTCOMES

Michael J. DeVivo

OVERVIEW

§ 4.1 Introduction

Spinal cord injury (SCI) has been the subject of extensive demographic and epidemiologic research during the past two decades. Much of what is known today about the epidemiology of SCI comes from the work of the Model Regional SCI Systems of Care funded by the National Institute on Disability and Rehabilitation Research in the United States Department of Education. The first model system was established in Phoenix, Arizona in 1970, and was quickly followed by several more located throughout the United States. A comprehensive national SCI database was established in Phoenix shortly thereafter to serve as the repository for prospectively collected standardized information on persons treated at these model systems. In 1983, this database was moved to the National Spinal Cord Injury Statistical Center (NSCISC) at the University of Alabama at Birmingham where it remains to this date. This database contains information on the injury itself, as well as the characteristics of persons who are injured, their acute care and rehabilitation experiences, their status at the time of discharge from rehabilitation, and their status at routine annual follow-up examinations. Over the years, three books have been published containing detailed information from this database, the latest in 1995.[1]

Recently, SCI has become a reportable condition in a number of states where SCI registries have been established, including but not limited to Arkansas, Colorado, Florida, Georgia, Iowa, Louisiana, Michigan, Mississippi, New Jersey, New York, Oklahoma, Utah, Virginia, and West Virginia. Initial results on the incidence, demographics, and causes of SCI from several states have now been published.[2] These registries have the advantage of being unbiased because they are population-based; however, they usually contain only limited information about each case and often do not contain any follow-up data beyond initial hospital discharge. Where follow-up data do exist, the data will only cover the first few years after injury because the registries have not been in existence for that long. However, the registries may provide useful information about similar cases in a particular geographic location. Nonetheless, given the limitations of current registry data for litigation purposes, in most instances the statistics presented herein will be derived from the NSCISC database. A more complete discussion of differences between the NSCISC database and state registry information is contained in the latest book from the model systems.[3]

§ 4.2 Incidence and Prevalence

There are no recent national studies of the incidence of SCI (number of new cases occurring each year) in the United States. However, based on regional

---

[1] Spinal Cord Injury: Clinical Outcomes from the Model Systems (S. Stover et al. eds., 1995); Univ. of Ala. at Birmingham, Spinal Cord Injury: The Facts and Figures (S. Stover and P. Fine eds., 1982); Good Samaritan Med. Ctr., Phoenix, Ariz., Spinal Cord Injury Statistics: Experience of the Regional Spinal Cord Injury Systems (J. Young et al. eds., 1982).

[2] C. Price et al., *Epidemiology of Traumatic Spinal Cord Injury and Acute Hospitalization and Rehabilitation Charges for Spinal Cord Injuries in Oklahoma,* 139 Am. J. Epidemiology 39–42 (1994); D. Thurman et al., *Surveillance of Spinal Cord Injuries in Utah,* 32 Paraplegia 666–68 (1994); B. Woodruff & R. Baron, *A Description of Nonfatal Spinal Cord Injury Using a Hospital-based Registry,* 10 Am. J. Preventive Med. 11–12 (1994); P. Acton et al., *Traumatic Spinal Cord Injury in Arkansas, 1980 to 1989,* 74 Archives Physical Med. & Rehabilitation 1037–38 (1993); K. Gerhart, *Spinal Cord Injury Outcomes in a Population-based Sample,* 31 J. Trauma 1530–31 (1991).

[3] B. Go et al., Spinal Cord Injury: Clinical Outcomes from the Model Systems 26–50 (S. Stover et al. eds., 1995).

studies and state registries, it appears that the incidence of SCI is approximately 10,000 new cases in the United States each year.[4] This figure does not include an estimated 5000 additional persons who die at the scene of the injury-producing event.[5] The prevalence of SCI (number of persons who are alive today and who have such injuries) is approximately 200,000 persons.[6] Moreover, the prevalence of SCI is increasing as a result of reduced mortality rates.

§ 4.3 Causes of SCI

Overall, the leading cause of SCI has been automobile crashes, resulting in 35.8 percent of all new SCI cases since the inception of the NSCISC database in 1973. Falls have ranked second (18.1 percent), followed by gunshot wounds (14.6 percent), diving incidents (8.5 percent), motorcycle crashes (6.1 percent), and being hit by a falling or flying object (3.7 percent). No other cause accounts for more than 1 percent of SCI cases. A complete listing of causes of SCI and their frequencies is contained in the latest book from the model systems.[7]

Over the past 20 years, there has been a trend toward increasing percentages of spinal cord injuries occurring as a result of acts of violence (gunshots, stabs, person to person contact, and explosions). From 1973 to 1977, acts of violence were the cause of only 13.8 percent of spinal cord injuries. However, from 1990 to 1994, acts of violence caused 30.4 percent of all spinal cord injuries enrolled in the NSCISC database.[8] Conversely, motor vehicle crashes caused 45.7 percent of spinal cord injuries from 1973 to 1977, but only 35.0 percent from 1990 to 1994, and sports-related spinal cord injuries decreased from 14.8 percent to 8.1 percent during that same time.

---

[4] C. Price et al., *Epidemiology of Traumatic Spinal Cord Injury and Acute Hospitalization and Rehabilitation Charges for Spinal Cord Injuries in Oklahoma,* 139 Am. J. Epidemiology 39–42 (1994); D. Thurman et al., *Surveillance of Spinal Cord Injuries in Utah,* 32 Paraplegia 666–68 (1994); B. Woodruff & R. Baron, *A Description of Nonfatal Spinal Cord Injury Using a Hospital-based Registry,* 10 Am. J. Preventive Med. 11–12 (1994); P. Acton et al., *Traumatic Spinal Cord Injury in Arkansas, 1980 to 1989,* 74 Archives of Physical Med. & Rehabilitation 1037–38 (1993); K. Gerhart, *Spinal Cord Injury Outcomes in a Population-based sample,* 31 J. of Trauma 1530–31 (1991); J. Kraus et al., *Incidence of Traumatic Spinal Cord Lesions,* 28 J. Chronic Disease 476–78 (1975).

[5] J. Kraus et al., *Incidence of Traumatic Spinal Cord Lesions,* 28 J. Chronic Disease 476–78 (1975).

[6] C. Harvey, *New Estimates of Traumatic SCI Prevalence: a Survey-based Approach,* 28 Paraplegia 540 (1990); M. DeVivo, *Prevalence of Spinal Cord Injury: A Reestimation Employing Life Table Techniques,* 37 Archives Neurology (1980).

[7] B. Go et al., Spinal Cord Injury: Clinical Outcomes from the Model Systems 36 (S. Stover et al. eds., 1995).

[8] National Spinal Cord Injury Statistical Ctr., Univ. of Ala. at Birmingham, Spinal Cord Injury: Facts and Figures at a Glance (1995).

Unfortunately, interpreting these proportional trends is not as simple as it seems. For example, an increase in the percentage of spinal cord injuries caused by acts of violence could result from a decrease in the actual number of violence-related injuries as long as other causes were decreasing at an even faster rate. However, it is more likely that the number of injuries caused by acts of violence is in fact increasing. It is not possible to distinguish between these or other competing hypotheses because the NSCISC database is neither all-inclusive nor population-based. Ultimately, trends in underlying incidence rates determined from the state registries will resolve this important question.

Although further details concerning the exact nature of the injury-producing events are not contained in the NSCISC database, this information is occasionally available from other published studies. For example, P. Fine and associates reported a detailed accounting of a series of 48 spinal cord injuries resulting from gunshot wounds, including the exact nature of each event as well as an epidemiologic profile of the entire series.[9] J. Kraus and associates and E. Wigglesworth have reported extensive analyses of neurologic outcomes as well as vehicle and crash factors in motor vehicle-related spinal cord injuries.[10] Information on alcohol and drug involvement as well as safety belt usage at the time of injury has also recently been reported from several state registries.[11]

§ 4.4 Epidemiology of SCI

Since 1973, 58.5 percent of all spinal cord injuries occurred between the ages of 16 and 30, with 21.1 percent between ages 31 and 45, 9.7 percent between ages 46 and 60, 4.9 percent between ages 61 and 75, 4.5 percent before age 16, and 1.3 percent after age 75. The mean (arithmetic average) age at time of SCI is approximately 31, and the median (50th percentile) age is 26.[12] Motor vehicle crashes are the leading cause of SCI among younger persons, while falls are

[9] P. Fine et al., *Gunshot Wounds of the Spinal Cord: a Survey of Literature and Epidemiologic Study of 48 Lesions in Alabama,* 13 Ala. J. Med. Sci. 176–79 (1976).

[10] E. Wigglesworth, *Motor Vehicle Crashes and Spinal Injury,* 30 Paraplegia 544–46 (1992); J. Kraus et al., *Neurologic Outcome and Vehicle and Crash Factors in Motor Vehicle Related Spinal Cord Injuries,* 1 Neuroepidemiology 226–34 (1982).

[11] C. Price et al., *Epidemiology of Traumatic Spinal Cord Injury and Acute Hospitalization and Rehabilitation Charges for Spinal Cord Injuries in Oklahoma,* 139 Am. J. Epidemiology 40–42 (1994); D. Thurman et al., *Surveillance of Spinal Cord Injuries in Utah,* 32 Paraplegia 666 (1994); B. Woodruff & R. Baron, *A Description of Nonfatal Spinal Cord Injury Using a Hospital-based Registry,* 10 Am. J. Preventive Med. 12 (1994); P. Acton et al., *Traumatic Spinal Cord Injury in Arkansas, 1980 to 1989,* 74 Archives Physical Med. & Rehabilitation 1037–38 (1993); K. Gerhart, *Spinal Cord Injury Outcomes in a Population-based Sample,* 31 J. Trauma 1530 (1991).

[12] B. Go et al., Spinal Cord Injury: Clinical Outcomes from the Model Systems 27 (S. Stover et al. eds., 1995).

the leading cause among the elderly. The percentages of SCI due to both sports and acts of violence decrease dramatically with advancing age.

Approximately 82 percent of persons with SCI are men. Motor vehicle crashes are the leading cause of SCI among both men (41.9 percent) and women (56.3 percent).[13]

Nonwhites are at higher risk for SCI than whites. Since 1990, 28.3 percent of persons enrolled in the NSCISC database have been African American.[14] However, according to the 1990 United States census, only 12.1 percent of persons in the general population are African American. Since 1990, acts of violence have caused approximately 46 percent of all spinal cord injuries that occurred among African Americans, approximately 52 percent of all spinal cord injuries that occurred among Hispanics, but only about 8 percent that occurred among whites.[15]

Spinal cord injuries occur in cycles, with the fewest injuries occurring in February, followed by a steady increase until July and a steady decrease until the next February. Twenty percent of spinal cord injuries occur on Saturday, followed by 18.6 percent on Sunday, and 14.5 percent on Friday. The fewest spinal cord injuries occur on Tuesdays and Wednesdays.[16]

Since spinal cord injuries are the result of traumatic physical impact (car crashes, gunshot wounds, and so forth), it is not surprising that they are often accompanied by other associated injuries. These associated injuries are sometimes quite severe and can have long-term consequences affecting functional capabilities. When SCI is caused by a motor vehicle crash, there is a concomitant loss of consciousness at least briefly in 42.5 percent of cases, a relatively severe associated head injury in 18.4 percent of cases, at least one nonvertebral fracture in 39.7 percent of cases, and a traumatic pneumothorax/hemothorax in 16.6 percent of cases.[17] Other causes of SCI are generally associated with fewer concomitant injuries.

The most common injury level is C5 (15.7 percent), followed by C4 (12.7 percent), C6 (12.6 percent), T12 (7.6 percent), C7 (6.3 percent), and L1 (4.8 percent). Overall, 52.9 percent of persons enrolled in the NSCISC database have tetraplegia from cervical (neck) injuries, while 46.2 percent are classified as having paraplegia from either thoracic, lumbar, or sacral (chest or back) injuries. The remaining 0.9 percent experience complete neurologic recovery by the time of discharge from rehabilitation. Spinal cord injuries are almost equally divided

[13] *Id.* at 28 and 39.

[14] National Spinal Cord Injury Statistical Ctr., Univ. of Ala. at Birmingham, Spinal Cord Injury: Facts and Figures at a Glance (1995).

[15] T. Elliott et al., *Spinal Cord Injury Model Systems of Care: the Legacy and the Promise,* 4 NeuroRehabilitation 87 (1994).

[16] B. Go et al., Spinal Cord Injury: Clinical Outcomes from the Model Systems 41–42 (S. Stover et al. eds., 1995).

[17] *Id.* at 44.

between those that are neurologically complete (51.7 percent), and those that have some residual neurologic sparing below the injury level and are classified as incomplete (48.3 percent).[18] Additional information on neurologic level and extent of SCI appears in the chapters on basic anatomy and classification of spinal cord injuries.

LONG-TERM CONSEQUENCES OF SCI

§ 4.5 Place of Residence

Historically, many persons with SCI were forced to live out the remainder of their lives in institutional settings such as nursing homes. Today, however, 94.1 percent of all persons with SCI who are discharged from a model system are sent to a private noninstitutional residence within the community (in most cases their home before injury). Four percent are discharged to nursing homes, 1.5 percent are discharged to another hospital, and 0.4 percent are discharged to other locations. Moreover, 98 percent of persons who are still alive 10 years after injury continue to reside in private residences within the community.[19] Over age 60, however, the likelihood of nursing home residence begins to rise sharply, reaching 22 percent in the over-75 age group.[20]

§ 4.6 Rehospitalization

Since 1973, rehospitalization rates for treatment of secondary medical complications have been relatively high among persons with spinal cord injuries, ranging from 398 hospitalizations per 1000 persons per year for the 16-to-45 age group to 535 hospitalizations per 1000 persons per year for persons over the age of 75.[21] More recently, however, rehospitalization rates and lengths of stay per rehospitalization have been declining due to improved methods of prevention and management of secondary medical complications as well as the changing nature of health care cost reimbursement practices.[22] Although several statistically significant predictors of

---

[18] *Id.* at 45–48.

[19] M. DeVivo et al., *Spinal Cord Injury: Rehabilitation Adds Life to Years,* 154 W.J. Med. 604 (1991).

[20] M. DeVivo et al., *A Cross-sectional Study of the Relationship between Age and Current Health Status for Persons with Spinal Cord Injuries,* 30 Paraplegia 823–24 (1992).

[21] *Id.*

[22] M. DeVivo et al., Spinal Cord Injury: Clinical Outcomes from the Model Systems 243–44 (S. Stover et al. eds., 1995); C. Ivie III & M. DeVivo, *Predicting Unplanned Hospitalizations in Persons with Spinal Cord Injury,* 75 Archives Physical Med. & Rehabilitation 1184–86 (1994).

the likelihood of rehospitalization for individuals have been identified, the resulting predictive models are still not very accurate.[23] Therefore, the individual's own postinjury pretrial experience is probably the best predictor of future rehospitalization rate. The usual causes of rehospitalization are respiratory complications, urinary tract complications, and decubitus ulcers.

§ 4.7 Postinjury Employment and Indirect Costs

Although many persons with SCI obtain employment after injury, most remain unemployed indefinitely.[24] Those who return to work within the first year after injury almost always return to the same job with the same employer they had prior to injury. After the first year, those who become employed almost always obtain a different type of job with a different employer, often for less money than they were making prior to injury.[25] Moreover, those who do obtain postinjury employment often have difficulty sustaining that employment.[26]

Many predictive factors are associated with increased likelihood of becoming employed after SCI. These include younger age, being male, being white, being functionally independent and ambulatory, having strong motivation, having a good preinjury work history, being a college graduate, and having sufficient social support.[27] Reasons for the low postinjury employment rate include inaccessible workplaces, lack of accessible transportation, negative attitudes of employers, low self-expectations, and strong economic disincentives including potential loss of compensation and medical benefits.[28]

---

[23] C. Ivie III & M. DeVivo, *Predicting Unplanned Hospitalizations in Persons with Spinal Cord Injury,* 75 Archives Physical Med. Rehabilitation 1184–86 (1994).

[24] M. DeVivo et al., Spinal Cord Injury: Clinical Outcomes from the Model Systems 260–63 (S. Stover et al. eds., 1995); M. James et al., *Postinjury Employment Outcomes among African-American and White Persons with Spinal Cord Injury,* 38 Rehabilitation Psychology 154–58 (1993); J. Kraus, *Employment after Spinal Cord Injury,* 73 Archives Physical Med. Rehabilitation 164–67 (1992); M. DeVivo et al., *Spinal Cord Injury: Rehabilitation Adds Life to Years,* 154 W.J. Med. 605 (1991); M. Berkowitz et al., The Economic Consequences of Traumatic Spinal Cord Injury 121–29 (1992); M. DeVivo et al., *Employment after Spinal Cord Injury,* 68 Archives Physical Med. & Rehabilitation 494–97 (1987).

[25] M. DeVivo et al., Spinal Cord Injury: Clinical Outcomes from the Model Systems 259 (S. Stover et al. eds., 1995).

[26] A. El Ghatit & R. Hanson, *Variables Associated with Obtaining and Sustaining Employment among Spinal Cord Injured Males: Follow-up of 760 Veterans,* 31 J. Chronic Disease 364–68 (1978).

[27] M. DeVivo et al., Spinal Cord Injury: Clinical Outcomes from the Model Systems 260–63 (S. Stover et al. eds., 1995); S. McShane & J. Karp, *Employment Following Spinal Cord Injury; a Covariance Structure Analysis,* 38 Rehabilitation Psychology 33–35 (1993); M. DeVivo et al., *Employment after Spinal Cord Injury,* 68 Archives Physical Med. Rehabilitation 495–96 (1987).

[28] C. Britell, *Why Aren't They Working?,* 14 J. Am. Paraplegia Soc'y 1–2 (1991); S. Better et al., *Disability Benefits as Disincentives to Rehabilitation,* 57 Milbank Memorial Fund Q. 416–422 (1979); R. Walls et al., *Negative Incentives to Rehabilitation,* Rehabilitation Literature 143–50 (1977).

Additional information on postinjury employment prospects is contained in the vocational analysis chapter, **Chapter 11.**

Estimates of the average present value of indirect costs associated with lost wages and fringe benefits as well as methodologies for assessing these losses on an individual basis are available using the human capital approach.[29] For example, in 1992 dollars, M. DeVivo and associates estimated the value of average annual lost wages and fringe benefits for persons with SCI to be $37,876 from the time of injury until age 65. These estimates do not include any determination of social costs and lifestyle impacts. Alternative measures of indirect losses based on willingness to pay could be developed that would include these social costs; however, this approach has several major methodological limitations, particularly when applied to SCI, and therefore, is not often used to project future losses after SCI.[30]

It is particularly difficult to estimate indirect losses for children with no work history. Given the typical age at which many of these injuries occur, educational plans are often interrupted and not subsequently completed. M. Berkowitz and associates reported that the educational plans of 41 percent of persons in their study were altered as a result of SCI.[31] Therefore, future earnings potential will be underestimated. Alternatively, basing the estimate of indirect losses on planned educational achievement is equally inappropriate because plans are not always fulfilled.

§ 4.8 Lifetime Direct Costs

The direct costs of SCI are somewhat easier to determine. Average charges for acute care and rehabilitation and all other expenses up to the first anniversary of injury in 1992 dollars for persons treated in federally-designated model SCI systems of care were $417,067 for persons with relatively complete injuries between C1 and C4, $269,324 for persons with relatively complete injuries between C5 and C8, $152,396 for persons with relatively complete thoracic or lumbosacral spinal cord injuries, and $122,914 for persons with functional motor sparing below the injury regardless of actual injury level.[32] However, by the time of trial, actual costs for acute care and rehabilitation will almost always already be known. What is more important is to estimate annual charges that

[29] M. DeVivo et al., Spinal Cord Injury: Clinical Outcomes from the Model Systems 263–65 (S. Stover et al. eds., 1995); M. Berkowitz et al., The Economic Consequences of Traumatic Spinal Cord Injury 129–34 (1992).

[30] M. DeVivo et al., Spinal Cord Injury: Clinical Outcomes from the Model Systems 258 (S. Stover et al. eds., 1995).

[31] M. Berkowitz et al., The Economic Consequences of Traumatic Spinal Cord Injury 177–81 (1992).

[32] M. DeVivo et al., Spinal Cord Injury: Clinical Outcomes from the Model Systems 237–38 (S. Stover et al. eds., 1995).

will be incurred thereafter, and the number of years over which those charges will be incurred.

Average annual charges after discharge from rehabilitation for the same four neurologic categories in 1992 dollars are $74,707, $30,602, $15,507, and $8,614, respectively.[33] Similar but slightly lower estimates have been developed by M. Berkowitz and associates using a slightly different neurologic grouping scheme.[34] Included in these figures are all charges for rehospitalizations, nursing home stays, attendant care, outpatient physician and therapy visits, outpatient lab fees, home and environmental modification charges, equipment (purchase, rental and repair), medications, supplies, household assistance, and other miscellaneous charges directly resulting from the SCI. In addition, estimates of the value of unpaid attendant care and other goods and services provided by friends and family members are included in these annual cost figures. Individual estimates for each cost category are provided in both references.[35]

Because there is so much variability in direct costs for each person, it is not recommended that averages such as these be applied in any given case. Rather, it is preferable to develop a life care plan along the lines described in **Chapter 8.** In this way, the person's actual needs can be met and prevailing community prices of necessary goods and services can be used rather than national averages. However, average figures such as these might be used to help assess the reasonableness of life care plans once developed. Significant departures in either direction from these average figures should be thoroughly justified based on the physical condition and living situation of the person as compared to average individuals in the same neurologic group.

§ 4.9 Long-term Survival

There are two commonly used statistical measures of the length of potential future survival. One is the median (50 percent) survival time. This is the point in time at which an individual is equally likely as not to still be alive. It is determined from a standard life table analysis of a large sample of individuals who are as similar to the person in question as possible. The other measure is life expectancy, which is the arithmetic average number of remaining years of life for that same large sample of comparable persons. Often, median survival and life expectancy are the same; however, there are times when they may be different by as much as 2 or 3 years. A simple example will illustrate this point. If three individuals experience survival of one year, two years and nine years, the median survival for members of the group would be two years, but the average life

---

[33] *Id.*

[34] M. Berkowitz et al., The Economic Consequences of Traumatic Spinal Cord Injury 140 (1992).

[35] *Id.*; M. DeVivo et al., Spinal Cord Injury: Clinical Outcomes from the Model Systems 237–38 (S. Stover et al. eds., 1995).

expectancy for members of the group would be four years [(9 + 2 + 1) divided by 3]. Therefore, understanding this distinction can be very important when determining economic damages.

There is a common misconception that both life expectancy and median survival following SCI are not significantly reduced from that which would be expected in the absence of SCI, particularly for those persons who survive the first year postinjury. This myth is typically based on the physician's perception of clinical practice and the fact that the physician is aware of only a few deaths occurring among patients. Unfortunately, most physicians do not treat enough persons with SCI to make such assessments, and often lose track of patients over time. Therefore, while physicians can often estimate quite accurately the short-term case fatality rate for hospitalized conditions such as pneumonia based on their clinical practice, it is not appropriate to estimate the life expectancy of persons with SCI in this way. Instead, well-designed long-term studies of large numbers of persons with SCI are necessary to answer this question.

Fortunately, several such studies exist.[36] The following abridged **Table 4–1** reflects the most current data on life expectancy after SCI for persons who survive the first postinjury year by age and neurologic category:

Table 4–1

Life Expectancy (Years)

Age	Normal	Any Level Ventilator Dependent	C1–C4 ASIA A,B, or C	C5–C8 ASIA A,B, or C	T1–S5 ASIA A,B, or C	Any Level ASIA D
20	56.3	19.9	32.8	38.6	44.8	49.0
40	37.6	12.4	20.9	23.6	28.8	31.7
60	20.5	6.6	11.0	11.2	13.8	15.9[37]

In this table, ASIA categories A, B, and C represent neurologically complete injuries or incomplete injuries with either sensory sparing only or nonfunctional motor capability below the injury level. ASIA category D represents incomplete injuries with functional motor capability below the injury level.

36 M. DeVivo & C. Ivie III, Life Expectancy of Ventilator-dependent Persons with Spinal Cord Injuries, 108 Chest 227-229 (1995); M. DeVivo and S. Stover, Spinal Cord Injuries: Clinical Outcomes from the Model Systems 289–98 (S. Stover et al. eds., 1995); M. DeVivo et al., *Prognostic Factors for 12-year Survival after Spinal Cord Injury,* 73 Archives Physical Med. & Rehabilitation 156–62 (1992); G. Whiteneck et al., *Mortality, Morbidity, and Psychosocial Outcomes of Persons Spinal Cord Injured More than 20 Years Ago,* 30 Paraplegia 617–30 (1992); W. Geisler et al., *Survival in Traumatic Transverse Myelitis,* 14 Paraplegia 262–75 (1977).

37 M. DeVivo & C. Ivie III, Life Expectancy of Ventilator-dependent Persons with Spinal Cord Injuries, 108 Chest 227-229 (1995); M. DeVivo and S. Stover, Spinal Cord Injuries: Clinical Outcomes from the Model Systems 298 (1995).

The table reveals substantial differences in life expectancy based on both neurologic status and age. The life expectancy of a 20-year-old ventilator-dependent person with SCI who is at least one year postinjury is reduced from 56.3 years (average survival to age 76.3) to only 19.9 years (average survival to age 39.9). However, for 20-year-old persons who have very incomplete motor functional injuries, life expectancy is indeed almost normal.

These estimates are meant for illustration purposes only. They are helpful when tracking progress in treatment practices over time. However, they should not be applied in specific cases because the neurologic categories are too broadly defined, do not take race or gender into account, and do not account for other preexisting conditions or associated injuries that might affect life expectancy. Instead, more precise estimates should be obtained from samples of persons that are matched more closely to the characteristics of the individual case. Such estimates can be obtained from the NSCISC for a modest fee, and may also be available from other sources.

The major limitation of survival analyses is that they must of necessity be conducted on persons injured some time ago so that sufficient follow-up may occur. In other words, assessment of 20-year survival must be based on persons injured 20 years ago when medical care and survival rates were quite different. An alternative approach is to use more recently injured persons followed for shorter periods of time, compare their experience with that of the able-bodied population of comparable age, gender, and race, and extrapolate those findings into the future. While this has the advantage of using more recently injured persons, it is necessary to assume that the relationship between short-term mortality rates for persons with SCI and their able-bodied peers will remain constant into the future. Such an assumption may not always be warranted. In any event, since there has been a trend toward increasing survival rates after SCI, any projection based on previously injured persons will be at least slightly conservative. Moreover, the impact of new treatments that might be developed in the future cannot be taken into account.

Nonetheless, despite limitations, current life expectancy projections do provide an impartial objective basis for determining damages. As was the case with comparing costs determined from life care plans with national average cost estimates, the same can be done with average life expectancy projections. If an expert suggests that an individual will do substantially better or worse than average, justification of that opinion should be required in terms of how this person differs from other persons of comparable age, gender, race, neurologic level, degree of injury completeness, ventilator status, and so forth, in a way that would meaningfully affect survival.

It should be emphasized that these figures represent averages for a group of comparable individuals. No one can say with any degree of certainty exactly how long any particular individual will live. Fatal car crashes, heart attacks, and other factors are unpredictable and can occur without warning at any time.

However, the exact probability (chance) of living to each successive year can be calculated for any individual and may be of assistance in describing future survival prospects more clearly to jurors.

Several causes of death occur much more frequently among persons with SCI than other individuals of the same age, gender, and race, including pneumonia and other respiratory diseases, pulmonary emboli, septicemia, urinary tract complications, and suicide.[38] Increased mortality from ischemic heart disease, stroke, and bladder cancer also occurs among persons with SCI, but not until at least 20 years postinjury.

---

[38] M. DeVivo & S. Stover, Spinal Cord Injuries: Clinical Outcomes from the Model Systems 298–313 (S. Stover et al. eds., 1995); M. DeVivo et al., *Causes of Death during the First 12 Years after Spinal Cord Injury,* 74 Archives Physical Med. & Rehabilitation 248–54 (1993).

CHAPTER 5

FUNCTIONAL EXPECTATIONS FOR THE SPINAL CORD INJURED PATIENT

Karen Tomec Schmitz, R.P.T.

§ 5.1 Introduction

This chapter describes the functional expectations of spinal cord injured patients as related to injury level. It covers various activities and the degree to which the patient will need assistance or the degree of independence demonstrated and required for each activity. Activities include ADLs (dressing, eating, personal hygiene), bronchial hygiene, pressure relief, bed mobility, driving (for high-level quadriplegics and paraplegics), and functional ambulation for paraplegics.

Functional status descriptions for each classification relates to patients with complete lesions. Incomplete lesions at identical levels retain sporadic sensation and function below the level of the injury.

§ 5.2 Quadriplegics

C1–C3

Patients injured at any of these levels are considered low-level quadriplegics because they retain a low level of functional ability. These patients have use of the face and neck musculature. They are able to talk, eat, sip, and blow, but are totally dependent with respect to all activities of daily living (ADLs). C1–C3 quadriplegics must rely on an attendant for all ADLs including bathing, dressing, skin inspection, transfers, bed mobility, and coughing to clear secretions in the lungs. They are respiratory dependent. A phrenic nerve stimulator (an electrode that causes the diaphragm to contract) can be used during the day to assist in respiration.

An electric wheelchair is a requirement and can be outfitted to allow the patient to control it by one of many types of devices: breath control (sip-and-puff) that utilizes breathing in and breathing out to control movement of the wheelchair, tongue control that utilizes the tongue on a joystick to maneuver the chair, or a chin control that employs a pad in front of the chin to maneuver the chair. For pressure relief, a reclining wheelchair is necessary. This allows low-level quadriplegics some degree of independence in performing pressure relief.

They also need an environmental control unit. An environmental control unit can be attached to a sip-and-puff controller or to a joystick. It allows patients to control appliances, light switches, or answer a telephone.

C4

These patients have the added use of the diaphragm and trapezius muscles (allowing them to shrug the shoulders). They are still limited in many ADLs. C4 quadriplegics can move from supine to sitting by use of an electric bed, however they will not be able to use the upper extremities for control. They are able to provide occasional minimal assistance using head and scapular movements with other bed mobility such as rolling. They have the ability to direct all bed mobility. C4 level quadriplegics must still rely on attendant care for many of the ADLs, including bathing, dressing, skin inspection, transfer, bed mobility, and coughing assistance to clear secretions in the lungs. They have the ability to direct bronchial hygiene.

Eating can be accomplished independently with the assistance of splints and adaptive eating utensils. An electric typewriter or computer can be controlled by the use of a joystick operated by the head or mouth, by sip-and-puff controls, or by using a rubber-tipped stick held in a splinted hand accompanied by a mobile arm support. Page turning devices are available that can be operated by an environmental control device. Wheelchairs can often be controlled manually with the proper arm supports and hand splints in a joystick-controlled chair. C4 quadriplegics can enjoy a few forms of recreation given the proper equipment. For instance, cards, checkers, or chess games may be adapted for recreation with built-up playing pieces and special hand splints. Drawing and painting is also possible using the mouth or hand (utilizing a hand and elbow splint and powered arm braces).

C5

Patients with an injury at this level have the use of all of the muscles previously discussed plus the additional use of muscles that allow patients to flex (bend) the elbow and supinate the forearm (that is, turn the palm up). External rotation of the shoulder (rotate arm away from the body), abduction of the shoulder (90 degrees), and limited shoulder flexion are also possible for C5 quadriplegics. C5 quadriplegics need assistance from an electric bed to move from supine to sitting, but they may demonstrate some upper extremity control. They are able to assist moderately with other bed mobility by using head, scapular movements, or shoulder movements. As with C4 quadriplegics, C5 quadriplegics are able to direct all bed mobility.

C5 quadriplegics can accomplish the same tasks as C4 quadriplegics while using less adaptive equipment. C5 quadriplegics are able to perform these tasks with more skill and ease. In addition, these patients can feed themselves with adaptive utensils and hand braces. They still do not have the use of their hands to hold utensils independently. They are able to assist a caregiver in upper body dressing and can perform a few personal hygiene tasks such as face washing with a wash mitt, and brushing teeth with an adaptive toothbrush. They will be able to direct and assist with bronchial hygiene.

They are also capable of self-locomotion in a wheelchair equipped with handrim projections (knobs on the outer rim of the chair's wheels), although an electric wheelchair is a more appropriate option depending on the individual patient's ability to propel the wheelchair. If an electric wheelchair is necessary, a hand joystick can be used in conjunction with a yoke or armrest to support the arm controlling the chair.

C6

These patients retain function of the muscles that allow C6 quadriplegics to use the arms to raise the arms forward (shoulder flexion), backward (extension), across the body (rotation and adduction), over their head (scapular abduction and upward rotation), turn the hand so that the palm faces downward (forearm pronation), and bend wrist upward (wrist extension). With an injury at this level, the fingers are nonfunctional. However, by extending the wrist, patients can make the fingers flex (curl toward the palm) resulting in a *tenodesis grasp.*

C6 quadriplegics can perform many more ADLs, including self-feeding with adaptive utensils, self-dressing by utilizing momentum and clothing with button hooks and zipper pulls. C6 quadriplegics are able to perform all bed mobility independently with or without side rails on the bed. Skin inspection and pressure relief can be performed independently. They have the ability to assist with and perform bronchial hygiene. Patients are also able to cough manually by pressing on the abdomen to stimulate the cough mechanism and clear secretions from the lungs.

Locomotion is independent with a manual wheelchair. Transfers are independent with the aid of a sliding board. Driving is also possible for some patients depending on the level of spasticity. Driving is accomplished through the use of hand controls and a U-shaped cuff attached to the steering wheel. They require assistance putting wheelchairs into vehicles, or must have access to vans equipped with a lift.

C7

C7 quadriplegics retain function of muscles that allow them to straighten the elbow (elbow extension), bend the wrist down (wrist flexion) and straighten the fingers (finger extension). With the use of these additional muscles, C7 quadriplegics can perform more ADLs independently, including bathing with the use of a shower chair, adaptive shower head, and adaptive handles in the bathroom. C7 and C8 quadriplegics are able to independently perform bed mobility without any special equipment. Bowel and bladder management is more independent with a digital stimulator, suppositories, a raised toilet seat, and a catheter. Housekeeping chores can be accomplished independently. Patients are independent with regard to bronchial hygiene.

Locomotion is independent with just the addition of a friction surface on the wheelchair handrim. Handrim knobs are not necessary for C7 quadriplegics. Finally, driving is even more independent since patients can load a wheelchair without assistance.

C8–T1

At this level patients retain full use of all upper extremity muscles including the hand muscles. Patients are fully independent with personal hygiene. Wheelchairs can be operated manually without any adaptive hand rims. Patients can also perform light housekeeping duties and meal preparation with the aid of some adaptive equipment such as a reacher. Living in a wheelchair accessible environment, including lowered work surfaces (for example, countertops, stove top, and sink) is necessary for complete independence. Driving is possible with hand controls. Employment is also possible in buildings without architectural barriers.

§ 5.3 Paraplegics

T4–T6

These paraplegics benefit from improved trunk control and increased respiratory reserve secondary to retention of the top half of the intercostal muscles (rib cage muscles) and the long muscles of the back. Patients are able to perform ADLs independently (bronchial hygiene, housekeeping duties, meal preparation). Locomotion in the wheelchair is fully independent, including the ability to climb curbs and other obstacles using the "wheelie" approach. They can also participate fully in wheelchair sports and many other forms of recreation. Ambulation may be possible, but is not practical for functional purposes. Patients are able to stand using knee and ankle braces attached to a brace around the lower trunk.

T6–T8

T6–T8 paraplegics are independent with all ADLs, bronchial hygiene, housekeeping, and meal preparation in a wheelchair-accessible home. Employment is possible in buildings without architectural barriers.

T6–T8 paraplegics are able to ambulate independently with a knee-ankle-foot orthoses (KAFOs) in the parallel bars, but require supervision during gait for short distances with a walker. Therefore, T6–T8 paraplegics are not good candidates for functional walking. This is due to poor strength and poor control of the trunk musculature making balancing and trunk stability inadequate for functional ambulation. They are, however, independent in donning and doffing the orthosis, moving forward, backward, sideways, and turning in narrow spaces.

T9–T12

Patients retain function of lower abdominals and all intercostal muscles allowing nearly normal respiration, which results in increased endurance. Locomotion by wheelchair is still necessary for energy conservation. However, ambulation is possible in a limited area (such as around the house with braces and crutches). T9–T12 paraplegics are independent with gait utilizing KAFOs and forearm crutches or a walker on level surfaces. They become skilled with the swing-to or swing-through gait pattern. However they need assistance with ambulation on rough terrain and elevations. Patients need supervision in managing stairs, curbs, elevators, and escalators. They also require supervision with falling and getting up from the ground.

T12–L3

The T12–L3 paraplegics are independent with ambulation with KAFOs and forearm crutches on all terrain, curbs, and stairs. They are also independent falling safely and getting up from the floor unassisted. However, the wheelchair is still the main source of mobility secondary to the energy expenditure required with ambulation.

L2–L4

L2–L4 paraplegics retain the use of muscles that allow hip flexion and adduction and knee extension. Functional ambulation is possible with braces and crutches, however, the energy expended is high, thereby requiring the paraplegic to use the wheelchair for extended periods of locomotion.

L4–L5

These patients retain the use of low back muscles, and some muscles that allow weak knee flexion. Ambulation is possible with braces and crutches, and in some cases just a cane. L4–L5 paraplegics can ambulate with AFOs (ankle foot orthosis), forearm crutches, conventional crutches or canes on all surfaces, stairs, and ramps. They are able to fall independently and safely get up from the floor unassisted.

CHAPTER 6

ACUTE AND CHRONIC COMPLICATIONS OF SCI

Joan M.K. Fox, M.D.

Michael P. Pietrzak, M.D.

Mark R. Kosieradzki

§ 6.1 Introduction

Until recently, SCI (spinal cord injury) was associated with poor long-term survival. Modern medical developments have made SCI less life-threatening. Long-term disability and immobilization, however, create a different set of issues. As a result, there has been a gradual change in focus from simply attempting to sustain life, to trying to improve quality of life. This change in focus presents medical personnel with a new challenges; treating the complications and sequelae. This chapter provides an overview of the many complications that impact the lives of SCI patients.

§ 6.2 Pressure Sores

Pressure sores (also known as bed sores, pressure ulcers, decubitus, or ischemic ulcerations) are defined as cellular-necrosis of tissue stemming from pressure as a result of extended immobilization.[1] The effect of prolonged pressure over the same spot on the body destroys the tissue, creating sores. These sores, if allowed to progress unchecked, can develop into massive open wounds. Pressure sores are generally believed to have the greatest impact on the quality of life of SCI victims.[2]

Pressure sores are classified by grades; grade I being the least severe, with grade V being the most. Grade I is evidenced by redness (erythema) or hardening (induration) of the skin over a bony prominence. Grade II is a superficial ulceration that extends into the skin. Grade III is an ulceration that extends below the level of the skin (subcutaneous), but not into the musculature. Grade IV is a deep ulceration extending into the musculature, down to a bony prominence. Grade V exhibits extensive ulceration extending into joints or body cavities.[3]

Level

Pressure sores affect SCI victims injured at any level. The only difference the level of the lesion makes is that the higher the level of the lesion, the less able the patient is to take preventative precautions independently.

Incidence

Numerous studies of SCI victims show that 20 to 33 percent of SCI victims develop at least one pressure sore per year.[4] In a 1993 study, 140 SCI victims were examined on one day and 33 percent presented one or more ulcers, with 27 percent of those being severe (grade III or higher).[5]

---

[1] J. DeLisa, Rehabilitation Medicine, Principles and Practice 716 (2d ed. 1993).

[2] F. Frost, *Role of Rehabilitation after Spinal Cord Injury,* 20 Urol. Clinic of N. Am. 549–59 (1993).

[3] J. DeLisa, Rehabilitation Medicine, Principles and Practice 721 (2d ed. 1993).

[4] *Id.*

[5] *Id.*

Etiology

Pressure sores result from the effects of prolonged pressure on soft tissue resulting in a breakdown, and eventually destroying it. SCI victims are in particular danger of developing pressure sores because of their impaired sensation. In individuals with normal sensation, the brain subconsciously recognizes when a certain area of the body has been subjected to prolonged pressure and periodically directs shifts of position.[6] Since SCI victims may have little or no sensation below the level of their injury, they don't perceive pressure areas of their body because they feel no discomfort. Therefore, it is imperative for every SCI victim to change positions at least every two hours and constantly examine the skin for signs of redness or hardening that signal the onset of a pressure sore. Depending on the level of the injury, the SCI victim may or may not be capable of performing these functions independently.

Pressure sores most commonly appear in the areas of the heels, the ischial tuberosities (the elevated round process of the lower pelvis), the posterior inferior iliac spines (lower, rear pelvic bones), and the bony prominences below the head of the femur around the hip.[7] However, pressure sores can appear anywhere below the level of the injury. Many factors contribute to the development of pressure sores:

1. Compression that results in deprivation of the tissue of oxygen and nutrients (vascular ischemia)
2. Moisture
3. Age
4. Altered sensation
5. Psychological factors.[8]

In addition, researchers have recognized seven factors that help identify persons who are at particular risk for developing pressure sores:

1. The level of the injury
2. Completeness of the cord lesion, both motor and sensory
3. Etiology of the SCI
4. Race
5. Employment status

---

[6] P. Gutierrez, R. Young & M. Vulpe, *Spinal Cord Injury: An Overview,* 20 Urol. Clinic of N. Am. 373–82 (1993).

[7] J. DeLisa, Rehabilitation Medicine, Principles and Practice 724 (2d ed. 1993).

[8] Rothman & Simeone, The Spine 1237 (3d ed. 1992).

6. Level of education
7. Familiarity with SCI care needs.[9]

For the attorney, identification of one or more of these factors that apply to your client can be helpful in analyzing the cost of future medical care.

Care and Management

Pressure sores are treated as any other open wound, but with an eye toward prevention of reoccurrence. Those with less severe pressure sores can be treated conservatively by removal of the destroyed tissue, infection control, and regular wound cleaning and dressing. For more severe pressure sores, surgery is required. Depending on the location and severity of the pressure sore, the surgery may involve skin grafts, skin flaps, muscle flaps, or musculocutaneous flaps. Flaps are used in the most severe cases and involve mobilizing a piece of skin or muscle to connected to a blood vessel to close the wound. Inherent to all SCI victims are the costs of caring for SCI patients who develop pressure sores and for preventing the development of pressure sores. A frequently cited study reveals that patients who develop no pressure sores during their initial hospitalization had an average hospital stay of less than four months. On the other hand, for those patients who developed severe pressure sores the average hospital time from injury to discharge was eight months.[10] Additional costs are incurred for patients who develop pressure sores following their initial hospitalization and reentry into the community. Lesions classified as grade III or higher most frequently require hospitalization and plastic surgery, but grade I or II may be able to heal without surgery if properly treated. For pressure sores that have progressed to the point where hospitalization becomes necessary, the average cost of that hospitalization and treatment ranges between $50,000[11] and $70,000.[12] These costs present a strong argument towards adopting methods of preventing the development of pressure sores. Most texts on the subject recommend the patient be turned or position shifted at least once every two hours. Additionally, at every turning, the skin should be meticulously inspected for any sign of redness, hardness, or heat. For the quadriplegic, these tasks must be performed by another, usually necessitating outside attendant care. Depending on the presence and ability of the family to provide some of these services, 24-hour attendant care may be the only viable option.

---

[9] J. DeLisa, Rehabilitation Medicine, Principles and Practice 719–20 (2d ed. 1993).

[10] *Id.* at 716.

[11] *Id.* at 730.

[12] Hochschuler, Cotler & Guyer, Rehabilitation of the Spine, Science and Practice 326 (1993).

§ 6.3 Spasticity

Spasticity is an abnormal condition that is a reaction to SCI. It is characterized by symptoms ranging from increased muscle tone to severe spasms that can throw a person from the bed or wheelchair. Mild to moderate spasticity is actually beneficial to most SCI patients as it helps the patient retain muscle tone and bulk that in turn provides pad-like protection against pressure sores and contractures of joints.[13] Severe spasticity, however, can be a significant problem because it affects independent functioning, contributes to the development of pressure sores, and can be painful.[14]

Severe spasticity greatly interferes with daily functioning. It is especially troubling for those who have retained a high level of motor function since the spasticity may preclude them from becoming more independent. Activities such as operating an automobile with hand controls, transfers, or wheelchair mobility may be inhibited or prevented by severe spasticity.[15]

Spasticity also affects rehabilitation efforts. A common form of therapy for SCI patients is passive muscle stretching. However, muscle stretch often elicits spastic contractions.[16] Most patients experience one of two types of muscle stretch reflexes, either phasic or tonic.[17] Muscle stretch reflexes are contractions of the muscles in response to an external stimulus, in this case stretch. Phasic muscle stretch reflexes are short-lived contractions, usually ceasing within seconds.[18] They occur when rapid movement of the muscle is attempted either through passive stretch or tendon tap.[19] Slow movement of the muscle, however, will not cause spastic contractions of the muscle.[20] Tonic reflexes, on the other hand, can be precipitated by either rapid or slow movement of the muscle, and the accompanying contraction will be sustained as long as stretch is maintained.[21] Tonic reflexes have a more severe negative impact on the level of function attained by an SCI patient. Increased spasticity is a concern for both the patient and the medical team. Not only does it interfere with rehabilitation efforts and independent functioning, it may be indicating some other underlying problem. What causes increased spasticity is still unknown for the most part. It often is related to some other

---

13 R. Davis *Spasticity Following Spinal Cord Injury,* 112 Clinical Orthopedics & Related Res., 66–75 (1975).

14 J. DeLisa, Rehabilitation Medicine, Principles and Practice 666–67 (2d ed. 1993).

15 *Id.*

16 *Id.*

17 *Id.*

18 *Id.*

19 *Id.*

20 J. DeLisa, Rehabilitation Medicine, Principles and Practice 666–67 (2d ed. 1993).

21 *Id.*

complication affecting the patient at the time, such as a bladder infection, severe pressure sores, kidney stones, or even a blocked catheter.[22] Some researchers have theorized that increased spasticity may even be a substitute pain response, however, solid scientific evidence is lacking.[23]

Level

Spasticity affects patients most frequently with cervical injuries and thoracic injuries, but far fewer patients with lumbar and cauda equina injuries will experience spasticity.

Incidence

Spasticity, to some degree, affects nearly all cervical cord injured patients and most thoracic cord injuries. Spasticity is present in less than half of lumbar injured patients and in less than one quarter of cauda equina injured patients. Spasticity is likely to be more severe in an incomplete spinal cord lesion than in a complete lesion.

Etiology

Spasticity arises in SCI patients once the period of spinal shock wears off following the trauma. Spinal shock refers to the condition when the body is completely unresponsive below the level of the lesion. The patient experiences no sensation, has no reflex response, and has no voluntary movement. Spasticity is the result of reflex responses that are built into the spinal cord and therefore is absent during the period of spinal shock.

Once the period of spinal shock wears off, however, the spinal reflexes return and become hyperactive. The hyperactivity of these reflexes is due to the inability of the brain to connect with the reflex arc in the spine responsible for the reflex. In a neurologically intact person, the suprasegmental tracts connect the brain to the reflex arc and the brain modulates the degree of reflex activity. In the SCI patient, the suprasegmental pathways are interrupted between the brain and the spinal cord as a direct result of the lesion. Therefore, the spinal reflexes go unregulated below the level of the lesion, resulting in spasticity. While the degree to which a person experiences spasticity varies widely, there is no known scientific explanation.

---

[22] R. Davis, *Spasticity Following Spinal Cord Injury,* 112 Clinical Orthopedics & Related Res. 66–75 (1975).

[23] *Id.*

Care and Management

As noted above, increased spasticity is often a signal of some underlying problem. Therefore, the treatment of spasticity generally involves an attempt to diagnose the underlying problem, and treat it with the assumption that once the underlying problem has been resolved, the accompanying spasticity will also resolve.

Although increased spasticity may indicate some underlying complication, severe spasticity is present in some individuals without any secondary causation.[24] For individuals with severe spasticity, a number of drug options are available. The most common and most popular drug given to control spasticity is Baclofen.[25] It can be administered orally or through the use of a pump installed in the body. The discovery of drug treatments to control spasticity has greatly improved the quality of life for many SCI patients, however, for some, surgical intervention becomes necessary to control their spasticity. In extremely severe situations, thermal rhizotomy (cutting the nerve roots), is performed in an attempt to control spasticity.

§ 6.4 Autonomic Dysreflexia

Autonomic dysreflexia (a.k.a. hyperreflexia) is a life-threatening condition due to extremely high blood pressure, that results from excessive sympathetic discharge from the autonomic nervous system.[26] The result of the patient's rapidly rising blood pressure may be life-threatening. Autonomic dysreflexia presents itself with symptoms ranging from pounding headache, blurred vision, flushing, sweating dilated pupils, and atrial fibrillation (rapid and irregular contractions of the upper chambers of the heart that often lead to excessively low blood pressure known as hypotension), congestive heart failure, angina (pain and feeling of constriction around the heart), or thromboembolism.[27]

Level

Autonomic dysreflexia is common among SCI with lesions above T6, either complete or incomplete lesions.

---

[24] *Id.*

[25] R. Rothman & Simeone, The Spine 1240 (3d ed. 1992).

[26] R. Erickson RP, *Autonomic Hyperreflexia: Pathophysiology and Medical Management,* 61 Arch. Phys. Med. Rehabilitation 431–40 (1980).

[27] A. Pine, S. Miller & J. Alonso, *Atrial Fibrillation Associated with Autonomic Dysreflexia,* 70 Am. J. Phys. Med. & Rehabilitation 271–73 (1991).

Incidence

It usually appears between two and 15 months postinjury. Incidence peaks within three years postinjury, and then subsides. However, it may appear at any time. Cervical cord injured patients are at particular risk of developing this syndrome (60 percent), but thoracic cord injured patients also are at risk (20 percent).[28]

Etiology

Autonomic dysreflexia results from uninhibited autonomic spinal cord reflexes. Noxious afferent stimuli (bladder distension, impacted bowel, severe decubiti ulceration, deep vein thrombosis, or urinary tract infection) enter the spinal cord below the level of the lesion, initiating various segmental, intersegmental, and autonomic vasoconstrictor (blood vessel constriction) reflexes. The lesion then blocks the ascending impulses from reaching the brain and blocks descending mediating impulses from the brain allowing the reflexes to continue unchecked, resulting in exaggerated vasoconstriction below the level of the lesion. This may dramatically increase blood pressure (up to 300 mm Hg. systolic), potentially causing severe pounding headache and putting the patient at significant risk for cerebral hemorrhage or seizure.[29] Baroreceptors (blood pressure receptors) in the chest and neck sense the increased blood pressure, and trigger parasympathetic vasodilator reflexes above the level of the lesion and decrease the heart rate.

Care and Management

Treatment generally consists of trying to control the patient's blood pressure through the use of changed body position and/or drug therapy. At the same time, discovery and resolution of the underlying cause is sought, relieving bladder distension is often successful. For those patients who suffer from frequent episodes, drug therapy is available to help moderate the condition.

§ 6.5 Syringomyelia

Syringomyelia is the development of a fluid-filled cavity (cyst) in the spinal cord. Most often in SCI patients this spinal cord cyst causes no problems due to the neurologic impairment from which the patient already suffers. Occasionally, however,

---

[28] A. Selzman & N. Hampel, *Urologic Complications of Spinal Cord Injury,* 20 Urol. Clinic of N. Am. 453–62 (1993).

[29] M. Hanak & A. Scott, Spinal Cord Injury: An Illustrated Guide for Health Care Professionals 31 (1983).

a cyst will affect a part of the patient's spinal cord that was unaffected by the trauma. Cysts can also develop in SCI patients who had minimal neurologic deficits. Those situations are characterized by ascending neurological findings accompanied by pain, hyperhidrosis (excessive sweating), and increased spasticity.[30]

Level

Paraplegics develop posttraumatic syringomyelia at a rate nine times higher than complete quadriplegics.[31]

Incidence

It develops in SCI patients between 0.3 percent and 3 percent.[32] Complete quadriplegics account for only 8 percent of the total numbers of patients who develop syringomyelia.[33]

Etiology

There is no known cause for the disorder.

Care and Management

Since most patients experience no symptoms due to syringomyelia, most physicians choose not to treat it. However, if symptoms begin to arise as a result of the cyst, surgery is generally required to remove or drain the cyst from the cord. A recent article, however, suggests shunting the cyst early before the cord is too severely damaged, even if it is causing no symptoms for the patient.[34]

§ 6.6 Pain

Chronic pain is a surprising complication of spinal cord injury. Most SCI patients experience two different types of pain. The first is musculoskeletal pain, and the second is nerve root pain.[35]

---

[30] J. DeLisa, Rehabilitation Medicine, Principles and Practice 895 (2d ed. 1993).

[31] Rothman & Simeone, The Spine (3d ed. 1992).

[32] J. DeLisa, Rehabilitation Medicine, Principles and Practice 895 (2d ed. 1993).

[33] Rothman & Simeone, The Spine 1589 (3d ed. 1992).

[34] L. Robinson & J. Little, *Motor Evoked Potentials Reflect Spinal Cord Function in Posttraumatic Syringomyelia,* 69 Am. J. Phys. Med. & Rehabilitation 307–310 (1990).

[35] J. DeLisa, Rehabilitation Medicine, Principles and Practice 895 (2d ed. 1993).

Musculoskeletal pain is often secondary to the trauma. Many patients report pain localized to the level of the injury. It is often described as being a throbbing, aching pain. Another common form of musculoskeletal pain is shoulder pain.[36]

Nerve root pain can manifest itself either above or below the lesion. When it appears above, it is described as a sharp pain or possibly like an electric shock.[37] When it appears below the level of the injury (sometimes called phantom pain), it is often described as a cold, burning pain.[38]

Level

Pain affects SCI patients regardless of the level of the lesion.

Incidence

Musculoskeletal pain is experienced by nearly all SCI victims, and is especially common in persons injured from a puncture trauma, for example, from gunshot or stabbing. Shoulder pain is one of the more frequent complaints. For instance, most studies report shoulder pain in 50–78 percent of quadriplegics.[39] Nerve root pain most often appears six months following the injury, and some studies have reported an incidence of diffuse burning pain as high as 90 percent.[40]

Etiology

Musculoskeletal pain is most often related to the original trauma that damages the spinal cord. Shoulder pain can also develop from overuse, especially in paraplegics when it stems from manual wheelchair use. Shoulder pain also develops in patients who do not use a manual wheelchair. This is sometimes the result of severe spasticity or heterotopic ossification. However, many quadriplegics experience shoulder pain without either spasticity or heterotopic ossification.[41] Many believe this pain is the result of degeneration, contracture, and rotator cuff tendinitis.[42]

---

[36] Hochschuler, Cotler & Guyer, Rehabilitation of the Spine, Science and Practice 358 (1993).

[37] J. DeLisa, Rehabilitation Medicine, Principles and Practice 895 (2d ed. 1993).

[38] *Id.*

[39] J. Silfverskiold & R. Waters, *Shoulder Pain and Functional Disability in Spinal Cord Injury Patients,* Clinical Orthopedics & Related Res. 141–45 (1991).

[40] J. DeLisa, Rehabilitation Medicine, Principles and Practice 895 (2d ed. 1993).

[41] J. Silfverskiold & R. Waters, *Shoulder Pain and Functional Disability in Spinal Cord Injury Patients,* Clinical Orthopedics & Related Research 141–45 (1991).

[42] *Id.*

Care and Management

Treatment for chronic pain is as difficult in the SCI population as it is in the general population. Reassurance, relaxation techniques, transcutaneous nerve stimulation, antidepressants, and biofeedback are all used to treat pain.

§ 6.7 Gastrointestinal Dysfunction

SCI affects gastrointestinal functioning in nearly every respect. It affects the ability of the bowel to empty, the proper function of the colon, and causes gastritis and ulcers. Gastrointestinal (GI) dysfunction has one of the most negative impacts on the quality of life for victims of SCI. In addition, gastrointestinal dysfunction often results in morbidity (disease) and is potentially life-threatening.

The neurogenic bowel refers to the loss of the ability to empty the bowel normally.[43] In some patients it results in severe constipation, while in others the result is incontinence (inability to retain feces). In either case, the neurogenic bowel impacts the quality of an SCI victim's life immensely.

Gastrointestinal bleeding is a frequent complication in the acute phase following SCI. Stress ulceration is an especially high risk for patients with lesions above T5.[44] The stress most newly injured SCI patients are experiencing is often linked to this complication. SCI patients also experience more frequent and more severe pain in the GI tract. This is generally due to esophageal disease. SCI patients are at higher risk for esophageal disease, which results in pain and gastric ulceration.[45] Chronic constipation and changes in metabolism may be causative factors, but the cause has not been decisively determined.[46]

Level

Gastrointestinal dysfunction is seen consistently in all patients who have a lesion above S3.[47]

---

[43] J. Banwell, C. Creasey, A. Aggarwal & J. Mortimer, *Management of the Neurogenic Bowel in Patients with Spinal Cord Injury,* 20 Urol. Clinic of N. Am. 517–25 (1993).

[44] J. DeLisa, Rehabilitation Medicine, Principles and Practice (2d ed. 1993).

[45] L. Stinneford, A. Keshavarzain, B. Nemchausky, M. Doria & M. Durkin, *Esophagitis and Esophageal Motor Abnormalities in Patients with Chronic SCI,* 31 Paraplegia 384–92 (1993).

[46] *Id.*

[47] J. Banwell, C. Creasey, A. Aggarwal & J. Mortimer, *Management of the Neurogenic Bowel in Patients with Spinal Cord Injury,* 20 Urol. Clinic of N. Am. 517–25 (1993).

Incidence

Gastrointestinal dysfunction is a complication that affects persons injured above the level of S3.

Etiology

Normal fecal continence is the result of a balance between two opposite forces: expulsion forces and resistance. The balance between these is compromised after SCI, particularly in those with lesions in the cervical spine or high thoracic spine. Expulsion forces stem from abdominal pressure, rectal contraction, and gravity.[48] Abdominal pressure and rectal contraction are controlled voluntarily. Therefore, the ability or inability to effectively evacuate the bowel is directly related to the level of the lesion. Any lesion above L1 affects the abdominal muscles, and a lesion above S3 will compromise the rectum.

Resistance forces stem from the internal and external sphincter, the anorectal angle, and friction.[49] The internal and external sphincters are subject to autonomic control, and are regulated by the parasympathetic nervous system that is innervated between S2 and S4. Therefore any lesion above this level will impair the ability of the patient to retain fecal continence.

Care and Management

In those patients who suffer from severe constipation, a bowel program is needed to assure proper emptying of the bowel to prevent fecal impaction and the necessity for manual disimpaction. The need for manual disimpaction should be avoided if at all possible because of the risk of injury to the patient.[50] Therefore SCI patients have their nutrition monitored very closely to insure they receive enough dietary fiber to retain fecal bulk. In conjunction with a regular schedule for emptying the bowel, this factor can make the loss of bowel control less traumatic.

§ 6.8 Urinary Dysfunction

The anatomy of the lower urinary tract consists generally of the bladder (the whole anatomical unit that stores and discharges urine), the detrusor (the smooth muscle in the bladder wall), the internal urethral sphincter (smooth muscle

---

[48] J. DeLisa, Rehabilitation Medicine, Principles and Practice (2d ed. 1993).

[49] *Id.*

[50] J. Banwell, C. Creasey, A. Aggarwal & J. Mortimer, *Management of the Neurogenic Bowel in Patients with Spinal Cord Injury,* 20 Urol. Clinic of N. Am. 517–25 (1993).

continuation of the detrusor), the external urethral sphincter (striated muscle), and the urethra. The detrusor is unique because it is controlled voluntarily while most smooth muscles are controlled by the autonomic system. When the detrusor contracts, the bladder is reduced in size in all dimensions, and is responsible for helping the bladder empty. The internal urethral sphincter is located at the bladder neck and is the primary muscle responsible for sustaining continence. It is controlled by the autonomic nervous system. The external urethral sphincter is responsible for opening and closing the urethra to allow voiding.

Acutely following injury, during the spinal shock period, the bladder is totally flaccid (unresponsive), and there is no desire to urinate because the bladder is not responding to distension. The patient is therefore unable to relieve bladder pressure without a catheter. Such inability to empty the bladder is often referred to as a type of neurogenic bladder. The most common complication of the neurogenic bladder is the urinary tract infection.

Urinary tract infection describes a condition where there has been microbial invasion of the tissue of the urinary tract. Individuals may also present with asymptomatic bacteriuria or as a colonization. *Asymptomatic bacteriuria* refers to bacteria that is present in, but has not caused any symptoms. Until recently, asymptomatic bacteriuria was believed to increase the risk factor for urinary tract infections and treated with antibiotics. However, the most recent research has shown that asymptomatic bacteriuria has no harmful effects on the genitourinary system.[51]

Symptomatic bacteriuria refers to a bacterial infection that has accompanying symptoms that may include fever, sweating, chills, nausea, vomiting, heightened spasticity, or abdominal tenderness.[52] Colonization is bacteriuria without any tissue invasion.[53]

Incontinence is another common problem for SCI victims. Incontinence is the inability to retain urine in the bladder. Although incontinence is not life-threatening the way many of these other urinary complications are, incontinence continues to be an important problem for SCI victims and their caregivers.[54] Incontinence causes a number of problems, especially moisture that contributes to skin care problems, pressure sore development, and infection. Many patients elect or require surgical intervention to minimize or eliminate the problem.

---

[51] A. Selzman & N. Hampel, *Urologic Complications of Spinal Cord Injury,* 20 Urol. Clinic of N. Am. 453–62 (1993).

[52] *Id.*

[53] *Id.*

[54] P. Van Kerrebroeck, E. Koldewijn, S. Scherpenhuizen & F. DeBruyne, *Morbidity Due to Lower Urinary Tract Function in Spinal Cord Injury Patients,* 31 Paraplegia 320–29 (1993).

Renal (kidney) failure results from a number of factors working either independently or in concert including chronic pyelonephritis (inflammation of the kidney), vesicoureteral reflux, hydronephrosis (collection of urine in the renal pelvis due to obstruction of outflow), and kidney stone formation.[55] Renal failure is a frequent cause of death in SCI patients.

SCI patients are also at risk for bladder cancer. Indwelling catheters are the most frequently cited cause due to the persistent irritation and nidus for infection.[56] Recent advances in urologic care have reduced the risk of bladder cancer. However, any patient who has had an indwelling catheter for longer than 10 years is still at a statistically higher risk of contracting bladder cancer and should be checked regularly.

Level

Urinary dysfunction may occur in any patient with a lesion at or above S3.

Incidence

Dysfunction of the urinary system and the complications that result are the most frequent problem encountered by SCI victims.[57] According to the National Spinal Cord Injury Data Research Center, urinary tract infections have been reported in as many as 66 percent of paraplegics and 70 percent of quadriplegics.[58] Data further reveals that as many as 34 percent of women complain of incontinence as being a major source of discomfort in their lives.[59] In men, 25 percent present cases of severe incontinence.[60] In addition, 30 percent of the deaths in SCI patients since WW II can be attributed to renal failure.[61]

Etiology

The neurogenic bladder in SCI results from lost voluntary control of the external sphincter that inhibits the ability to empty the bladder completely, or in some cases at all. Urinary tract infections are the result of the patient's

---

[55] A. Selzman & N. Hampel, *Urologic Complications of Spinal Cord Injury,* 20 Urol. Clinic of N. Am. 453–62 (1993).

[56] *Id.*

[57] Hochschuler, Cotler & Guyer, Rehabilitation of the Spine, Science and Practice 319 (1993).

[58] *Id.*

[59] P. Van Kerrebroeck, E. Koldewijn, S. Scherpenhuizen & F. DeBruyne, *Morbidity Due to Lower Urinary Tract Function in Spinal Cord Injury Patients,* 31 Paraplegia 320–29 (1993).

[60] *Id.*

[61] A. Selzman & N. Hampel, *Urologic Complications of Spinal Cord Injury,* Urol. Clinic of N. Am. 453–62 (1993).

exposure to one or more of the following risk factors: overdistension of the bladder, backward flow of urine during voiding (vesicoureteral reflux), high voiding pressure, large postvoiding residual volumes, stones, or other types of outlet obstruction, or enlargement of the prostate.[62] Incontinence is simply a direct result of damage to the spinal cord—it is a lost function. Renal failure and bladder cancer are secondary complications that are further complications of the lost function.

Care and Management

For patients with the neurogenic bladder, catheterization is required to prevent overfilling of the bladder.[63] Unfortunately, the catheter is often the source of urinary tract infections, especially during the acute treatment phase when it is necessary to place an indwelling catheter that is only changed weekly.[64] Indwelling catheters are passed through the urethra to the bladder to drain the bladder. The presence of an indwelling catheter often causes infection because it provides a continuous opening into the body for bacteria and yeast to enter the body.

Incontinence is most often treated with a combination of behavioral treatment and pharmacologic therapy. Two common behavioral treatments are scheduled times for voiding and bladder training. Various drugs are also used to either block receptors that trigger the voiding response or for their anesthetic effect on the bladder. Surgical intervention is also used effectively in some cases for treatment of incontinence. It is mainly used in connection with excessive urine retention due to loss of sphincter control.

§ 6.9 Sexual Dysfunction

As the survival rates of SCI victims have risen dramatically since WW II, concerns for improving the quality of life have gained importance. Sexual functioning tends to be a high priority for SCI victims. This is especially true since the mean age of SCI victims is 26 years old.[65]

For most SCI victims, there are two hurdles that must be cleared to regain adequate or satisfactory sexual functioning: the first is physical, and the second is psychological. It is just as important for the SCI to adjust to a new sense of his or her own sexuality as it is to discover how to perform physically postinjury. Most SCI

---

[62] *Id.*

[63] Hochschuler, Cotler & Guyer, Rehabilitation of the Spine, Science and Practice 319 (1993).

[64] A. Selzman & N. Hampel, *Urologic Complications of Spinal Cord Injury,* 20 Urol. Clinic of N. Am. 453–62 (1993).

[65] E. Smith & D. Bodner, *Sexual Dysfunction after Spinal Cord Injury,* 20 Urol. Clinic of N. Am. 532–42 (1993).

patients report no change in their desire for sex, although it is also common for SCI patients to feel sexually inhibited due to their injury. In addition to the psychological factors at work, such as diminished self-image and performance fears, there are the problems associated with incontinence that must be dealt with by either the patient or the partner.

Sexual performance in males is achieved through erection, ejaculation, and orgasm. After SCI all three are generally affected. In a neurologically intact male, erection is achieved in one of two ways. The first way is reflexogenic. Reflexogenic erections result from direct tactile stimulation. However, such erections are generally short-lived unless accompanied by continual stimulation.[66] The second type of erection is psychogenic. Psychogenic erections result from impulses originating in the brain.[67] In an SCI male, the ability to achieve either type of erection is significantly impaired. However, reflex erections are more commonly experienced than psychogenic erections. Ejaculation/orgasm is even less common than erections. Therefore, successful fertilization is rare.

Much less is known about the effect of SCI on women and their sexuality. Nevertheless, it is known that SCI affects women's sexuality due to impaired or absent sensation below the level of the lesion. However, some women have reported increased sensation above the level of the injury, especially in the T4–T5 area. This increased sensation has occasionally been reported to produce paraorgasm.[68] Paraorgasm is described as sexual pleasure that is consistent with a female's normal orgasmic sensations but does not occur in the groin and abdomen area.[69]

Vaginal lubrication is often affected after SCI. Sufficient lubrication is especially uncommon in women with complete lesions, while it is more common in women with incomplete lesions.[70] Intercourse is still an option for most women, although extreme spasticity and/or contractures may make intercourse impractical, if not impossible. Intercourse is also altered due to decreased mobility.

There is good news for women who have sustained SCI since fertility in women is far less affected by SCI than it is in men. Most women resume normal menstrual cycle function after the period of spinal shock wears off.[71] Pregnancy is often as possible for women with SCI as for those without. Additionally, labor and childbirth is basically unchanged for SCI women,[72] although some autonomic dysreflexia can be a childbirth complication for some

---

[66] *Id.*

[67] *Id.*

[68] J. DeLisa, Rehabilitation Medicine, Principles and Practice 771 (2d ed. 1993).

[69] E. Berard, *Sexuality of Spinal Cord Injured Women: Physiology and Pathophysiology: a Review,* 27 Paraplegia 99–112 (1989).

[70] J. DeLisa, Rehabilitation Medicine, Principles and Practice 771 (2d ed. 1993).

[71] *Id.*

[72] *Id.*

women.[73] For most pregnant SCI women the only heightened risk is that she may have an unsupervised birth because of her inability to detect the beginning of labor.[74] For this reason, an SCI pregnancy must be carefully monitored by doctors.

Level

The ability to achieve erection after SCI is largely dependent on the level of the injury. In patients injured at the cauda equina level, usually no reflex erections occur and psychogenic erections occur rarely. In patients injured at either the level of the cervical or thoracic spine, reflex erections are generally possible, but psychogenic erections are very rare.[75]

The level of the lesion affects sensation in women. The higher the level of the lesion, the smaller the area of the body in which the woman experiences any sensation.

Incidence

Somewhat surprisingly, most men (70–80 percent) can achieve some form of erection. However, ejaculation and fertility results are much smaller. Although currently ejaculation is possible for only 5 percent of SCI patients, progress is being made with fertility potential.[76]

Some degree of sexual dysfunction applies to all women with SCI. The differences are related to the amount of sensation retained.

Etiology

Sexual dysfunction is another direct result of injury to the spinal cord; both impaired sensation and loss of function contribute to sexual dysfunction.

Care and Management

As noted above, very few SCI males can achieve ejaculation. However, recent studies have dramatically changed the outlook when it comes to fertility options for men who are otherwise unable to ejaculate after SCI. Two options available

---

[73] E. Berard, *Sexuality of Spinal Cord Injured Women: Physiology and Pathophysiology: a Review,* 27 Paraplegia 99–112 (1989).

[74] J. DeLisa, Rehabilitation Medicine, Principles and Practice 773 (2d ed. 1993).

[75] E. Smith & D. Bodner, *Sexual Dysfunction after Spinal Cord Injury,* 20 Urol. Clinic of N. Am. 535–42 (1993).

[76] S. Seager & L. Halstead, *Fertility Options and Success after Spinal Cord Injury,* 20 Urol. Clinic of N. Am. 543–47 (1993).

for SCI men who wish to become biological fathers are vibratory stimulation and electrostimulation by rectal probe. Vibratory stimulation involves holding a vibrator to the penis for three to four minutes, allowing a brief rest, then repeating until ejaculation occurs. Generally, SCI patients with lesions above T8 benefit from this procedure more than those with lower lesions. Electrostimulation involves insertion of a rectal probe inside the anus so that the electrodes are in contact with the prostate gland and the seminal vesicles. Although most men are able to produce ejaculate through one of the two methods, the quantity and quality of the semen produced varies greatly.[77] Nevertheless, more men with SCI are becoming biological fathers because of these two procedures.

Sexual dysfunction in women is more difficult to treat because the dysfunction relates directly to lost motor function and lost sensation, neither of which can be restored by medical treatment. Pregnancy and delivery is basically unchanged for SCI women, however for those women who find pregnancy increases their risk of autonomic dysreflexia, caesarean sections have proven to be a satisfactory alternative to natural childbirth.[78]

§ 6.10 Heterotopic Ossification

Heterotopic ossification (HO) is the growth of bone in soft tissue areas surrounding joints. It eventually leads to reduced range of motion and contracture. It is the result of calcium being lost from the bones and then reappearing in areas of soft tissue.[79] SCI victims lose a considerable amount of bone and calcium from their bones in the first three to six months following their injury.[80] This is related to the lack of mobility and the absence of normal weight-bearing activities. As a result, the body releases the calcium and bone that it feels is no longer necessary.

Heterotopic ossification is first detected by swelling and heat in the affected area. As the bone continues to form, the swelling becomes firm and more localized.[81] HO can also present itself as decreased range of motion without the swelling or heat. HO is often difficult to diagnose early because it presents itself

---

[77] *Id.*

[78] E. Berard, *Sexuality of Spinal Cord Injured Women: Physiology and Pathophysiology: a Review,* 27 Paraplegia 99–112 (1989).

[79] M. Hanak & A. Scott, Spinal Cord Injury: An Illustrated Guide for Health Care Professionals 113 (1983).

[80] K. Ragnarsson & G. Sell, *Lower Extremity Fractures after Spinal Cord Injury: a Retrospective Study,* 62 Arch. Phys. Med. Rehabilitation 418–23 (1981).

[81] Hochschuler, Cotler & Guyer, Rehabilitation of the Spine, Science and Practice 357 (1993).

much the way in which deep vein thrombosis does. It is most common in hip joints, shoulders, knees, and elbows.[82]

Level

Heterotopic ossification affects SCI patients regardless of lesion level. It also affects patients regardless of whether their paralysis is complete or incomplete and whether spastic or flaccid. It appears to present more often in males than females,[83] however this may be related to the disparity in the number of SCI males to females.

Incidence

Heterotopic ossification occurs between 16 percent and 53 percent.[84]

Etiology

There is no widely accepted theory for why HO occurs, but some believe it may be related to decreased tissue oxygenation.[85] More recently, researchers have theorized that HO may be linked to passive motion exercises in paralytic limbs.[86] O. Daud and associates found that heterotopic ossification occurred only in patients when the start of passive motion exercises were started more than seven days following the injury.[87] This result heightens the necessity to get SCI victims transferred to a spinal cord injury center as soon as possible after injury. Those patients that are admitted early appear to have a statistically lower risk of developing HO than those that are delayed.

Care and Management

Heterotopic ossification is best treated and prevented by an early and aggressive range of motion program. Additionally, drugs such as disodium etidronate have proven effective in limiting ossification. If the condition has progressed to the point where range of motion is severely affected and joints are frozen (ankylosis), surgery is generally the only option.

---

[82] *Id.*

[83] V. Nixon, Spinal Cord Injury: a Guide to Functional Outcomes in Physical Therapy Management 197 (1985).

[84] J. DeLisa, Rehabilitation Medicine, Principles and Practice 894 (2d ed. 1993).

[85] *Id.*

[86] O. Daud, P. Sett, R. Burr & J. Silver, *Relationship of Heterotopic Ossification to Passive Movements in Paraplegic Patients,* 15 Disability & Rehabilitation 114–18 (1993).

[87] *Id.*

§ 6.11 Osteomyelitis

Osteomyelitis involves inflammation (infection) of the bone, especially the bone marrow and surrounding areas. Osteomyelitis presents symptoms of pain in the affected area, fever, sweats, leukocytosis (increased white blood cell count), unusual rigidity of the overlying muscle, and skin inflammation.

In SCI patients, osteomyelitis has been linked to delaying the healing of severe pressure sores.[88] Pressure sores, as noted above, are generally thought to stem from prolonged pressure, spasticity, and other factors, but not directly from osteomyelitis. Nevertheless, osteomyelitis has an adverse affect on the treatment of pressure sores.

Level

Osteomyelitis affects patients at any level of injury.

Incidence

A 1994 study showed that osteomyelitis is much more common than originally thought. When patients are properly diagnosed using scanning equipment, incidence levels have been reported as high as 33 percent.

Etiology

Osteomyelitis is caused by pathogenic (disease-causing) bacteria.

Care and Management

Early diagnosis allows osteomyelitis to be treated by antibiotics. However, surgical intervention accompanied by high doses of antibiotics may become necessary if the abscess in the bone worsens. One of the problems facing the medical team is that osteomyelitis is very difficult to diagnose in patients also suffering from severe pressure sores. For that reason, it often goes untreated and becomes an underlying inhibitor to the healing process of pressure sores. A 1994 study showed that, when properly diagnosed and treated, pressure sores with accompanying osteomyelitis heal at a comparable rate compared to patients without the underlying osteomyelitis.[89] Unfortunately, osteomyelitis is often not diagnosed by the treating physician.

---

[88] R. Darouiche, G. Landon, M. Klima, D. Musher & J. Markowski, *Ostoemyelitis Associated with Pressure Sores,* 154 Arch. Internal Med. 753–55 (1994).

[89] *Id.*

§ 6.12 Charcot Joints

Charcot joints refers to a diseased joint. In SCI patients this generally occurs in the spinal column joints. Another name for Charcot joints is neuropathic joints. In SCI patients, the loss of sensitivity results in the failure of proper muscle contractions to protect the spine.[90] As a result, the spine suffers minute fractures of the joints and eventually sclerosis (hardness) forms. The typical patient with Charcot spine will present swelling and deformity of the joint.[91] In the beginning the condition is painless, and is difficult to detect until bone and joint destruction is well underway, which is why it rarely gets treated early. Charcot joints also evolve in different ways in different persons. In some, total destruction of the joints may occur in weeks, while in others it may take years. Spinal joints however usually evolve slowly, which gives medical personnel the time and warning to treat the condition.

Level, Incidence, and Etiology

Very little is known about why spinal column joints become diseased in SCI victims and the level of the lesion does not appear to be related to its occurrence. However, the incidence is generally reported between 5 percent and 10 percent.[92]

Care and Management

Treatment for Charcot joints usually requires surgery.[93] Operating on a spine with Charcot joint is extremely dangerous, because stabilization of the spine is necessary both anteriorly and posteriorly.[94]

§ 6.13 Fractures

Most fractures occurring in the SCI population occur in the lower extremities, with fractures of the femoral neck and subtrochanteric region being the most difficult to treat effectively.

---

[90] M. Harrison, M. Sacher, B. Rosenblum & A. Rothman, *Spinal Charcot Arthropathy,* 29 Neurosurgery 273–76 (1991).

[91] *Id.*

[92] *Id.*

[93] *Id.*

[94] Hochschuler, Cotler & Guyer, Rehabilitation of the Spine, Science and Practice 344 (1993).

Level

All SCI patients are at risk for bone fractures. Level of the lesion has little impact physiologically speaking on the risk. However, level of lesion will have an effect due to other factors. For instance, paraplegics who are able to perform transfers independently are at higher risk for sustaining fractures due to falls.[95] Especially in the learning stage, falls during transfers are quite common.[96]

Incidence

SCI patients are at higher risk for suffering fractures as a result of their injury. Most studies report an incidence of 2–6 percent of the SCI population suffering fractures in the lower extremity areas.[97] The femur is most often the site of fractures.

Etiology

There are many factors that contribute to the increased risk of fractures in the SCI population, but osteoporosis (loss of calcium and bone mass) may be the most significant factor as the bone becomes weaker and more brittle. The loss of bone mass below the level of the lesion occurs almost immediately after the injury, especially during the period of spinal shock.[98]

Additionally, as patients are subjected to falls during transfers and other stresses during physical rehabilitation, fractures occur with more frequency. In addition, as patients with SCI grow older, the effects of osteoporosis and prolonged immobilization make lower extremity fractures possible even when performing simple tasks such as turning the patient in bed.

Care and Management

Treatment for fractures in the SCI population is similar to treatment for any other person. Closed treatment with splints is generally recommended.[99] However, circumferential plaster casts are avoided because of the potential for pressure sores resulting from frequently poor padding beneath the plaster.[100]

---

[95] J. DeLisa, Rehabilitation Medicine, Principles and Practice 895 (2d ed. 1993).

[96] *Id.*

[97] *Id.* at 894.

[98] Hochschuler, Cotler & Guyer, Rehabilitation of the Spine, Science and Practice 357 (1993).

[99] J. DeLisa, Rehabilitation Medicine, Principles and Practice 895 (2d ed. 1993).

[100] *Id.*

§ 6.14 Respiratory Dysfunction

For most SCI patients, there is a high risk of developing one of the vast number of potential complications due to respiratory dysfunction. The process of breathing consists of two steps. After SCI, there is the possibility that either or both of these steps have been compromised. The first is inspiration, in which the muscles of the chest wall (intercostal muscles) and the diaphragm contract to compress the abdominal cavity and expand the thoracic cavity.[101] This decreases the pressure in the lungs, and air fills the lungs in an attempt to restore the pressure balance.[102] During expiration, on the other hand, the intercostal muscles and diaphragm relax, allowing the abdominal cavity to expand, increasing the pressure in the lungs, and thereby forcing air out.[103] Coughing is also a critical part of the respiratory process. Coughing is a forced expiration that is accomplished by a forceful and sudden contraction of the muscles of the abdomen.[104] The consequences of not being able to perform any of these processes is potentially life-threatening.

Level

SCI patients who have been injured in the cervical spine area are at the highest risk for developing respiratory complication since any injury above C4 inhibits all of the above respiratory processes.[105] SCI victims with spinal cord lesions between C6 and T12 are at risk of developing pulmonary complications even though diaphragmatic function has been spared.[106] At any level of injury above T12, the ability to cough is inhibited, if not completely absent.[107]

Incidence

Mortality is still relatively high during the first three months to one year following injury to the cervical spine. Studies reveal that 15–18 percent of patients with lower cervical spine injuries die due to acute respiratory failure.[108]

---

[101] M. Hanak & A. Scott, Spinal Cord Injury: an Illustrated Guide for Health Care Professionals 57 (1983).

[102] *Id.*

[103] *Id.*

[104] *Id.*

[105] *Id.* at 58.

[106] M. Hanak & A. Scott, Spinal Cord Injury: an Illustrated Guide for Health Care Professionals 58 (1983).

[107] Hochschuler, Cotler & Guyer, Rehabilitation of the Spine, Science and Practice 318 (1993).

[108] J. Spinal, L. Michel & P. Westbrook, *Pulmonary Dysfunction Following Traumatic Quadriplegia,* 243 JAMA 528–31 (1980).

More common problems are the incidence of pneumonia and atelectasis (potentially collapsed lung). In a recent study conducted over a five-year period from 1985–1990, of 261 patients who were admitted to Model Regional Spinal Cord Injury Care Systems, 175 (67 percent) experienced some type of respiratory complication.[109] The most common being atelectasis (36 percent), pneumonia (31 percent) and ventilatory failure (22 percent).[110]

Etiology

The diaphragm is innervated by nerves stemming from C3–C5. When the diaphragm has been affected, both inspiration and expiration are inhibited. Without the use of the diaphragm, the ability to contract the abdominal cavity and decrease the pressure in the lungs is seriously impaired.[111]

Care and Management

Many quadriplegics must be ventilated immediately after the injury. With therapy, however, most patients who have lost diaphragmatic function learn to breathe on their own by learning to use their accessory neck muscles.[112] Nevertheless, few are ever able to regain the level of inspiratory volume they had preinjury.[113] Many patients with high level lesions will require a ventilator for the rest of their lives. If patients have retained movement of their arms, they can be instructed in how to manually cough.[114] If not, patients may require 24-hour attendant care.

§ 6.15 Orthostatic Hypotension

Orthostatic hypotension (OH) is a condition in which both systolic (maximum blood pressure during contraction of the ventricles) and diastolic (the point of least pressure) blood pressure drops below normal due to postural changes. It is most common when a patient arises from a lying down position to a sitting

---

[109] A. Jackson & T. Broomes, *Incidence of Respiratory Complications Following Spinal Cord Injury*, 75 Arch Phys—Med. Rehabilitation 270–75 (1994).

[110] *Id.*

[111] M. Hanak & A. Scott, Spinal Cord Injury: an Illustrated Guide for Health Care Professionals 58 (1983).

[112] Rothman & Simeone, The Spine 1238–39 (3d ed. 1992).

[113] *Id.*

[114] V. Nixon, Spinal Cord Injury: A Guide to Functional Outcomes in Physical Therapy Management 45 (1985).

or standing position.[115] The symptoms include dizziness, lightheadedness, or loss of consciousness.[116]

Level

The sympathetic nervous system is innervated by nerves stemming from the spinal cord between T1 and L2. Therefore, any lesion above the level of L2 will affect the sympathetic nervous system and the patients may be at risk for orthostatic hypotension.

Incidence

Orthostatic hypotension occurs frequently after the injury due to immobilization during the first six to eight weeks.

Etiology

The damage to the spinal cord and its affect on the sympathetic nervous system is often cited as the underlying cause leading to OH.[117] The damage to the sympathetic system leads to loss of vasoconstrictor control. Due to this impairment, blood tends to pool in dependent regions.[118] The net effect is lower than normal blood pressure when the patient changes to a more upright position.[119]

Care and Management

Preventative measures that are frequently used include wearing an abdominal binder, elastic support stockings, tilt-table tolerance training, and use of a reclining wheelchair with elevating footrests.[120]

---

[115] S. O'Sullivan & T. Schmitz, Physical Rehabilitation: Assessment and Treatment 556–57 (2d ed. 1988).

[116] *Id.*

[117] *Id.* at 556.

[118] *Id.* at 556–57.

[119] *Id.* at 556.

[120] M. Hanak & A. Scott, Spinal Cord Injury: an Illustrated Guide for Health Care Professionals 55–56 (1983).

§ 6.16 Deep Vein Thrombosis (DVT)

SCI patients are at high risk for developing DVT. A DVT is a blood clot within the vanous system. It most often appears in the calf, thigh, or pelvis, but it can appear anywhere. It is particularly dangerous because of the possibility the clot can break loose and travel through the blood stream. A floating blood clot is referred to as an embolus. A large embolus which blocks a pulmonary artery can result in death.[121]

Level

DVT occurs at all levels of injury. However, because it is related to lack of muscle tone, those patients who are spastic, especially spastic soon after injury, may be at less risk than patients with flaccid paralysis or an extended period of spinal shock.[122] Incidence DVT is also particularly difficult to diagnose because it resembles many other complications. For that reason, the rate of incidence reported by various researchers has varied widely depending on the type of diagnostic method used. Those researchers who have used advanced techniques to diagnose often cite incidence between 50 percent and 75 percent.[123] DVT occurs most frequently within the first two months following the injury.[124]

Etiology

DVT results from the development of an abnormal blood clot within a vessel. Lack of normal muscle contractions in the lower extremities impairs the normal venous pumping mechanism,[125] slowing blood flow, thus resulting in higher concentrations of procoagulants causing the formation of a clot.[126] Age and prolonged pressure due to immobilization (sitting or lying) increase the risk of DVT.[127]

---

[121] S. Gunduz, *Deep Vein Thrombosis in Spinal Cords Injured Patients,* 31 Paraplegia 606–10 (1993).

[122] J. DeLisa, Rehabilitation Medicine, Principles and Practice 671 (2d ed. 1993).

[123] S. Gunduz, *Deep Vein Thrombosis in Spinal Cords Injured Patients,* 31 Paraplegia 606–10 (1993).

[124] S. O'Sullivan & T. Schmitz, Physical Rehabilitation: Assessment and Treatment 557–58 (2d ed. 1988).

[125] *Id.*

[126] *Id.*

[127] *Id.*

Care and Management

Most treatment programs are related to early preventive procedures, including drug therapy (prophylactic anticoagulants), frequent turning to relieve pressure on the large vessels, range of motion, elastic support stockings, pneumatic compression devices, and positioning of the lower extremities to facilitate venous return.[128]

§ 6.17 Pulmonary Embolism

Pulmonary embolism is an obstruction of a vessel by a clot in the pulmonary arteries. As noted, it is the result of a deep vein thrombosis that breaks off and travels into the pulmonary arteries. It may be a life-threatening condition if it disrupts enough of the flow of blood into the lungs.

Level

Pulmonary embolism occurs at all levels of injury.

Incidence

A March 1994 study revealed that pulmonary embolism occurs in 3.1 percent of the patients examined.[129]

Etiology

A pulmonary embolism is a blood clot that breaks free and lodges in a pulmonary vessel.

Care and Management

Treatment for pulmonary embolism involves pharmacologic therapy, including anticoagulation (prevents further clotting), throbbolytics (clot dissolvers), increased oxygen administration to relieve the effects of hypoxemia (lack of oxygen in the blood), and reassurance and relaxation to relieve the pain and stress often experienced by the patient.[130] See also § **6.16.**

---

[128] *Id.*

[129] A. Jackson & T. Groomes, *Incidence of Respiratory Complications Following Spinal Cord Injury*, 75 Arch. Phys. Med. Rehabilitation 270–75 (1994).

[130] S. O'Sullivan & T. Schmitz, Physical Rehabilitation: Assessment and Treatment 557–58 (2d ed. 1988).

CHAPTER 7

ACUTE CARE OF THE SPINAL CORD INJURY PATIENT

Michael P. Pietrzak, M.D.

OVERVIEW

§ 7.1 Introduction

Comprehensive care of spinal cord injuries (SCI) involves several important aspects. In evaluating the care given to the patient with spinal cord injury it is useful to understand these principle aspects of care. Included are:

1. Overall proactive injury prevention programs (example: safety programs, protective gear, and so forth)
2. Recognition of potential injury (awareness of which mechanisms of injury are likely to be associated with SCI)
3. Limitation of any further damage after a potential injury is recognized (example: immobilizing the cervical spine after a fall)
4. Curtailment of progression of the injury (example: pharmacologic agents to retard further swelling of the cord after injury)
5. Definitive treatment to reverse any aspect of the injury that can potentially be corrected (example: emergency surgery to remove or fix fragments of bone that are impinging on the spinal cord)
6. Supportive care during the recovery phase
7. Rehabilitation
8. Chronic care.

Acute care involves these aspects of care to varying degrees (the exceptions being rehabilitation, chronic care, and prevention), although even prevention programs are significantly effected by information on injury patterns and epidemiology data gathered during acute care. All the above aspects of care affect each other and may often occur simultaneously. Obviously taking steps to prevent further injury will be important during all phases of care. Similarly proper initial care may lead to more successful rehabilitation.

Treatment in the acute phase will have a major impact on the later treatment and contribute significantly to the final outcome. Acute care of spinal cord injuries can be readily viewed in a temporal fashion. These temporal phases for practical purposes can be identified as:

1. First aid or "buddy care"
2. Formal prehospital care or EMS
3. Emergency department care
4. Emergency surgery.

Each of these phases involve some degree of the aspects of care outlined. This chapter will approach acute care by concentrating on the temporal phases of care separately while addressing the important aspects and principles of care in each.

§ 7.2 General Concepts and Principles of Acute Care

A full understanding of appropriate acute care for the SCI patient is not possible without some knowledge of the general principles of trauma care systems and mechanisms of injury.

Role of the Trauma System

In the 1960s and 1970s the American College of Surgeons began to organize and develop a systematic integrated approach to trauma care. It became evident that the outcome of injured patients was not only affected by the care rendered by the physician, but also was highly dependent on an integrated system that could ensure the patient would be promptly treated by the appropriate level of provider and facility. This system involves prehospital care, transportation, communication, and a system plan that guarantees patients are delivered to the appropriate level of facility. The concept of trauma centers was developed to care for multiple or complicated trauma patients. Spinal cord injury patients require expert care for optimal outcome. It would be inappropriate for an ambulance to transport a spinal cord injury patient to an minor urgent care center. It is incumbent on the responsible authorities to make certain that prehospital and trauma systems are appropriately designed to meet these needs. Furthermore, in spite of the most sophisticated hospital care, if prehospital care is substandard, SCI injuries can be irreparably worsened.

Mechanisms of Injury

As described in **Chapter 1,** the spinal column includes skeletal structures, connecting ligaments, and the spinal cord. This skeletal structure provides protection for the cord as well as the articulating framework that permits mobility. Excessive flexion, extension, rotation, compression, distraction (pulling apart), or penetrating trauma may lead to injury of the cord or its supporting structures. The degree of force or motion necessary to cause injury will vary depending on a number of factors including age, flexibility, previous injuries or surgery, presence of disc disease, muscle strength, and the anatomical variations that may be present in the spinal column. This can be illustrated by cases of patients with spinal stenosis (narrowing of the spinal canal) when severe spinal cord damage may occur with injuries that normally would have done little or no damage. Spinal cord injuries are not limited to high energy mechanisms. Even excessively vigorous neck extension during endotracheal intubation has been reported to cause SCI. Sophisticated acute care management includes consideration of these factors in the evaluation and treatment.

An understanding of all the mechanisms and associated potential injuries is beyond the scope of this chapter. It is sufficient to be aware that excessive motion or force in any direction has injury potential. Certain injury patterns are characteristic for different mechanisms of injury. Classic examples are hyperflexion (neck forcefully bent too far forward) and hyperextension (neck bent backwards, for example whiplash) injuries. In flexion injuries the neck is forced forward. The supporting posterior ligaments are stretched and then torn. The forward flexion may place excessive force on the anterior portion of the vertebral body causing compressions or fracturing a fragment of bone off the anterior lip. If the flexion occurred with sufficient force, instability and subluxation (displacement) of the vertebral body can occur. If these structures impinge on the cord, damage is likely. Extension injuries affect the anterior ligamentous structures. Physicians expert in the acute care of SCI seek the mechanism of injury to help predict the injury pattern before definitive diagnoses can be made. This is more than a mere academic exercise as many injuries involve only the ligaments and may lack radiologic evidence of bone injury. In fact in some cases the history of the mechanism may be the only evidence to suspect cervical injury since the patient's mental status may be altered (for example, by intoxication), making the individual unaware of neck pain or injury. Failure to recognize this potential can lead to premature excessive motion and a preventable SCI.

§ 7.3 Prioritization of Care

Since injuries of the spinal cord are often accompanied by other threatening injuries or complications, the successful management of trauma is highly reliant on the appropriate prioritization of treatment. In general guidelines in the Advanced Trauma Life Support manual published by the American College of Surgeons are accepted national standards for evaluation, prioritization, and treatment of injuries. Deviation from these guidelines and standards do occur in certain clinical situations, however, such deviation should be justified by the clinician. Even in isolated spinal cord injuries, assuring adequate airway and breathing takes priority over treatment of the cord injury. Presence of other injuries such as severe bleeding might also take priority. The principal priorities established by consensus of professional organizations are airway, breathing, and circulation (ABCs). The procedures and interventions used to stabilize the ABCs may pose a risk to the patient with spinal column injury. Those trained in the management of trauma are aware of the potential dangers to the cord and necessary precautionary measures while instituting priority life saving procedures or ABCs. Some of this will be discussed later in **§§ 7.6** and **7.7.**

ACUTE CARE

§ 7.4 First Aid Care

The primary goal of first aid is to recognize that the potential for SCI has occurred, leave the patient immobile, provide comfort, and seek emergency professional help. In some communities CPR is widely taught to the general public. Some of the airway interventions taught in CPR can be of significant risk to the cervical SCI patient. Basic CPR courses focus on cardiac care and do not fully address protection of the spine. Organizations involved in high risk activities such as football, high diving, auto racing, and so forth generally provide more advanced first aid capability that might include spinal immobilization and extrication procedures. Ideally first aid providers might be able to keep the airway open and the patient breathing while keeping the spine immobilized. This usually means leaving the patient where the patient was found. However, leaving the potential SCI patient underwater or in a vehicle that is burning in order to avoid risk of injury to the cord would be obviously inappropriate. The risks to the rescuer also need to be considered. The degree to which a rescuer is expected to intervene and the standards to which the person can be held are dependent on the individual's specific medical training.

§ 7.5 Prehospital Care

Usually the recognition of potential spinal injury and proper stabilization begin with the arrival of formal prehospital care or EMS (Emergency Medical Services). All EMS personnel have some knowledge of spinal immobilization techniques. Standards for prehospital care in the United States have been developed to provide immobilization in all potential cases of injury. This is often viewed as annoying to patients who may feel fine and cannot understand the necessity of these measures. However, the protocols have been designed to err on the side of preventing further injury, especially before formal medical evaluation has taken place. The unconscious patient found on the ground should usually be immobilized. Anyone not recalling the nature of the accident and even cardiac patients who have fallen to the floor are potential SCI patients. The capability of evaluation in the field is limited, therefore the categories of patients immobilized are very broad. In most cases no injury is uncovered, but the practice is defended on the basis of the severe consequences of failure to immobilize.

There are many acceptable techniques for immobilization in the field. These include (but are not limited to) rigid collars, rolled towels or blankets, tape, and combinations of these. Whatever technique is used, the general goals are the same. Rotation, flexion, extension, and distraction are to be minimized for the entire transfer process. At the same time an adequate airway is maintained. Soft collars usually cannot provide adequate support to immobilize the injured neck. Furthermore whatever immobilization process is used should allow advanced airway interventions if necessary. A perfectly immobilized cord will be of little use to the patient who could not be intubated and subsequently dies.

Generally any potential SCI patient, after having the ABCs addressed, have a collar applied and are placed on some type of rigid apparatus (that is, a spine board or chair in the case of automobile extrications) for movement or transport. The techniques used to place patients on the apparatus are critical and usually require more than one person in unison to move the body as a unit with relatively minimal movement of the spinal column. The "log roll" technique is the most commonly accepted by the EMS community and the ACS. However, a few studies have shown this technique to allow a significant amount of movement in patients with unstable injuries.[1] Once the patient is on the board, further securement procedures can take place. After immobilization is completed the airway should be reevaluated. Vital signs should be periodically assessed enroute. Spinal shock can be difficult to assess in transit. However, fluids can be readily administered to maintain blood pressure. Conclusive studies on which fluid type to give in the field do not exist, although circulatory volume expanders such as .9 normal saline and lactated ringers are generally accepted. Likewise the use of oxygen while generally employed lacks definitive scientific evidence of benefit. The prehospital delivery of pharmaceutical agents that may be beneficial to SCI patients if given early (that is, steroids to prevent further swelling and thus minimizing further damage) is controversial and requires further study.

EMS systems should be developed to take the spinal cord patient to an appropriate medical facility experienced in the management of trauma, bypassing other hospitals unless the condition of the patient requires lifesaving interventions. Adequate prehospital care is not judged simply by the care given by the attendants when the ambulance arrives, but involves the appropriate design of the system.

EMERGENCY DEPARTMENT CARE

§ 7.6 Initial Care and Evaluation

When the patient arrives at the emergency department, the objective of the medical team is to identify the injuries and stabilize the patient. If a patient is seriously injured with surgically correctable injuries, as little time as possible must be spent in the emergency treatment ward in order to deliver the patient to the operating room (OR) quickly. The primary survey is accomplished first. This is an examination of the patient that should take less than two minutes. The survey should not be interrupted other than to immediately solve the problems it is designed to find in the order that these problems are addressed. The

---

[1] R. McGuire, *Spinal Instability and the Log-rolling Maneuver,* 27 J. Trauma No. 5 at 525–31 (May 1987).

first consideration is the airway. Can the patient get air into the lungs? Options available for restoring the patient's airway include: positioning, intubation, a nasopharyngeal or oral airway (a small plastic piece that fits in the mouth and nose), or a cricothyrotomy (an incision or puncture in the patient's neck to bypass the upper airway). Whichever technique is used, measures should be taken to insure the stability of the spine. The second aspect the primary survey addresses is breathing. Can the patient move air in and out of the lungs unassisted? If not, why not? Potential reasons include neurologic impairment from a head injury or spinal cord trauma. The final part of the primary survey is circulation. Is the heart beating? Is there a significant source of bleeding somewhere? The purpose of the primary survey is to assess and stabilize the patient's vital organs (lungs, heart, and brain). An amputation of the leg may also be cricital, but if immediate attention is given to that procedure, the patient may die from respiratory failure in the meantime. Most primary surveys now include a further priority (D), which stands for a brief assessment of disability.

A more thorough secondary survey is accomplished after the primary survey and its appropriate interventions have been completed. This is a full examination of the patient. It should include rolling the patient as a unit and inspecting everything. More detailed spinal and neurologic exams (addressed in **§ 6.8**) are performed at this time. The overall goal of the secondary survey is to systematically identify and address all the injuries present. The secondary survey often includes a standard series of x-rays: cervical spine, chest, and pelvis x-rays. Additional studies are ordered as indicated by the survey.

§ 7.7 Evaluation of the Spine

Central to the discussion of acute care of SCI is the evaluation of the spine with special attention to the cervical spine. This evaluation requires both physical examination and imaging techniques. The history or circumstance surrounding the injury will often indicate the direction and focus of the evaluation. If an obvious neurologic deficit exists, the steps to be taken are usually clear. However, most patients presenting to emergency departments from accidents arrive with cervical collars but no neurologic deficits. The evaluation of the neck and spine will then be designed to identify any potential injuries while protecting the spine. The general practice has been to keep all potential spinal injury patients securely immobilized until radiologic studies show an absence of injury. However, in some cases expertly trained physicians may clinically clear the patient without radiologic studies. Adequate definitive studies establishing the exact criteria to determine whether to x-ray or not do not exist. However, reasonable criteria used by experienced clinicians to clear the patient include:

1. Absence of high energy injury
2. Full mental capacity and alertness (that is, the patient is not groggy or intoxicated)
3. No other significant injuries that could mask the pain (for example, a broken femur could cause enough pain that a patient may not be aware of pain in the neck area)
4. Absence of midline neck tenderness
5. Full range of motion of the neck without pain.

This last step should only be attempted after the first four conditions are met. Furthermore, the range of motion of the neck should be actuated by the patient (not the examiner) and curtailed at any moment neck pain or other symptoms are encountered. While it is impossible to rule out spinal injury with total certainty, reasonable practitioners may release such selected patients without x-ray studies.

In cases where these criteria are not met, proper radiographic imaging is in order. The universal initial choice is standard plain film x-ray. For most of the spine, two views are usually adequate for screening. The number of views necessary to evaluate the cervical spine is a matter of considerable debate and ranges from one-to-five views. Common errors in imaging the cervical spine include failure to image C7 and T1 where 5–10 percent of cervical injuries occur. Special techniques need to be employed to properly evaluate these levels of vertebrae. Another misconception is that a normal x-ray study implies that injury is not present. There are many soft tissue injuries that may not be evident on initial x-rays. These may include unstable ligamentous injuries. Such injuries could be suspected if significant midline neck pain were present even with negative initial x-rays. Prior to clearing such a patient flexion-extension tests could be performed to identify whether subluxation (the shifting of one or more vertebrae out of position) is present. Extreme caution is required since flexion or extensions could lead to initial neurologic injury. Therefore any motion should be self actuated by the fully alert patient and curtailed if increased pain or neurologic symptoms occurs. Occasionally patients will have such significant neck muscle spasm that the cervical vertebrae will not properly flex. In such cases the study is invalid and cannot rule out an unstable injury. Finally, the use of flexion-extension films when a potentially unstable fracture is present should be limited to specialists expert in this area. At any point the emergency treatment that a physician identifies an unstable fracture or ligamentous injury, the patient should be securely immobilized and appropriate specialists consulted.

If standard x-rays are inconclusive, unobtainable, or in any way inadequate other imaging techniques may be employed, including tomogram, computed tomography (CT), fluoroscopy, and magnetic resonance imaging (MRI). These studies will help clarify and delineate injuria suspected or partially seen on plain film studies. The CT and MRI have the additional advantage of delineating soft tissue more clearly than x-ray and therefore are more useful to evaluate spinal cord involvement. Often a combination of studies is required. Ultimately the clinician must combine the information from the physical examination of the spine and imaging studies with neurologic examination to determine the full extent of spinal cord injury.

§ 7.8 Neurologic Examination

While the radiologic studies identify structural lesions, functional problems are primarily addressed by the neurologic examination. The neurologic evaluation in the acute setting assists the treatment decision process, establishes a baseline from which progress can be evaluated, and provides significant prognostic information. The initial steps of the neurologic assessment occur during the primary survey. For example spontaneous breathing implies that something is neurologically intact (C3–C4 supplying stimulus to the diaphragm). Gross disability (that is, inability to move extremities) is also often noted in the primary survey. More detailed neurologic examination is accomplished during the secondary survey. The degree of exam detail required in the emergency setting is variable but is driven primarily by the information needed to assist in the decision process of patient care. Additionally, sufficient information is needed to establish a baseline exam so that deterioration or improvement can be assessed. In some cases the exam may be curtailed if priority surgery is indicated. At a minimum, an attempt should be made to have sufficient information to establish the level and grossly describe the degree of disability (for example, complete motor and sensory loss below the level of the umbilicus). If time and the patient's condition allows, greater detail of neurologic exam is warranted.

There are many aspects of the neurologic examination that may be accomplished and recorded in the acute setting. The standard elements include motor, sensory, and reflex testing. Motor exam is usually graded from one through five by the patient's ability to move against various resistances. Grade five is full strength. Four indicates ability to push against resistance, but not with full strength. Grade three strength can lift against gravity, but not against resistance. Two indicates the ability to move, but insufficient strength to lift the extremity against gravity. One is muscle contraction but no motion, while zero is no evidence of voluntary contraction. The sensory exam may be very complex and subjective in interpretation. Elements often tested take into account pain, pressure, light touch, position, vibration, and heat. These sensations are transmitted to the brain via anatomically distinct tracts in the spinal cord. As described in the **Chapter 1,** the posterior columns of the spinal cord carry fibers responsible for deep pressure, vibration, and position. Therefore a patient with an injury isolated to the posterior portion of the spinal cord may have sufficient strength to walk but difficulty and awkwardness doing so due to lack of positional sense.

Checking reflexes, while almost universally done, is not always useful unless correlated with other findings in the neuro exam. Reflexes often assessed in the SCI patient include the deep tendon reflexes and the bulbocavernosus reflex.

The combination of motor, sensory, and reflex exams indicates the functional loss and can also categorize the findings into recognized cord syndromes that help direct treatment and establish prognosis. For example, the presence of the sacral sparing with paralysis in the arms greater than paralysis in the legs could indicate a central cord syndrome seen with hyperextension and occasionally in flexion injuries. The significance is that central cord syndromes have a better prognosis (statistically significant chance of better outcome) than anterior cord syndrome.

§ 7.9 Emergency Department Interventions

Interventions in the emergency department setting are designed to stabilize the patient, protect the cord from further injury, curtail any progression of injuries already present, and treat anything that is feasibly correctable in the emergency department. Most of the spinal immobilization techniques have been discussed in the §§ **7.4** and **7.5.** In the emergency department setting there may be some additional more definitive types of immobilization available. The clinical situation will drive these interventions. Traction may be applied to stabilize the spine. This is often accomplished with tongs and weights and should be done in cooperation with appropriate specialists. Traction is rarely applied until the extent of injury is appreciated.

Medications used in the emergency treatment of SCI are based on the principle minimizing progression of the damage. High doses of intravenous steroids (methylprednisolone), if given within eight hours of injury, believed to minimize edema (swelling) in the injured cord, have shown some promise. Further study is required before this can be established as a standard. Newer agents including the 21 amino-ketosteroid, GM-1 ganglioside, and others that might stimulate regeneration of damaged neurons are under investigation.[2]

Supportive care in the emergency department should include placement of a nasogastic tube to reduce abdominal distention, foley catheterization to prevent bladder distention and autonomic stimulation (which may lead to dysreflexia), treatment of spinal shock as indicated, and initials steps to prevent pressure necrosis as outlined in **Chapter 5.**

---

[2] F. Giesler et al., *Recovery of Motor Function after Spinal Cord Injury: A Randomized Placebo-controlled Trial with GM-1 Ganglioside,* 324 New Eng. J. of Med. No. 26 at 1829–38 (June 27, 1991).

Some lesions can be definitively managed in the emergency department setting by the appropriately trained physician. Some unilateral facet dislocations may be manually reduced and placed in a stabilizing device without going to the OR. However, most definitive corrective interventions are done in the OR setting.

§ 7.10 Definitive Care: Surgical versus Nonsurgical

Stabilization and immobilization of spinal fractures are accomplished either surgically or nonsurgically depending on the circumstances of the fracture. The goal of surgical treatment of the spine is to prevent further injury through stabilization of unstable structures and removal of potentially dangerous fragments and to facilitate the return of neurological function by abating neurologic impingement or correction of deformities. Physicians hope that the treatment helps the patient attain a painless, balanced, and stable spinal column. Non-surgical treatment of the spine is designed to either immobilize the spine in its posttraumatic position, or to reduce the posttraumatic deformity and provide subsequent external immobilization.

Before discussing specific treatments for the different types of fractures, it is important to be aware of the difference between reduction and fixation. Reduction means taking a bony injury and eliminating the deformity, most often by realigning the two pieces of bone so that they can heal together. Open reduction is done by surgically opening the body and placing the pieces back together. Closed reduction is done by manipulation without an incision. Fixation is taking the reduced bone fragments and immobilizing them. Fixation may be accomplished either internally or externally. Internal fixation involves surgically placing plates, screws, or wires into the bone. External fixation is a cast, splint, or other immobilizer placed on the outside of the body to hold the underlying bony pieces in place.

The surgical approach varies depending on the area of the spinal cord that is to be instrumented. There are different curvatures to each part of the spine and differences in the relationship between the canal size and the size of the cord. Timing of the surgery is also a consideration that is different with each patient. Two indicators that indicate immediate surgery are progressive neurologic deterioration and acute spinal dislocation with residual neurologic function. However, delay of the surgery may facilitate stabilization of the patient's general condition, resolution of spinal edema (swelling), organization of fracture hematoma, and reduction of intraoperative blood loss, all desirable results. Many surgeons advocate a 7-to-10 day waiting period prior to surgery for these reasons. Each case may have mitigating circumstances and the experience of the surgeon involved will have an impact on the decision.

Regardless of whether the patient is treated surgically or nonsurgically, there are a multitude of complications that can affect the recovery and life of the spinal cord injury patient. The complications that most often threaten the acute spinal cord injury patient include loss of sympathetic tone, neurogenic shock, deepvein thrombosis, pulmonary embolism, autonomic dysreflexia, respiratory failure, pneumothorax, pneumonia, ARDS (adult respiratory distress syndrome), stress gastritis, fecal impaction, urinary tract infection, kidney infection (pyelonephritis), and spread of infection into the blood stream (urosepsis). See **Chapter 3** for complete descriptions of these and other complications encountered by the spinal cord victim.

§ 7.11 BIBLIOGRAPHY

American College of Surgeons Committee on Trauma. Advanced Trauma Life Support Handbook, 1993.

Browner, Bruce. *Skeletal Trauma—Fractures, Dislocations, and Ligamentous Injuries.* W.B. Saunders Co., 1992.

Fenstermaker, R.A. "Acute Neurologic Management of the Patient with Spinal Cord Injury." *Urologic Clinics of North America* 20 (August 1993): 413–21.

Grant, Harvey. *Emergency Care.* 6th ed. Brady Co., 1994.

Heckman, James. *Emergency Care and Transportation of the Sick and Injured.* 5th ed. Park Ridge, Illinois: American Academy of Orthopedic Surgeons, 1992.

Meyer, P.R. "Spinal Cord Injury." Neurologic Clinics 9 (1991): 625–61.

Rosen, Peter. *Emergency Medicine Concepts and Clinical Practice.* 3d ed. Mosby Co., 1992.

Sonntag, V.K.H. & R.A. Douglas. "Management of Spinal Cord Trauma." *Neurosurgery Clinics of North America* 20 (August 1993): 373–82.

CHAPTER 8

PHYSICAL THERAPY

Karen Tomec Schmitz, R.P.T.

§ 8.1 Role of the Physical Therapist

The physical therapist (PT) occupies a crucial role in the rehabilitation of a newly injured spinal cord injury (SCI) patient. The PT is responsible for helping the SCI patient recover maximum strength and function and, in conjunction with the occupational therapist, achieve the highest level of independence possible. To accomplish these goals, the therapist must assess the patient's current and potential functional level. With this information, the therapist determines how to assist the patient achieve such potential by developing a rehabilitation plan, including a determination about what type of equipment, mechanisms, and/or adaptive devices are needed.

To properly develop a rehabilitation plan, the PT must thoroughly evaluate the patient's current neurological impairment status. This involves assessing muscle strength, muscle tone, respiratory function, sensory impairment, skin integrity, range of motion (ROM), flexibility, and overall functional assessment.

Muscle strength is assessed by manual resistance testing and graded on a scale of zero-to-five. Tone assessment is accomplished by a determination of the presence or absence of abnormal tone: flaccidity, spasticity, or clonus (repetitive muscle bouncing). Respiratory function is determined by observing the patient's breathing pattern, chest expansion, use of accessory musculature, and cough effectiveness. Sensory impairment involves three determinations:

1. Ability to detect light touch
2. Ability to discriminate painful stimuli and temperature
3. Proprioception (self awareness of body parts in space).

Skin assessment is performed by checking for changes in skin color, tissue hardness, tissue breakdown over bony prominences, and heat. ROM and flexibility assessment involve a determination of the normal motion of the joint and the flexibility of the muscles around those joints. Overall functional assessment is a determination of the patient's ability to use the retained muscles to perform multiple functions, including activities of daily living (ADLs).

ADLs refer to functions that need to be performed on a daily basis to achieve independent living. For most quadriplegics, a home attendant is required to carry out many ADLs. Nevertheless, the more ADLs that can be performed by the patient, the better both psychologically and physically for the patient. ADLs include feeding, grooming, personal hygiene, cooking, phone use, dressing, bed mobility, transfers, bowel and bladder management, skin inspection, and pressure relief.

§ 8.2 Respiration

Respiration is the process of moving oxygenated air into the lungs (inspiration) and removing carbon dioxide out of the lungs (expiration). During inspiration the diaphragm and intercostal muscles contract to expand the thoracic cavity and the rib cage. When the diaphragm contracts, the abdominal muscles relax, allowing the thoracic cavity to expand further. Meanwhile the intercostal muscles contract between the ribs, lifting the rib cage up and out further allowing the thoracic cavity to expand. The net effect is decreased pressure in the lungs, which causes air to move into the lungs to restore the pressure balance. Expiration is achieved by allowing the diaphragm and intercostal muscles to relax while simultaneously contracting the abdominal muscles, which results in increased pressure on the thoracic cavity and forces air out of the lungs.

The diaphragm is innervated by the phrenic nerve, which stems from the spinal cord between C3 and C5. The intercostal muscles are innervated from the spinal cord between the T1 and T12 levels. Therefore, any SCI above T12 may result in paralysis of the intercostal muscles and any injury above C5 may result in diaphragmatic paralysis. With the loss of the intercostal muscles and diaphragm, reduced respiratory function occurs. It is generally expressed in terms of reduced vital capacity.

Vital capacity is defined as the maximum amount of air that can be forcibly expelled after a maximum inhalation and is expressed as a volume measurement (mL). Normal vital capacity is approximately 4600 mL. The greater the vital capacity, the more likely the patient can breathe independently (without a respirator) and clear secretions. Any patient with a vital capacity under 800 mL generally requires mechanical support (respirator) to sustain adequate ventilation.

In addition to adequate ventilation, the SCI patient must be able to cough to clear secretions. Coughing is forced expiration accomplished by the sudden contraction of the abdominal and intercostal muscles. Impairment of the ability to cough is especially dangerous because it increases the risk of developing upper respiratory infections (URI) such as pneumonia. A vital capacity of at least 1500 mL is required for the patient to be able to cough adequately. Coughing is generally classified either as functional (able to clear secretions without assistance), weak functional (requires some manual assistance), or nonfunctional (requires suctioning to clear secretions).

A physical therapist must be aware of the respiratory impairment of each patient treated and work to improve each patient's respiratory and muscular function. The therapist performs a number of tests to determine the patient's current respiratory functional ability.

Respiratory muscle function. To assess function, the therapist checks for muscular strength and tone in the abdominals, the diaphragm, and intercostal muscles, as well as respiratory rate (the speed at which the patient breathes).

Chest expansion. Using a tape measure around the patient's chest, the therapist can assess chest expansion. Normal chest expansion is between 2.5 and 3 inches, but many SCI have no chest expansion and some even have a negative difference due to weak musculature in the abdominals and intercostals.

Breathing pattern. Checking the breathing pattern determines which muscles are functioning and whether the patient is efficiently using those muscles that have been spared. This is done by palpating the muscles to feel for muscle contraction and function.

Cough. Assessing the patient's ability to cough determines if the patient is independently able to clear secretion from the lungs, or if the patient needs assistance to cough. Depending on the patient's coughing strength (functional, weak functional, or nonfunctional), the therapist teaches the patient assistive coughing techniques.

Vital capacity. This is used as a baseline for determining weakness in the respiratory muscles. A patient's vital capacity is measured by having the patient blow into a hand held incentive spirometer.

In addition, the therapist must take into account factors that may be affecting respiratory function. This includes the trauma sustained at the time of injury (fractures of the ribs, sternum, or extremities, lung contusions, or soft tissue damage), or preexisting pulmonary problems (pulmonary disease, allergies, asthma, or a history of smoking).

For most patients, the goals in respiratory management include increasing the vital capacity for improved bronchial hygiene (increased effectiveness of cough), prevention of chest tightness and of ineffective substitute breathing patterns, and learning to coordinate good breathing skills with functional activities. Range of motion exercises are used to prevent contractures of the chest wall that can compromise respiratory function. Upper extremity exercises are used to stretch the pectorals and shoulders muscles; other exercises are designed to rotate and elongate the trunk. Respiratory exercises are used to develop diaphragmatic breathing, chest expansion, and normal timing.

To achieve these goals the following treatment activities are employed by the therapist to assist the patient.

Deep breathing exercises. Diaphragmatic breathing helps increase vital capacity. To accomplish this, the therapist applies gentle pressure to the patient's abdomen during inspiration and expiration. This allows the patient to concentrate on deep breathing patterns. Expiration can be facilitated by applying pressure to the thorax (rib cage). This compressive force assists in a more forceful expiration and thus more efficient inspiration. In conjunction with deep breathing exercises, therapists utilize incentive spirometry and inflation hold exercises. The incentive spirometry technique uses a hand held spirometer, a device that measures forced expiration volumes. The patient is asked to blow into the apparatus, providing both an external resistance force and visual feedback to assist in learning. The inflation hold technique is an exercise in which the patient breathes in and holds his or her breath for a few seconds. This helps the patient maximize their inspiratory volume.

Glossopharyngeal breathing. This technique is essential for patients with poor respiratory reserve. Patients with high-level cervical lesions need to utilize this form of breathing. This also helps alleviate the patient's anxiety over mechanical malfunctions of an artificial life support system. The patient is able to turn off the respirator for short periods of time and breathe unassisted using this technique. Patients are taught to use accessory muscles to assist in respiration and to improve vital capacity. The therapist instructs the patient to repeatedly breathe in small amounts of air, using a sipping or gulping pattern. This forces the patient to utilize available facial and neck muscles to assist in respiration. Using this technique permits a gradual increase of inspired air to improve chest expansion despite paralysis of the primary muscles of respiration.

Airshift Maneuver. This technique provides the patient with an independent method of chest expansion. It is accomplished by having the patient breathe in maximally, close the glottis (back of the throat), relax the diaphragm, and allow the air to shift from the lower thorax to the upper thorax. This airshift maneuver can increase chest expansion by 0.5 to 2 inches.

Strengthening exercises. Strengthening can be done for the following muscles: diaphragm, abdominals, and accessory musculature (if they are innervated). To exercise the diaphragm, progressive resistive exercises are used. This is done by applying manual pressure to the abdomen (just below the sternum) or by use of weights. The patient tries to breathe against the resistance of the weights or hand pressure.

Assisted coughing. There are several techniques to assist with coughing. The level of the injury determines if the patient can cough independently. Coughing is necessary to clear the lungs of secretions. The therapist or attendant can assist the patient in coughing by applying pressure to the epigastric area in a quick upward and inward fashion as the patient attempts to cough. A patient with upper extremity strength can perform this technique alone while in a seated position. If the patient does not have upper extremity strength, this is done by the therapist or caregiver in a supine, sidelying, or sitting position. When the patient is in a sidelying position, counter rotation is used to assist with coughing. The patient inhales when the shoulders are forward, the pelvis is then moved quickly forward and upward as the patient exhales. Quadriplegics can facilitate coughing while in a prone-on-elbows position. The patient extends the head while breathing in, then quickly flexes forward while exhaling. In a sitting position, the patient bends backward while inhaling, and then quickly flexes forward while exhaling.

Abdominal support. An abdominal binder or corset can be helpful to assume some of the function of the weak or absent abdominal muscles. The abdominal corset supports the abdominal contents and improves the resting position of the diaphragm. Pushing the diaphragm up to a higher resting position within the chest cavity in turn allows for maximal inferior and lateral excursion of the diaphragm and increased vital capacity. The abdominal binder also assists in maintaining intrathoracic pressure and decreasing postural hypotension.

Stretching. Chest mobility is important in assisting in the aforementioned respiratory approaches. Manual stretching of the pectoral and other chest wall muscles facilitates mobility and compliance of the thoracic wall. Passive manual stretches and mobilization of the rib cage can be incorporated in the treatment. Many of these stretches can be included in the patient's mat program. An example is rolling on the mat, utilizing trunk rotation, and thus stretching the thoracic wall.

Additional Techniques. These include instructing the patient in postural drainage positions and chest percussion techniques to assist in mobilizing and eliminating secretions. These techniques are especially important with a weak or nonfunctional cough.

Respiratory function varies depending upon at what level the SCI patient is injured. The following is a description of the functional capabilities of the different levels.

C4 Quadriplegic. Patients have the ability to direct bronchial hygiene and coordinate respiration with functional activities such as using sip-and-puff controls and directing ADLs. They are expected to achieve from 30 percent to 50 percent of the vital capacity of the expected norm.

C5 Quadriplegic. Patients are able to direct and assist with bronchial hygiene. They can coordinate respiration with operating sip-and-puff controls and/or hand controls, along with assisting and directing all ADLs. C5 quadriplegics will have a vital capacity of 40 percent to 60 percent of the expected norm.

C6 Quadriplegic. Patients have the ability to assist and perform bronchial hygiene and coordinate respiration by assisting with or performing all ADLs. Their vital capacity is from 60 percent to 80 percent of the expected norm.

C7–C8 Quadriplegic. Patients have the ability to perform bronchial hygiene and coordinate respiration with all ADLs. Vital capacity is also from 60 percent to 80 percent of the expected norm.

Paraplegics. Patients have the ability to perform bronchial hygiene independently and coordinate respiration with all functional activities. They can achieve a vital capacity of 80 percent of the expected norm.

§ 8.3 Regaining and Preserving Muscle Function

During the acute phase (early stage) the primary emphasis is on respiratory management, maintaining range of motion, prevention of secondary complications, and facilitating active movement in the intact musculature. During this stage it is also important to assess the patient's tolerance to an upright or vertical position. Once the physician has cleared the patient orthopedically (that is, fractures are stable), the patient is ready for upright activities.

Since the patient has been immobilized for some time, the patient may experience postural hypotension when moving upright. *Postural hypotension* is a decrease in blood pressure that occurs when a patient is moved from a horizontal position to a vertical position.[1] Therefore a very gradual acclimation to a vertical position is necessary. An abdominal binder and elastic stockings help deter venous pooling in the lower extremities. The progression of these upright activities involves initially raising the head of the bed, progressing to a recliner wheelchair with elevating leg rests, and then to a tilt table on which a full upright position can be obtained. A tilt table is a good device to orient the patient to an upright position because of its capacity to have a patient start in a supine position (lying on the back) and move to a vertical (standing) position in a gradual and smooth manner. Once the patient has acclimated to the vertical position, the patient can progress to the next stage (subacute phase) of treatment.

In the subacute phase, the emphasis will not only be on respiratory management, range of motion, and positioning, but also on expanding the patient's program to resistive exercises for the muscles that remain intact. Many devices can be utilized to assist in strengthening, such as PNF (proprioceptive neuromuscular fascilitation), PRE (progressive resistive exercises) using manual resistance (that which is given by the physical therapist), weights, wall pulleys, sling suspension, and group exercise classes. During this phase, the patient works on developing motor control and muscle reeducation techniques to the appropriate musculature for strengthening. The patient also works on regaining postural control and balance by substituting upper body control and vision for lost proprioception.

§ 8.4 Mat Exercise

Mat activities are a very important component of the rehabilitation phase. This phase involves a sequence of activities that works on stability within a posture (for example, lying supine or on the side) and progressing to controlled mobility. This is transferred into a functional movement (that is, moving from a supine position to a sitting position in a controlled manner while maintaining balance).

Mat activities incorporate individual components of a more complex and functional skill. The progression is from easy to difficult movements, progressing from a symmetrical motion to an asymmetrical motion to weight shifting and movement within a posture. The appropriate activity also depends on the patient's level of injury and medical status. Mat activities are initiated as soon as the patient has been cleared for activity.

The progression of mat activities helps develop improved strength and functional ROM, improves awareness of the patient's new center of gravity, promotes

---

[1] S. O'Sullivan & T. Schmitz, Physical Rehabilitation: Assessment and Treatment 556 (1988).

postural stability, facilitates dynamic stability, and assists with determining the most functional and efficient methods for accomplishing specific tasks. Furthermore it allows the patient to develop functional patterns of movement for innervated musculature, and momentum to move body parts that lack active movement.

Rolling. This is one of the first mat exercises that the patient learns. It is important for bed mobility, dressing of the lower extremities, and preparation for independent positional changes in bed to assist in pressure relief. With the quadriplegic patient, this activity requires the patient to use the head, neck, and arms, as well as momentum to move the trunk and legs. For the paraplegic this activity is easier because of available upper extremity strength.

Prone-on-elbows. This position is used for improved bed mobility and preparation for assuming the quadriped (on hands and knees) and sitting positions. It facilitates head and neck control as well as proximal stability of the shoulder and scapular muscles. The position may be hard to tolerate for a patient with a thoracic or lumbar injury because it causes an increased stress on the low back; therefore gradual acclimation may be necessary. Many activities can be done in this position to work and strengthen the upper body. For paraplegics, prone-on-elbows helps the patient effect hyperextension of the hips and low back. This flexibility is required during ambulation, standing from a wheelchair, and rising from the floor with crutches and leg braces.

Supine-on-elbows. In this position the patient lies on the back and is propped up on elbows. The position is used to assist with bed mobility and prepare the patient to assume a long sitting position. It is an important shoulder and scapular strengthening exercise.

Pull-ups. This is an important exercise (with quadriplegics, C5 and lower) to strengthen the biceps and shoulder flexor muscles in preparation for wheelchair propulsion. This is accomplished with the assistance of the therapist. The patient is lying on the back with the therapist at the hips. The therapist holds on to the patient's wrists while the patient pulls himself up off the mat.

Sitting. There are two positions for sitting: long sit (patient's legs are straight) and short sit (knees are bent and feet are off the mat). Both are important for many ADLs: dressing, self-ROM, transfers, and wheelchair mobility. For the paraplegic, it is essential that the patient have good sitting balance and the ability to move within this posture as it will be used later while standing. With regard to long sitting, the quadriplegic requires a minimum of 100 degrees of straight-leg ROM to assume the position. Without this amount of flexibility the patient will be sitting on the sacrum and will stretch the low back musculature, possibly increasing spinal instability.

The sitting position will vary depending on the level of the patient's lesion. Patients with a lumbar or lower thoracic level lesion sit in an erect sitting position. Patients with a low cervical or high thoracic lesion sit in a forward flexed or slouched position with the head forward. Those patients with a high cervical lesion will have poor sitting posture. Assuming the sitting position will not be difficult for the paraplegic patient because these patients have abdominal and tricep (elbow extensor) musculature. The quadriplegic can assume a stable sitting position by leaning back onto outstretched arms. The patient can assume this position from either the prone-on-elbow or the supine-on-elbow position. Initially, adaptive equipment may be necessary to facilitate movement into sitting. This may include an overhead trapeze, rope ladders, or graduated loops hanging from an over-bed frame.

Many exercises can be done in the sitting position. One important activity is working on balance, progressing from both arms to maintain a base of support to one or no upper extremity support. For the paraplegic, high-level balance exercises can be performed to challenge the patient's dynamic balance (for example, ball throwing between the patient and therapist).

Sitting push-ups is another important exercise that is used as a preliminary activity for transfers and ambulation. The quadriplegic patient can perform this exercise with elbows locked and arms positioned behind. By leaning forward and depressing the shoulders the patient can lift the buttocks from the mat. For the paraplegic, this activity will be easier as the patient can use more of the upper extremity muscles (triceps and forearm muscles) to lift the body. By changing the height of the push-up blocks this exercise becomes more challenging. This activity is also important so that adequate clearance of the buttocks during transfers for skin protection can be accomplished.

Quadriped position (in paraplegia). This all-fours position is an important functional activity that leads up to ambulation. It is one position that allows weight bearing through the hips and helps facilitate initial control of the available musculature of the hips and lower trunk. In this position, many activities can be done to promote balance and strength, develope equilibrium responses, to facilitate contraction of the proximal muscles to help stabilize the joints, to facilitate tonic holding of the available postural muscle (trunk muscles) by alternately freeing one arm from the weight bearing position, and finally to facilitate dynamic balance reactions and to improve coordination and timing.

Kneeling (in paraplegia). For the paraplegic patient this is an important lead-up activity to ambulation utilizing crutches and bilateral knee ankle foot orthoses (KAFOs). This position works on trunk and pelvic control and promotes upright balance control. It is assumed from the quadriped position. The patient can maintain this position with the use of mat crutches (short adaptive crutches). In the kneeling position the patient can continue to work on static and dynamic balance with emphasis on lower trunk and pelvic control.

§ 8.5 Transfers

Transfer training is initiated once the patient has adequate sitting balance. It is an important skill to be used for many other functional activities such as tub transfers, ambulation, and driving. Bed transfers are often the first transfers that are taught. All transfers build on the skills that are developed during bed transfers.

Initially the mat is most frequently used since it has a firmer surface and is easier to learn on. Once the transfer has been learned, alternate surfaces such as a bed, toilet, bathtub, car, and chair to floor (plus the reverse) can be used.

Transfers are taught in steps, and the patient may spend a month just learning the components of the transfer. These components include the following: locking the brakes, removing the armrests, placing the sliding board, managing the legs, and moving to and from the wheelchair. Varying skills such as rotation, weight shifting, and balance are required to complete the transfer.

There are several different approaches to the components of the transfer. Some require more balance, others more ROM, and others more strength. Depending on the patient's skills, any of the various approaches can be used. Transfer training is a problem-solving activity and each patient develops a particular way of transferring.

Transfers are very time-consuming and require much energy, due to increased deficits in strength, from moving on and off different surfaces. A quadriplegic patient may spend as long as 20 minutes to complete initial transfers. Through practice and increased endurance the patient will be able to complete the transfer more quickly and efficiently. Once the patient is confident with transfer skills the patient can progress to more difficult transfers such as a bathroom transfer and car transfer.

Tub and toilet transfers are much the same as a bed transfer, however the initial positioning, approach, and the equipment differ. Bathrooms are often small and therefore positioning may be difficult. Equipment is needed for transfers, including raised toilet seats, various tub benches, grab bars, and a shower hose. The equipment used (such as bath bench or a commode) is less stable than the bed; therefore safety is a concern. Transfer approaches vary depending on the position of the toilet in the bathroom. The paraplegic can transfer directly onto the toilet with some variation of a lateral transfer. Transferring to the bathtub requires a tub bench. Paraplegics (T8 and sometimes T6 and below) can transfer in and out of the tub bottom. Upper thoracic and cervical injury patients need a bath bench and assistance to complete the transfers.

Car transfers can be difficult due to the limited space to which the patient is moving. Longer sliding boards are needed to perform the transfer. The car roof is comparatively low and the patient must consider the head when transferring. Paraplegics and often lower quadriplegic (C6–C8) can independently transfer into a car using a lateral approach. Some of those paraplegic patients (and some C8 patients) who are able to transfer into a car will also be able to put a wheelchair into the car. Quadriplegics need either assistance in transferring into a car or a van with a mechanical lift.

Cl through C4 quadriplegics require full assistance in performing a transfer. They will be able to direct the therapist or attendant on safe transfers to all surfaces. A C5 quadriplegic can direct and assist in safe transfers to all surfaces. A C6 quadriplegic can assist or perform transfers to all surfaces, but needs assistance with transfers to and from the floor. The C6–C8 quadriplegic will be independent with all transfers to all surfaces and can perform and/or assist with floor transfers. All quadriplegic patients need a sliding board to assist with transfers. Loops (straps that are attached around the patients thigh) may be used initially to help the quadriplegic patient to maneuver the legs during a transfer. A paraplegic will be independent with all transfers to all surfaces with or without orthosis or a sliding board.

§ 8.6 Wheelchair Mobility

For the spinal cord injured patient, a wheelchair will be the primary means of mobility. Even though some paraplegics are able to ambulate with crutches and orthoses, most will still opt to use the wheelchair for energy conservation and greater speed and safety.

Each patient will need to have a custom ordered wheelchair, according to level and extent of injury. Some general considerations in choosing a wheelchair are outlined below.

Seat depth. This is critical for proper weight distribution on the thighs and to prevent excessive pressure on the patient's ischial tuberosity (buttock).

Floor-to-seat height. This is important for erect posture.

Seat cushioning. All patients need a seat cushion for extra protection against pressure sores.

Sitting posture. The patient's knees should be at a right angle, thighs should be parallel to the floor, and the foot pedals should clear the floor.

Back height. A quadriplegic needs a higher back support for comfort and stability. A paraplegic has better trunk control and generally prefers a lower back support for added mobility and wheelchair propulsion.

Seat width. Wheelchairs come in different sizes and must fit the patient appropriately. If the patient is wearing an orthosis for trunk stabilization, a wider chair will be needed.

Other accessories. Heel loops or toe loops on the footrests may be necessary for patients with lower extremity spasticity. For patients with circulatory problems, elevating footrests are needed. Removable armrests and swing-away detachable leg rests are important components of the wheelchair that make transfers easier. There are several other accessories that are beneficial. A friction surface on the handrims of the chair (rubber tubing which is wrapped around the handrim) or vertical or horizontal handrim projections allow for improved grip on the handrim to control forward propulsion of the chair, especially for patients with poor hand control. Other helpful items include enlarged release levers on the leg rests, brake extensions, and antitipping devices to keep the patient from falling backward when ascending a ramp.

For high-level lesion quadriplegics (C4 and above) an electric wheelchair is essential. For the C5 quadriplegic, either a manual or electric wheelchair can be used, however these patients require an electric chair for long-distance travel. The control on an electric wheelchair is either a joystick or a sip-and-puff type. To allow independent reclining and pressure relief for the quadriplegics and high thoracic lesions, a hydraulic reclining unit is essential.

For active patients, more than one wheelchair will be needed. More and more patients are competing in wheelchair racing; for this a separate racing chair is needed. These chairs are smaller, lower to the ground (more aerodynamic), and much lighter than the normal wheelchair, allowing the patient more freedom, mobility, and speed.

The patient must be taught all the components of the wheelchair and how to manage the armrests, leg rests, and brakes. This is necessary for safe transfers. The patient also needs to be taught how to propel on level surfaces, ramps, and curbs. Patients with sufficient upper extremity strength (T1–L3 paraplegics) can be taught how to perform "wheelies." This skill is required for independent curb climbing, and maneuvering on rough terrain such as gravel and mud. Because the casters (small wheels in the front of the wheelchair) can get caught in the gravel or mud, or even prevent the patient from clearing the curb, doing wheelies is a very important skill to master.

The patient is also instructed on independent pressure relief while sitting in a wheelchair. This routine needs to be performed for every 10 minutes of sitting to help with pressure relief for tissue redistribution. It is critical for the prevention of pressure sores.

Another crucial part of wheelchair training is teaching the patient what to do if the patient should fall, and how to regain an upright position independently. This skill is primarily for the paraplegic patient. Those with quadriplegia will need assistance with resuming an upright position. For the quadriplegic patient who will be using an electric wheelchair, the knowledge of how to manage a joystick or the sip-and-puff units to maneuver the chair is necessary.

Those patients who will be driving need to be able to transfer into the car, fold the wheelchair, and move it in and out of the car, in addition to learning how to use hand controls to drive the car. To allow the quadriplegic patient to be more independent, a van with a powered platform lift will be necessary. The patient, too, will need to learn how to manage a car utilizing hand controls.

§ 8.7 Ambulation for Paraplegics

With higher level paraplegics, ambulation may be considered. Many factors need to be addressed before attempting ambulation and to determine whether it is feasible.

The patient will first need adequate muscle strength in the trunk, abdominals, and back muscles to help stabilize and control the trunk. Second, adequate range of motion is needed in the lower extremities (especially into hip extension). Third, sufficient cardiovascular endurance is necessary. The patient with an incomplete lesion who has some strength in one or both hip flexors or in the knee extensors will be more successful initiating walking. Fourth, the patient's weight, age, and upper body strength is important to consider along with any preexisting or current cardiovascular or respiratory problems. Other issues that may restrict ambulation are spasticity, loss of proprioception in the hip and knee joints, pain, bone deformity, and skin ulcers.

Energy expenditure is a further crucial consideration required for functional ambulators. For paraplegics, walking requires two-to-four times more energy than for the average person. Therefore endurance will be the determining factor as to whether the patient will be successful in a walking endeavor.

Cost is a factor. There is always a question of whether third-party payors are willing to underwrite or reimburse the patient for the costs of the equipment needed for ambulation. Learning to walk requires bilateral leg orthotics and crutches.

There are several types of braces available, referred to as KAFOs (knee ankle foot orthoses). The two most common leg braces are the conventional KAFO and the Scott-Craig KAFO. There are three different orthoses that can be used with the thoracic paraplegic. The hip guidance orthosis (HGO),[2] the reciprocating gait orthosis (RGO),[3] and the advanced reciprocating gait orthosis (ARGO).[4] The HGO is a hip-knee-ankle orthosis that is hinged at hip level with a rigid thoracic corset, and allows stabilization of the lower limbs in the sagittal or frontal plane. The RGO uses cables to help coordinate movement between the two lower extremities.[5] The more sophisticated model is the advanced RGO that allows the patient to unlock the knee joint during sit-to-stand

---

[2] F. Moore, *Parawalker: Walking for Thoracic Paraplegics,* 4 Physiother Pract 18–22 (1989).

[3] J. Beckham, *Louisiana State University Reciprocating Gait Orthosis,* 8 Physiotherapy 24–30 (1987).

[4] M. Lissene et. al., *Advanced Reciprocating Gait Orthosis in Paraplegic Patients,* (J. Zupko. ed. 7th World Congress, International Soc'y for Prosthetics and Orthotics (ISPO) 31 (Chicago, Ill. 1990)).

[5] S. O'Sullivan & T. Schmitz, Physical Rehabilitation: Assessment and Treatment 579 (1988).

maneuvers. Air pistons situated on either sides of the knee help store energy during sitting and is released during standing. However research by S. Lotta and associates showed that walking with these orthoses appeared to be a promising form of exercise rather than an alternative to wheelchair locomotion.[6]

To assist with balance the patient initially learns to walk in the parallel bars and then progresses to a walker. Once comfortable walking with the walker, the patient can progress to crutches, using the conventional crutches or Lofstrand crutches (forearm crutches). Forearm crutches attach around the forearm while the patient weight bears through the hands. These crutches permit more freedom for shoulder motion, are lightweight, and easier to transport. They also permit the patient to use the hands without disengaging the crutch from the forearm.

Learning to walk with the appropriate orthotics and crutches is time-consuming, and can require three-to-six weeks or longer to learn. However, giving an SCI patient the opportunity to walk helps the patient determine if walking is realistic and appropriate. The patient can go faster and use less energy using a wheelchair.

For an SCI patient to be considered a functional ambulator, the patient needs to be able to walk on all surfaces. This includes walking on level surfaces, tile, carpet, gravel, sidewalks, ramps, curbs, and stairs, both indoors and outdoors. The patient will have to learn how to don and doff (put on and take off) the braces and assume standing. The patient will also have to learn how to fall and be able to get up from the ground should this happen or be able to instruct others as to how to help the patient up from the ground. No matter how independent, SCI patients are susceptible to falling.

The type of gait pattern determines how much energy is expended. Three common gait patterns are the four-point gait pattern, the swing-to, and the swing-through gait pattern. The swing-through is harder to learn and requires greater upper body strength, good balance, and coordination. The four-point and swing-to gait patterns are easier to learn but require more energy. A patient initially becomes skilled with the four-point and swing-to gait pattern and progresses to the swing-through when capable.

Research has indicated that walking for the spinal cord injured patient is beneficial.[7] There is a high incidence of osteoporosis in the SCI patient because of calcium excretion from the bone. With the excretion of calcium from the bones, the bone weakens. This increase in calcium excretion has been postulated as a predisposing factor to ectopic bone and bladder stones. Weight bearing through the bones can help increase bone density and matrix, which will promote more protein to blend with calcium. Therefore it has been postulated that with standing there is increased pressure throughout the bones of the lower

[6] S. Lotta et al., *Restoration of Gait with Orthoses in Thoracic Paraplegia: A Multicentric Investigation,* 32 Paraplegia 608–15 (1994).

[7] Bergmann et al., *Study of Calcium and Bone Metabolism in Paraplegic Patients,* 15 Paraplegia 147–59 (1977–78).

extremity, and a decrease in calcium excretion from the bone occurs. Thus there are theoretically fewer incidences of osteoporosis, bladder stones, ectopic bone, and other problems related to calcium imbalances.

However, other research concludes that standing alone does not produce enough compressive pressure to stimulate bone growth.[8] More pressure is needed to produce bone growth. This pressure must come not only from weight bearing through the bone but also from muscle contraction and the shearing and torsion forces that result from the muscle action.

§ 8.8 Other Rehabilitation Modalities

Functional Electrical Stimulation (FES) FES has been utilized during rehabilitation for many different reasons. FES has been used for muscle strengthening (motor relearning and muscle reeducation), range of motion, increase sensory awareness (stimulating muscles during functional activities), muscle facilitation, orthotic substitution (used in conjunction with gait), management of spasticity, and decrease venous stasis (by stimulating the muscle pump).

FES is used to enhance standing and ambulatory activities with spinal cord patients.[9] It is employed in conjunction with cycle ergometry to help improve endurance. This is done by applying surface electrodes to the skin. By stimulating the muscles, the legs can peddle a stationary bike. Many rehabilitation clinics have cycle ergometers for clinical use. However, this type of treatment with continuous stimulation can cause muscle fatigue.

FES has been used to help stimulate muscles during different stages of gait. During the stance phase it can help stabilize the leg during weight bearing on that extremity. During the swing phase it can assist with bending the lower extremity to clear the ground.[10]

Functional Neuromuscular Stimulation (FNS) FNS is used in conjunction with diaphragmatic breathing, bladder function and training, immobility, deep vein thromboses (DVTs), contracture prevention, spasticity control, cardiovascular conditioning, and muscle bulk.

FNS is instrumental in assisting in diaphragmatic pacing for the chronic ventilatory insufficient patient. It allows SCI patients to be free from positive pressure ventilation (that is, the ventilator). This form of treatment is not for everyone who is ventilator dependent. The SCI patient who has ventilatory

---

[8] A. Abramson & E. Delagi, *Influence of Weight Bearing and Muscle Contraction on Disuse Osteoporosis,* 42 Archives of Physical Med. & Rehabilitation 147–151 (1960).

[9] S. O'Sullivan & T. Schmitz, Physical Rehabilitation: Assessment and Treatment 580 (1988).

[10] V. Nixon, Spinal Cord Injury: A Guide to Functional Outcomes in Physical Therapy Management 210 (1985).

failure due to interruption of the upper motor neuron of the phrenic nerve or due to respiratory control center malfunction will benefit from a phrenic nerve stimulator. However the patient must have a normal phrenic nerve, diaphragm, and lungs for this type of intervention.[11]

Bladder function is an area in which FNS has proven beneficial. It is used when traditional forms of bladder management have failed. The most successful is the sacral nerve root stimulator. An electrode is implanted at S2, S3, and S4 to stimulate voiding without prohibitive side effects. Other areas that can be stimulated to produce voiding is the spinal cord (conus medullaris), the bladder wall, the sacral nerve roots, and the pelvic floor.[12]

Studies have been done on the use of FNS to diminish the side effects of immobility of the SCI patient. FNS has been used to prevent and heal pressure sores, prevent DVT's, contractures, spasticity control, cardiovascular training, and muscle bulk increases. Two studies, by Carley and Wainapel[13] and by Alvarez and associates[14] found that low-intensity direct current improved healing; whereas, Kloth and Feeder[15] and Akers and Gabrielson[16] used high-voltage galvanic stimulation to increase the rate of healing. However, further studies need to be performed as these lacked sufficient numbers of subjects and appropriate control groups, thereby diminishing their efficacy.

By stimulating the calf muscles, FNS can help prevent deep vein thromboses (DVTs) in the acute SCI patient. Stimulation causes the calf muscles to contract and relax (muscle pump), thus helping to pump blood back toward the heart (venous blood flow). Electrical stimulation along with low doses of heparin (blood thinner) has also been effective.[17] However electrode placement can interfere with the activity required during rehabilitation (physical therapy).

Two other hypothesized benefits of FNS are contracture prevention and spasticity control. FNS can stimulate the muscle to correct contractures and help restore motion. Through reciprocal inhibition, stimulation of the antagonist muscle helps decrease spasticity in the agonist muscle.[18] An example of this is

---

[11] Yarkony et al., *Neuromuscular Stimulation in Spinal Cord Injury II: Prevention of Secondary Complications,* 73 Archives of Physical Med. & Rehabilitation 195–200 (1992).

[12] *Id.* at 196.

[13] P. Carley & S. Wainapel, *Electrotherapy for Acceleration of Wound Healing: Low Intensity Direct Current,* 66 Archives of Physical Med. & Rehabilitation 443–46 (1985).

[14] O. Alvarez et al., *Healing of Superficial Skin Wounds Is Stimulated by External Electric Current,* 81 J. Investigative Dermatology 144–48 (1983).

[15] L. Kloth, J. Feedar, *Accelleration of Wound Healing with High Voltage, Monophasic, Pulsed Current,* 68 Physical Therapy 503–08 (1988).

[16] T. Akers and A. Gabrielson, *Effect of High Voltage Galvanic Stimulation on the Rate of Healing of Decubitus Ulcers,* 20 Biomed. Sci. Instrumentation 99–100 (1984).

[17] G. Merli et al., *Deep Vein Thrombosis: Prophylaxis in Acute Spinal Cord Injured Patients,* 69 Archives of Physical Med. & Rehabilitation 661–64 (1988).

[18] M. Levine et al., *Relaxation of Spasticity by Electrical Stimulation of Antagonist Muscles,* 33 Archives of Physical Med. Rehabilitation 668–73 (1952).

to stimulate the quadricep muscle to decrease the spasticity of the hamstring muscle.

Cardiovascular (CV) conditioning is an area in which FNS can be beneficial. Through bicycle ergometry and arm crank ergometry, CV conditioning can be emphasized. Bicycle ergometry is a method of working the larger muscle groups of the lower legs to improve CV endurance without upper extremity musculoskeletal complications.[19] Arm crank ergometry (arm bicycle) is an effective way to strengthen the upper extremities and improve CV fitness. Increasing upper extremity strength assists patients with accomplishing ADLs. Arm crank ergometry has been shown to produce increase oxygen uptake, pulmonary ventilation, heart rate, and to lower oxygen consumption for each power output level.[20]

Lastly, studies have indicated that FNS can increase muscle bulk and strength.[21] In the Munsat and associates study,[22] an increased proportion of Type I (slow-twitch) fibers was observed. They noted an increase in the size of both Type I and II fibers with isometric contraction; whereas, with an isotonic contraction at a lesser resistance, Type I fibers decreased in number and size. Another study showed that anaerobic exercise produced a greater increase in muscle bulk than aerobic bicycle ergometry.[23]

§ 8.9 Long-range Planning

Once a patient has been discharged from the rehabilitation center, the patient's comprehensive multidisciplinary care does not end. It is essential that patients be monitored during transition to the community. This interaction helps the patient deal with psychosocial, medical, and functional issues related to the patient's disability. Issues such as aging and vocational and educational pursuits can be addressed. This is necessary to maintain an optimal state of health and function.

Periodic checkups with the physical therapist are required to assess the patient's functional status and upgrade skills when appropriate. The PT also needs

---

[19] K. Ragnarsson, *Physiologic Effects of Functional Electrical Stimulation-induced Exercises in Spinal Cord-injured Individuals,* 223 Clinical Orthopaedics 53–63 (1988).

[20] S. Hooker et al., *Acid-base Balance after Electrically Induced Leg Cycle and Voluntary Arm Crank Exercise in Paraplegics,* 16th Annual Scientific Meeting, American Spinal Cord Injury Ass'n (1990).

[21] A. Kralj & T. Bajd, Functional Electrical Stimulation: Standing and Walking After Spinal Cord Injury, 71 Archives of Physical Med. & Rehabilitation 201–06 (1989).

[22] T. Munsat, D. McNeal, & R. Waters, *Effects on Nerve Stimulation on Human Muscle,* 33 Archives of Neurology 608–17 (1976).

[23] P. Pacy et al., *Effect of Anaerobic and Aerobic Exercise Prompted by Computer Regulated Functional Electrical Stimulation (FES) on Muscle Size, Strength and Histology in Paraplegic Males.* 11 Prosthetics Orthotics Int'l 75–79 (1987).

to reassess the patient's equipment to see if something needs to be repaired, modified, or replaced. SCI patients are usually seen twice in the first year after discharge from the rehabilitation center, and then yearly. The primary goal of checkups with rehabilitation professionals is to provide preventative health care.

§ 8.10 Subsequent Musculoskeletal Injuries

Many SCI patients encounter subsequent musculoskeletal injuries. Repetitive stress injuries are prevalent with the increased involvement with wheelchair sports, and other occupational and recreational activities. Injuries such as carpal tunnel syndrome, as well as wrist, elbow, and shoulder tendonitis are common.

Spinal cord injury persons are currently surviving longer, and long-term effects of wheelchair use are of significant importance. The performance of ADLs places an tremendous load on the bones, joints, and soft tissues of the upper extremities, for those persons confined to a wheelchair.

Performing tasks from a seated position in environments designed for persons standing require repetitive activities such as wheeling, transfers, and elevating the shoulders. Such repetitive stress results in significant compression and impulse loads as well as shearing forces through the joint and muscles, often in biomechanically weaker ranges of upper extremity motion. Damage can occur from periods of high or long activity or stresses in ranges in which the tissues are unaccustomed. Without rest and healing, injuries can become chronic.

Pentland and Twomey's study suggests that long-term paraplegia and wheelchair use are associated with the development of upper limb pain and degeneration.[24] Reported pain prevalence for the paraplegic sample in Pentland and Twomey's study were: shoulder 39 percent, elbow 31 percent, and wrist and hand 40 percent. Upper limb pain is prevalent in 60 percent of SCI persons. They found that the most common tasks that caused upper limb pain were work and school, sleep, wheelchair transfers, outdoor wheeling, and driving. In another study, shoulder pain was reported in about half of the patients with spinal cord injuries.[25]

The upper extremity muscles are needed when lifting the body weight for wheelchair transfers and ischial pressure relief. These activities are important for independence and self-esteem. Therefore it is essential that persons with paraplegia be watched closely for the development of overuse-related problems and prevention.

Balanced strength and endurance of the muscles around the shoulder is essential for avoiding injuries and strains to the upper limbs. Preexisting disease,

---

[24] W. Pentland & L. Twomey, *Upper Limb Function in Persons with Long Term Paraplegia and Implications for Independence: Part I,* 32 Paraplegia 211–18 (1994).

[25] P. Aisen & M. Aisen, *Shoulder-hand Syndrome in Cervical Spinal Cord Injury,* 32 Paraplegia 588–92 (1994).

trauma, muscle imbalance, or musculoskeletal anomalies affect the integrity of the upper limbs. These preexisting problems plus the additional stresses of wheelchair use increase the risk of developing overuse-related problems. To minimize stress and maximize the SCI person's level of independence, it is essential for each to have ergonomically designed environments and equipment. It is also important for SCI patients to be educated about the care and conditioning of the upper limbs and to learn how to manage early signs of strain and overuse. Work simplification and knowledge of a variety of alternate activities of daily living techniques can decrease stress.

Prevention is critical for SCI persons when dealing with upper limb pain. It is important to maintain conditioning levels that correlate with what the person wants to do. It is necessary that the patient's environment and equipment do not require unusual or sudden loading. Careful progression of the activity intensity, attention to fatigue, and rest at early warning signs of pain or problems help minimize upper limb pain.

The main factors precipitating overuse in the shoulder include compression of the rotator cuff and muscle fatigue because of repetitive or static shoulder elevation, work posture, age, and compression and ischemia within the shoulder joint during weight-bearing activities through the upper limbs.[26]

Propulsion of a wheelchair requires the arms to abduct away from the body 40 degrees during the push phase. Nasca, Salter, and Weil's article indicates that by 45 degrees of abduction, there is already compression of the subscapularis, and supraspinatus tendons.[27] By 90 degrees of abduction, four of the rotator cuff tendons are being compressed.[28]

Rotator cuff tendonitis can occur in such sports as wheelchair racing because of the increased demand on the shoulder musculature. The repetitive shoulder motion needed to propel the wheelchair forward can put undue stress on the main stabilizing muscles of the shoulder. This irritation to the rotator cuff can lead to inflammation of the tendons and cause tendonitis. It is crucial for athletes to maintain proper strength in the rotator cuff muscles along with the shoulder girdle musculature. Coaches and trainers of wheelchair athletes must ensure that training progresses appropriately. Unlike able-bodied athletes, the SCI athlete cannot easily rest the upper limbs after a training session.

In recent years spinal cord injured persons have become more involved in recreational and competitive physical activities.[29] Many local, national, and

---

[26] W. Pentland & L. Twomey, *Upper Limb Function in Persons with Long Term Paraplegia and Implications for Independence: Part II,* 32 Paraplegia 219–24 (1994).

[27] R. Nasca et al., *Contact Areas of the 'Subacromial' Joint in Surgery of the Shoulders* 134–39 (J. Bateman & R. Welsh eds., 1989).

[28] *Id.*

[29] Y. Bhambhani et al., *Physiological Responses During Wheelchair Racing in Quadriplegics and Paraplegics,* 32 Paraplegia 253–60 (1994).

international track competitions include wheelchair races of various distances for SCI persons.

The International Stoke Mandeville Games Federation has set up seven competitive classes based on the level of impaired functional musculature of the individual. This permits individuals with SCI to compete on an equivalent basis from a functional standpoint.[30] The classes for quadriplegics are as follows: 1A (C6 spinal lesion or above), 1B (C7), and 1C (C8 spinal lesion). Paraplegics are assigned to class 2 (T1–T5 spinal lesion), 3 (T6–T10), 4 (T11–L3), and class 5 (L4–S2 spinal lesion).

In addition, wrist and elbow tendonitis can also occur from repetitive activities whether they are job-related or sports-related. This tendonitis may be more prevalent in SCI patients who have not regained full use of the upper extremity muscles, thus causing an imbalance in those muscles. Neck and back muscles may also be affected or strained, since most waking hours are spent in a sitting posture. If the patient does not maintain a proper posture while in the chair, additional stress on the back and neck musculature can occur. Every patient is different depending the level of lesion and the occupational and activity level at which the patient performs. Therefore, it is essential that SCI patients maintain functional skills and physical fitness.

§ 8.11 Bibliography

DeLisa, Joel A. *Rehabilitation Medicine, Principles and Practice.* 2d ed. Philadelphia: J.B. Lippincott Co., 1993.

Hanak, Marcia & Anne Scott. *Spinal Cord Injury: an Illustrated Guide for Health Care Professionals.* New York: Springer Publishing Co., 1983.

Hochschuler et al., *Rehabilitation of the Spine, Science and Practice.* St. Louis: Mosby-Year Book, Inc., 1993.

Nixon, Vickie. *Spinal Cord Injury: A Guide to Functional Outcomes in Physical Therapy Management.* Rockville, Md: Aspen Publications, 1985.

O'Sullivan, S.B. & T.J. Schmitz. *Physical Rehabilitation: Assessment and Treatment.* 2d ed. Philadelphia: F.A. Davis Co., 1988.

[30] R. Shephard, Fitness in Special Populations (1990).

CHAPTER 9

LIFE CARE PLAN

John E. Dahlberg

§ 9.1 Introduction

The *life care plan* is a document that analyzes all the extraordinary needs a disabled person will experience as a result of a disability and what costs the person will face in meeting those needs. The term life care plan has evolved over the last 10 to 15 years and generically refers to reports that summarize the anticipated extraordinary needs and costs over a person's lifetime. *Life care plans* are typically drafted for catastrophic disabilities, however, they may be used in other cases. As each person's disability is unique, the life care plan should be individualized to specific needs.

Historically the primary purpose for life care plans has been to assist in personal injury litigation. However, alternative uses have evolved in the areas of estate planning, setting reserves for third-party payors, and case management. The purpose of this chapter is to describe life care planning in the context of personal injury litigation, however, the concepts described can be readily applied to other uses for *life care plans.*

This chapter analyzes the special considerations for life care planning for spinal cord injuries. The trial attorney, or claims reviewer, should become familiar with the anatomy and physiology of spinal cord injury as well as with complications of spinal cord injuries described in detail in other chapters. With this information as a foundation, the attorney is better able to understand and anticipate the extraordinary needs a plaintiff will exhibit. Armed with this information the attorney will be better able to analyze a *life care plan* and conduct depositions of the plaintiff or life care planning expert.

Once an adult with a spinal cord injury has completed rehabilitation and returned to the home community, it can be anticipated that the disability will be stable unless there are significant contributing medical issues. Some of these special considerations would be ongoing neurological improvement, development of post traumatic cystic myelopathy, dual diagnoses (spinal cord injury and traumatic brain injury), and the late effects of aging with a spinal cord injury. A life care planner must review the medical records to identify any of these special considerations or any premorbid medical or personal issues that may complicate the life care planning process. Although some of these special considerations may make the life care plan more dynamic and therefore challenging to prepare, an attorney can and should account for special considerations.

A special case that is also challenging to analyze is the pediatric spinal cord injury. Fortunately pediatric spinal cord injuries are quite rare and make up a very small proportion of the total spinal cord injured population. However, depending on the age at which an individual sustains a spinal cord injury, it can be anticipated that there will be various ages and stages that the patient will grow through that will require specialized items of equipment and varying frequencies of therapy and medical contacts. Medications may also change as a young spinal cord injured person ages because the dosage will typically be adjusted according to the changing body weight.

Another challenging case to analyze is the ventilator-dependent quadriplegic. These individuals often have a much higher usage of medications, disposable supplies, durable medical equipment, and medical contacts. Additionally their attendant care needs typically require a higher acuity level of care.

§ 9.2 Medications

Medications, both prescription and over-the-counter, will typically be required for the individual with spinal cord injury. During the patient's initial hospitalization and rehabilitation program, various medications are explored to find which ones will be most effective for that individual. In most instances by the time the patient has completed rehabilitation, the types of medications that the patient will be using will have been identified and the patient will have begun to establish a routine usage. However, in some more problematic cases, ongoing adjustment of these medications may be necessary. Typically within the first one-to-two years the patient and physician have identified the type of medications that the patient will require for long-term maintenance. The medications used are generally for managing bowel, bladder, and spasticity; however, in some circumstances specialized medications may be required for specific complications.

Due to a neurogenic bowel the individual may require gastrointestinal agents to increase dietary bulk (and therefore bowel motility) to facilitate a bowel movement. A dietary bulk additive is used frequently to increase the motility of the digestive tract. In many instances stool softeners (with or without laxative agents) will be prescribed. Due to the individual's inability to volitionally control bowel movements, the patient will require a bowel program consisting of a suppository or mini-enema followed by rectal digital stimulation. This is sometimes referred to as a classic bowel program.

Similarly, due to a patient's neurogenic bladder, the patient may require medications to assist in safely managing renal function. These medications will be determined somewhat by the type of bladder management a patient is utilizing. If using an indwelling catheter for bladder drainage, a patient may require a medication to minimize spasticity (tone) of the bladder. An individual on intermittent catheterization may likewise require control of bladder tone to minimize urinary incontinence. For patients utilizing reflexive voiding with an external collection device, medications to enhance bladder tone can be used. Antibiotics are required in almost all cases. In most instances a person with neurogenic bladder experiences recurring urinary tract infections (UTIs). Although some of these UTIs may be treated conservatively (for example, by drinking additional fluids), on occasion the patient may require prescription antibiotics to combat microorganisms (usually once or twice per year). Antibiotics are generally used only for symptomatic presentation of a UTI and conservative measures for asymptomatic infections. Depending on the practice of the physician monitoring the patient, prophylactic antibiotics may be used to minimize the occurrence of urinary bacterial growth.

For many tetraplegics and even some paraplegics, spasticity can be a problem. When spasticity comprises the person's safety or function, medications may be used as a means to minimize it. Although there are several medications that can be used for this purpose, some have potential complications associated with them. The medication that is most commonly prescribed is currently baclofen.

The variability of each individual's needs and specific reactions to medications, dictates how the medication regime is individually tailored. However, once the medication or type of medication that the person will be requiring on a long-term basis has been established, it is then possible to project the annual cost. Although the dosage for adults usually remains fairly constant, dosages for pediatric spinal cord injuries will be adjusted as the child grows and the body weight changes. It is a relatively simple mathematical computation to calculate how many pills of any one medication an individual is taking in a year (365 days). Once this quantity is established, the cost for purchase of the medications in the appropriate quantity can be researched by contacting a local pharmacy or one of the national mail order pharmaceutical suppliers.

§ 9.3 Medical Supplies

A person will use various disposable supplies to assist in managing bowel, bladder, and skin concerns, and in some instances special considerations in managing menstruation.

Supplies for bladder management vary depending upon the type of bladder management utilized. An individual utilizing an indwelling catheter will need to change the catheter on a regular basis, generally monthly. This requires purchase of a new catheter, as well as a sterile insertion kit. To collect urine during the day the patient uses a disposable leg bag that can be cleaned and reused; however, it generally needs to be discarded every one-to-two weeks. At night the person on an indwelling catheter uses a larger bedside collection device to eliminate the necessity of emptying it in the middle of the night. When changing collection systems, the patient needs to clean and disinfect the catheter connections with alcohol or Betadine® swabs. Additionally, the collection devices need to be cleaned and disinfected in a solution such as bleach, vinegar, or a commercially available disinfectant. An individual utilizing reflex voiding through an external collector in a manner similar to the indwelling catheter, requires collection devices and cleaning solutions. However, the patient typically will not require alcohol or swabs. In place of the catheters and catheter kits, these individuals have an external collector, sometimes called a Texas catheter, which is usually changed on a daily basis. However, in the course of a week an individual may have a problem with an external collector breaking or slipping off that will require one or two more external collectors in addition to those of daily use. For the patient utilizing intermittent catheterization, the cost will vary depending on whether the individual has been established on a clean or sterile technique. Individuals using a clean technique ordinarily clean and reuse catheters; however, catheters should be replaced on a weekly basis. Most individuals do not require gloves but wash their hands thoroughly prior to catheterization. Such patients further require a surgical lubricant to assist in passing the catheter through the urethra into the bladder. Additionally, they may require baby wipes or swab sticks to clean the tip of the penis or the labia around the urethra prior to passing the catheter. The person who is utilizing a sterile technique generally needs a self-contained sterile catheterization kit. These kits include all of the items necessary for one catheterization and are disposed of following each use. Many individuals use adult diapers or diaper liners inside of clothing to contain urinary leaking between catheterizations. Leaking frequently increases during periods of urinary tract infections or during women's menstruation.

For bowel management the patient or the caregiver will require examination gloves for hygiene during a digital stimulation bowel program. Glove utilization for bowel program varies according to individual style; some individuals use as few as one or two gloves, and some as many as 10 or more per bowel program. A surgical lubricant or petroleum jelly is typically used for lubrication during a bowel program to minimize trauma to the rectal mucosa. Most patients make use of disposable underpads to prevent soiling of bed linens, wheelchairs, or floors. Following the bowel program, patients require disposable washcloths or baby wipes because cleanup is often too involved to use toilet tissue. For hygiene purposes and to control odor following a bowel program, patients use a plastic bag to dispose of stool and supplies. In spite of a regularly instituted bowel program, many individuals experience periodic bowel incontinence. It is, therefore, necessary to calculate the amount of supplies necessary to clean up following an involuntary bowel movement.

Some patients have a colostomy or surgically constructed bladder that requires different but easily identifiable supplies. The type and frequency of supplies required can be identified by consultation with the patient or an ostomy specialist.

As previously noted, the person with spinal cord injury is at risk of developing decubitus ulcers (bedsores). To minimize exposure to this risk, the person uses specialized bedding to protect the skin. Frequently a foam eggcrate mattress or artificial sheepskin is employed for this purpose. These devices need to be replaced periodically because of wear and soiling. To assist in positioning in bed, as well as to provide padding between bony prominences, the spinal cord injured person often uses additional pillows.

Many women with spinal cord injuries find that managing menstruation requires more supplies, particularly for a tetraplegic who has a more difficult time changing either pads or tampons. For individuals requiring additional supplies following spinal cord injury, the necessity, and therefore the cost, is eliminated once they reach menopause.

Once the supplies that a patient requires have been identified, the frequency of use can be determined and the total quantity used on an annual basis can be calculated. By contacting a local pharmacy or a national mail order medical supply house, the bulk purchase price can be readily established to assist in calculating ongoing costs for the person.

Patients who are maintained on a respirator require an extensive list of additional disposable supplies to care for pulmonary function. Disposable supplies are necessary for trach care, suctioning needs, and ventilatory support.

§ 9.4 Durable Medical Equipment

Durable medical equipment means the items of equipment a spinal cord injured person requires to facilitate mobility, activity of daily living function, or to minimize the person's disability. These items need to be purchased and replaced periodically and in many instances will require periodic repairs. Where possible, the patient's specific purchase price can be established from invoices. These may not be available in all cases because of the funding source. If the specific purchase price is not immediately available, contact a local vendor or research the national average purchase price as an alternative. In many instances this may be necessary because the person may not have sufficient funds or insurance to acquire necessary items of equipment. In addition to the purchase price of an item, the expected useful life of the item will be necessary to calculate the annualized or amortized cost. The person preparing a *life care plan* should have sufficient professional experience and background to specify what is the useful life expectancy of a piece of equipment. In some instances it may be helpful to use guides such as the American Hospital Association's *Estimated Useful Lives of Depreciable Hospital Assets* or by contacting local vendors.

The list of equipment needs to be individualized for each patient. This list can be extensive, particularly for tetraplegics who typically require more items of equipment than paraplegics.

A wheelchair, manual or power-driven, is the first and most obvious piece of equipment that paraplegics and tetraplegics require. In recent decades wheelchairs have undergone significant evolution demonstrating improvements for the users. Today most manual wheelchairs are made of lightweight and durable materials. Both manual and power-drive wheelchairs offer the potential for customized construction and fit to accommodate an individual's functional level. Furthermore, the customized prescription of these devices is targeted at improving the functional capability of an individual. Manual wheelchairs are generally used for an individual's primary mobility, however those who require power-drive wheelchairs will also require a manual wheelchair as a backup for occasional use. This use includes periods during which the primary power-drive wheelchair is being repaired or during visits to places that may not practically accommodate a heavier power-drive wheelchair.

Power-driven wheelchairs may be used in a standard format by a lower level tetraplegic (or in some rare instances paraplegic) with the standard joystick drive mechanism. The drive mechanism can be custom designed for the patient's functional level, including a joystick operation (either by hand or chin), or a sip and puff drive; in some instances head switches or ocular control mechanisms can also be integrated. For higher level tetraplegics that may not be able to do independent weightshifts, recline mechanisms can be attached to the standard frame to facilitate the patient's weightshifts. Additional adaptations such as arm and leg troughs for high-level tetraplegics or ventilator trays to transport a respirator-dependent tetraplegic's breathing apparatus can be attached. Sometimes the custom modifications of a power-drive wheelchair, particularly for a ventilator-dependent tetraplegic, may increase the cost of these chairs to a figure approaching $20,000 and in some cases more.

Shower chairs and commodes similar in design to manual wheelchairs are frequently used for both bowel program and showering requirements of spinal cord injured persons. These wheelchairs generally are constructed of rustproof materials with waterproof bearings to allow for use in wheel-in showers. For individuals who can transfer onto padded bath benches or raised padded toilet seats, wheelchair commodes may be replaced with these items.

Electric hospital beds are sometimes used by tetraplegics to enhance independent bed mobility or to facilitate the care given by attendants. Most rehabilitation programs discourage the use of these hospital beds unless required for enhancing a person's function or facilitating care. The reason is to allow the patient to function in the community without being reliant on an expensive and immobile piece of equipment such as a bed. If an individual who is unnecessarily reliant on an electric hospital bed wished to travel across country or visit a friend, the patient undoubtedly would not have access to a hospital bed at the destination. This would have the detrimental effect of discouraging the patient's ability to travel.

Modified vans are frequently required for the transportation of individuals with spinal cord injuries. Specifically, for those individuals reliant on power-driven chairs, the only safe and effective means of transportation is a fully modified van. Although a power-driven wheelchair can be broken down into various components that could fit inside of a car, it is not practical to utilize a wheelchair in this manner on a continuing basis. A modified van can accommodate a disabled passenger; with additional modifications it can accommodate a disabled driver. Generally, individuals injured at the C5–C6 level and lower are capable of driving such a van. In most instances individuals with injuries higher than C5 would be transported as a passenger only. A modified van may be necessary for persons who utilize manual wheelchairs to safely transport themselves and other passengers. Although a paraplegic, for instance, may typically transport a wheelchair in the backseat of a two-door car, this significantly compromises the space available for passengers and also the safety of backseat passengers. Transporting children under such conditions presents a potential hazard. Under these circumstances it is reasonable to equip the person with a fully modified van for safe and independent transportation of themselves and their family.

Environmental Control Units (ECUs) are remote-controlled devices that allow an individual to operate electrical appliances within their environment. Especially for tetraplegics, the availability of an ECU can enhance independence in activities of daily living, thereby reducing frequent reliance on caregivers. Enhancing the patient's independence by this method not only increases self esteem (by being able to perform more activities independently) but also reduces the risk of exhaustion on the part of the caregiver by minimizing requests for assistance. The sophistication, and accordingly cost, of these ECUs can vary from a basic unit available through a local business for approximately $200 to $400 to a much more sophisticated unit specifically designed for tetraplegics (varying in cost from $3,000 to as much as $16,000).

Very high-level tetraplegics may be unable to support themselves by independent breathing. In these instances a patient may require artificial support by respirators (sometimes called ventilators). It is necessary to purchase two ventilators to allow one to serve as a backup should a problem develop with the primary machine. Individuals who need to be maintained on a ventilator require numerous additional items of equipment, including suction machines, compressors, mist devices, and so forth.

Functional Electrical Stimulation (FES) has been adapted for use as a therapeutic exercise modality and functional improvement for spinal cord injuries. For those individuals who are capable of using this modality, the equipment and supplies to allow them access must be considered.

Cellular phones, like many high-tech items of equipment, have enhanced the lifestyle, capabilities, and safety of individuals with spinal cord injuries. Historically citizen's band radios have been used for emergency communication for individuals with disabilities. However, because of problems that have been demonstrated by relying on C.B. communications, cellular phone access has received broad support in recent years. The problems include reduced monitoring of some channels or monitoring of emergency calls by persons seeking to exploit the vulnerability of a disabled user. Cellular telephones have allowed more direct and safe access for emergency services to individuals with disabilities. Should a disabled person become stranded by equipment failure or weather-related problems, a cellular phone provides immediate access to police, ambulance, or towing services. Additionally, the disabled person is able to develop relationships with merchants facilitated by use of a cellular phone for pickups and delivery of dry cleaning or purchases. The provision of an appropriate cellular telephone and the cellular carrier connect charge should be considered in the development of a life care plan.

§ 9.5 Medical Procedures

The spinal cord injured individual requires periodic evaluations to monitor medical and functional status. Generally these reevaluations are conducted by a primary physician (usually a physiatrist), urologist, physical and occupational therapist, nurse, and counselor. Depending on specific needs that may be identified at any one evaluation, additional consultants may be required. When possible it is important to have these reevaluations conducted within a program that specializes in the care and rehabilitation of spinal cord injured persons. A model regional spinal cord injury care program can best serve the patient population of more complicated cases or higher level tetraplegics. Reevaluations are conducted on an outpatient or inpatient basis depending upon program design and the patient's needs. However, in the case of ventilator-dependent tetraplegics the reevaluation generally lasts longer, frequently as much as two weeks.

Due to the likelihood of recurring urinary tract infections, it is necessary for the spinal cord injured to have periodic urinalysis and urine culture and sensitivities to monitor the presence or severity of urinary tract infections. Therefore, it is necessary for a patient to have access to follow-up with a urologist (or other specialists) who can monitor the urinary tract function.

Spinal cord injured persons are at risk for multiple complications of their spinal cord injury. These include: urinary tract infections, decubitus ulcers, spasticity, respiratory compromise, autonomic dysreflexia, fractures, syringomyelia, pain, gastrointestinal dysfunction, sexual dysfunction, heterotopic ossification, osteoporosis, and others. It is likely that the patient will require treatment for some of these complications throughout his lifetime. Although the incidences of hospitalizations for complications are less frequent in the early years of a person's injury, as the individual ages with a spinal cord injury more frequent and lengthy complications can be anticipated. An averaged approach to predicting hospitalization costs can be calculated with the assistance of studies that have researched a representative sample population of spinal cord injured persons. Two sources for these statistics are *Spinal Cord Injury Facts and Figures* and *The Economic Consequences of Traumatic Spinal Cord Injury*.

§ 9.6 Therapy

Following a spinal cord injury the patient requires extensive physical and occupational therapy, and sometimes speech therapy. In most cases the maximum benefit from therapeutic intervention is achieved by the time the patient is ready to be discharged from the rehabilitation program. It is commonly understood that completion of the person's activities of daily living on a continuing basis after discharge is sufficient to maintain the patient's functional skills. In some instances it may be necessary for a person to continue to be involved in outpatient therapy (for example, continuing neurological change, participating in a gaiting program, and so forth).

In most instances, a pediatric spinal cord injured patient requires additional therapy following initial rehabilitation. As the young spinal cord injured person grows through various developmental stages, the patient will require therapy to enhance and maintain function, review and prescribe equipment, and prevent complications such as orthopedic deformities. From late adolescence to adult years, it can be anticipated that the pediatric spinal cord injured patient will similarly have achieved maximum benefit from therapy; however, the patient will require ongoing evaluations.

As previously indicated, a patient requires annual evaluations by therapists to monitor functional status, equipment, and any unfortunate effects of aging associated with spinal cord injury.

§ 9.7 Attendant Care and Household Assistance

A person who has compromised function of the upper extremities normally requires assistance to complete self-care and activities of daily living. Most tetraplegics (and in rare instances paraplegics) require attendant care on a regular and long-term basis. This assistance may involve help with bathing, toileting, dressing, feeding, transfers, transportation, and so forth.

In addition to the personal care that patients require, they also need assistance in managing their own households. Due to a person's paralysis, it is difficult (in some cases impossible) to do many of the common household chores and activities that a typical homeowner performs. Although the patient may be able to accomplish light household cleaning activities such as dusting, laundry, dishwashing, and so forth, heavier housecleaning like moving furniture, cleaning and organizing items in high places, cleaning bathrooms, and washing floors become impossible (or at least impractical). Additionally, the spinal cord injured person is unable to complete many of the minor plumbing, electrical, and mechanical repairs that most homeowners commonly do. Lawn care, snow removal, and house painting are likewise impossible for an individual with paralysis. Therefore, in addition to the personal attendant care that the individual may require, a handyperson or use of professional services to complete many of the household tasks may be necessary.

Due to a lack of resources, many patients rely on family or friends for assistance following discharge. Relying on family to perform the extraordinary care required in most instances will have detrimental effects on all members of the family. The spouse who must perform attendant care will not have the personal time previously available to complete typical daily activities. Additionally, the physical effects of performing transfers and other heavy care activities can have an unfortunate effect on the health of the caregiver. Role changes imposed by the disabiling condition can have a negative influence on self esteem of both partners and contribute to marital conflict. All of this is underscored by the occasional odious nature of the care involved in managing bowel program or involuntary bowel movements. A further consideration is the effect on the children within the family who no longer have the ready availability of either parent (the disabled parent as well as the caregiver parent) to attend to their emotional or physical needs. The combined negative effects of a family member providing this extraordinary care is well documented and leads to the recommendation of when possible to secure outside attendant care. Even in those instances when it is not possible to hire outside care, the economic contribution of a family member providing attendant care must be recognized.

The two most commonly used sources of hiring attendant care are private hire or a home health agency. Hiring privately requires the patient or a family member to place advertisements, screen calls and applications, interview potential candidates, train new attendants, establish and maintain appropriate employment records, and maintain good employer-employee relations. It is a rare person who possesses all of the skills and training of a personnel manager prior to a spinal cord injury. For this reason many individuals who opt for private hire encounter problems in the implementation of an attendant care program. Theft of personal property, neglect of duties, and high turnover are some of the common problems cited. Additionally, it requires employing several individuals so that a primary attendant receives time off and both primary and backup attendants are covered for illnesses and vacation time. Finally, the typically low rate of pay, lack of career advancement, and unpleasant nature of much of the care makes it difficult to attract quality employees. Although hiring privately allows a person to negotiate a lower direct cost, the indirect costs of hiring privately must be weighed into the equation.

In most communities there are home health agencies or nurses' registries that can provide attendant care on an ongoing basis. These agencies are responsible for screening, hiring, training, bookkeeping, and similar employer responsibilities thereby reducing the employer-employee responsibilities for the patient. Furthermore, the agencies maintain a pool of employees to cover sick time, vacation time, and turnover of attendants. The rate charged for attendants through a home health agency is normally higher than encountered when hiring privately, since the agencies charge an overhead for the responsibilities they assume. Although the problems encountered in securing attendant care cannot be totally eliminated, they are generally minimized by utilizing agencies.

Consistency is a very important part of an effective attendant care program. Most disabled individuals seek to find a primary attendant or attendants who will work steadily with them for years. Unfortunately this is the exception rather than the rule. However, the longer the spinal cord injured person can maintain a good attendant, the better the patient is served at many levels.

Home health agencies draft personnel policies in accordance with the Nurse Practice Act of the states they are located in. These policies describe the activities that caregivers of various skill levels can perform. Many spinal cord injured persons can be cared for by a home health aide or nurse aide. However, if invasive procedures such as catheterization, suctioning, tracheostomy change, or gastrostomy tube feedings are required, a skilled level of nursing, either LPN or RN (licensed practical nurse or registered nurse), is required.

Most tetraplegics have need for more intense levels of care in the morning when they get bathed, dressed, and transferred to the wheelchair and similarly in the evening as they return to bed. However, all patients will have other needs throughout the day. If able to be served by a home health aide level of care, frequently the home health agency can provide a live-in caregiver. This has the advantage of minimizing the number of people who need to be employed, thereby achieving better consistency in the caregiving routine. Typically a live-in attendant must be guaranteed eight hours uninterrupted sleep plus additional periods of personal time throughout the day. In most instances the care schedule can be worked out to the mutual satisfaction of the patient and the attendant. Additional consideration must be given to safeguard the privacy of the patient and the family in this situation while still ensuring ready availability of attendant care.

Unfortunately, if the patient requires skilled care, it is not possible to hire a live-in nurse through an agency. Therefore, it will be necessary to have more personnel involved on a shift basis. Typically, agencies will have some flexibility in scheduling shifts of up to 12 hours to help in achieving better consistency of personnel.

The ultimate goal of virtually every paraplegic and tetraplegic is to avoid the specter of institutional placement. Securing the appropriate attendant care on a reliable basis can avoid the necessity for a nursing home placement. However, in some rare and unfortunate instances institutional placement must be explored.

§ 9.8 Psychological Counseling

A spinal cord injury changes not only the person's physical status but also the patient's emotional and psychological well-being. Although not all individuals progress through the stages of one of the traditional adjustment models, experience shows that virtually all undergo a process of adjusting to their injury. With appropriate support most individuals have begun to adjust and cope with their injury by the time of discharge from the rehabilitation program. However, this adjustment process can continue for some months or even years.

Following discharge anticipate that the spinal cord injured person will experience various life changes or transitions that will be affected by his paralysis. These changes include: school transitions, adolescence, early dating experiences, marriage, childbirth, potential employment transition, and aging. The presence of a spinal cord injury may exacerbate the adjustment process during these life transitions. This may precipitate the need for counseling intervention during a transition adjustment crisis. It will be important to allow for the appropriate counseling support necessary during periods of transition.

Additionally, it may be necessary to involve the family in counseling to assist them in adjusting to periodic transitions. Because a good family support system is critical to a disabled person's adjustment process, the support of family members through their own transitions can aid in ensuring that the spinal cord injured person continues to enjoy the support necessary from family members.

§ 9.9 Recreation

Leisure time and recreational pursuits are important for the physical and mental well-being of all individuals, disabled or able-bodied. The effect of a spinal cord injury can frequently alter the person's previous leisure time choices. However, there are many leisure time and recreational options remaining for a disabled person. Frequently this involves the consideration of specialized pieces of equipment or supportive services to allow an individual entree into various activities. It is therefore necessary to consider the cost of specialized wheelchairs for sporting events (for example, wheelchair basketball, quad rugby, wheelchair tennis, and so forth) or other adaptive equipment. Individuals choosing to pursue activities such as swimming or horseback riding may require specialized therapeutic programs to assist in these pursuits.

§ 9.10 Case Manager

It is helpful for the spinal cord injured person to have a professional case manager available to him to assist in coordinating all aspects of care that he will require. This case manager, by definition, must stay abreast of the changes within the field that may affect the spinal cord injured person. Spinal cord injured persons should have the availability of meeting periodically with a case manager to ensure that they avail themselves of any new developments that may be of service to them and to guarantee that they achieve maximum benefit and coordination from all of the care and services that they require. The frequency of case management contacts will vary depending upon the extent of the spinal cord injury and the sophistication of the person living with spinal cord injury.

§ 9.11 Housing

A person with spinal cord injury will in almost all instances have need for specialized housing adaptations. Because of mobility limitations the individual will need a house that will accommodate a wheelchair. This requires the elimination of all steps, as well as widening of doorways and other passages. Some areas of the house need to be larger than those in the average home to facilitate specialized needs, for example, a larger bathroom with a wheel-in shower and a larger kitchen in which the spinal cord injured person can function. Additional durable medical equipment the individual uses requires storage space. Therefore the spinal cord injured person needs a house that is somewhat larger than the average home to accommodate specific needs. Furthermore, if the patient requires attendant care, it is appropriate to plan for separate space for the attendant's use when not immediately involved in the patient's care. This separate space provides the additional benefit of privacy for the patient and family as well as the attendant.

Although it is possible in some instances to modify an existing home, it is frequently difficult to retrofit such a structure to totally accommodate the spinal cord injured person's needs. When possible new construction designed around the specific needs of the patient more appropriately accommodates mobility and care needs. When planning new construction it is possible to design appropriate accessibility features while still allowing the house to blend into the surrounding neighborhood. If done well, the house remains attractive for resale, allowing the possibility of accumulated equity if the disabled person needs to move. Conversely, if a house is designed to look overly institutional it may be difficult to sell, decreasing equity and therefore suggesting additional costs when the disabled person moves.

§ 9.12 Bibliography

There are many publications available that are specifically written for the disabled consumer. Furthermore, many have carved out specialized niches focusing on a specific disability group. Such publications can be helpful and of interest to a spinal cord injured person and the patient's family. The cost for subscriptions to periodicals is an appropriate part of a life care plan.

Books

American Hospital Association. *Estimated Useful Lives of Depreciable Hospital Assets*. 1988.

M. Berkowitz et al. *The Economic Consequences of Traumatic Spinal Cord Injury*. Demos Publications: New York, 1992.

S.L. Stover. *Spinal Cord Injury: The Facts and Figures*. University of Alabama at Birmingham: Birmingham, AL, 1986.

Periodicals

Accent On Living. Bloomington, Ill.: Cheever Publications, Inc.

Disabled Outdoors. 5223 S. Lorel Ave., Chicago, Ill.

New Mobility. Culver City, Cal.: Miramar Publishers.

Paraplegia News. Phoenix, Ariz.: Paralyzed Veterans of Am.

Spinal Cord Injury Life. Cambridge, Mass.: National Spinal Cord Injury Ass'n.

Sports 'n Spokes. Phoenix, Ariz.: Paralyzed Veterans of Am.

CHAPTER 10

MEDICAL EXPERTS: COORDINATION OF WITNESSES

John Elliott Leighton

Steven C. Laird

§ 10.1 Introduction

The treatment of a spinal cord injury patient usually involves a myriad of types of health care providers. Although the paralysis aspect of the patient's condition may be obvious, it may still be necessary to utilize several different types of experts, both treating and nontreating, to create a clear picture. Not only will experts be able to explain why the spinal cord injury patient is paralyzed, but also be able to provide explanations concerning the care, treatment, susceptibilities, and consequences of various aspects of the patient's condition.

The seriousness of this type of injury often warrants the temporary retention of someone with a medical background, such as an experienced nurse consultant, who can help collect, review, and organize the massive amount of medical records usually involved in these situations. If such an individual (like a nurse consultant) is currently or temporarily retained, the person can also be of major benefit in communicating with the health care providers already involved in the patient's care and treatment. Often a health care provider is more receptive to someone in the health care field than to a legal representative of the patient. Another benefit of retaining someone such as a nurse consultant, is that the individual can often locate health care professionals who may be willing to give more detailed opinions or share expertise in a different area than the health care providers who are actually involved in the care and treatment of the patient. Even without such assistance, however, this chapter provides a brief overview of the likely health care providers involved in the care and treatment of a spinal cord injury patient.

Another consideration is the interfacing of medical care experts with other types of experts. For example, a biomechanical engineer may need information from an orthopedic surgeon or neurosurgeon concerning what specific activity led to the initial spinal cord injury. A life care planner or vocational expert may need information of the medical experts in order to determine projected costs concerning continued medical care and treatment. Although the relationship of nonmedical and medical experts should be kept in mind, the primary focus of this chapter is on the type of experts normally involved in the care and treatment of the spinal cord injury patient.

§ 10.2 Primary Care Physician

The primary care physician (PCP) comes in many shapes and sizes. In today's specialized medical climate, common primary care physicians include internists, cardiologists, and family practice physicians. For women sometimes the primary physician is a gynecologist. Primary care physicians assume a much more important role than most physicians expect. They must coordinate and oversee the various specialists treating the spinal cord injury patient.

The attorney should carefully examine the roles of the PCP before dismissing the individual as someone who cannot testify about the precise nature of the patient's damages. The PCP is frequently in the best position to explain the multidisciplinary aspects of the care and treatment of the patient, for it is this physician who interacts with the specialists and frequently refers the patient elsewhere. In this increasingly managed health care society the PCP is frequently referred to as the gatekeeper for the ability to decide what and which specialists will be seen.

It is the PCP who ultimately reviews the medications taken by the patient. The spinal cord injury patient is frequently administered a plethora of drugs, both prophylactically and remedially. Some may seem innocuous, but in combination with other medications may become virulent. Many physicians feel that the single greatest threat to chronic care patients today is the consequence of drug interactions.

More than anything else, the primary care physician is a resource for the practitioner. It is this provider who can best furnish information for the attorney to effectively present the patient's case.

§ 10.3 Neurologist

From the perspective of patients with spinal cord injuries, the neurologist is often the physician they tend to see the most. The neurologic involvement in such patients is evident. Since neurologists concern themselves with diseases of the brain and nervous system, spinal cord injury is directly within their field of specialty.

Neurologists, unlike neurosurgeons, do not generally perform surgery, so they are best suited for the primary management of the spinal cord patient after trauma and any surgery. Frequently a neurosurgeon or orthopedic surgeon will follow the patient until there is no longer an indication for future surgery, after which the neurologist manages chronic neurologic care. As a practical matter, neurosurgeons and orthopedic surgeons are most concerned with the surgical aspects of practice rather than the daily management of the patient. Neurologists may tend to make better witnesses as to daily care and treatment and alteration of activities of daily living.

Sometimes there is no internist or other primary care physician to manage the case, whereupon primary medical coordination will fall to the neurologist. Neurologists are highly skilled at treating the patient through medication or therapy.

Neurologists can explain to juries how the brain, as well as peripheral nerves and reflexes, can be affected by spinal cord injury. They can explain the effects of lack of activity of organs that can lead to a deterioration of muscle tone and atrophy of structures.

§ 10.4 Orthopedic Surgeon and Neurosurgeon

The orthopedist—orthopedic surgeon—is often the first surgical practitioner to care for the spinal cord injured. Many orthopedic surgeons routinely operate on spines, but generally limit surgeries to the bones and surrounding structures. Some do perform surgery that overlaps with that of the neurosurgeon.

Orthopedic surgeons tend to see a great deal of trauma in practice, and are probably involved in litigation-related cases even more so than neurosurgeons.

Orthopedic surgeons and neurosurgeons can be difficult to work with but can also be the best teachers for juries. They can be insightful and descriptive in explaining a particular injury. However, be aware of the potential for physicians to become jaded or skewed toward one particular philosophy. Since the vast majority of all trauma cases result in treatment by an orthopedic surgeon or neurosurgeon, these specialties demand more medico-legal attention than others. Some physicians may feel that this imposes upon them an unfair burden that detracts from the practice of medicine.

Inherent in the medical profession is an implied responsiblity to be a patient advocate, and part of what is in the patient's best interest is to assist in the legal aspects of care. Many times there cannot be proper medical care without the patient recovering damages for injuries if the injuries were caused or contributed to by another. Few patients can afford to be placed into expensive rehabilitation programs without significant funds. The orthopedic surgeons and neurosurgeons are often vital to the presentation of the SCI plaintiff's case.

There are other treatments orthopedic surgeons routinely perform for the SCI patient. Many who are paralyzed develop contractures that require release surgeries to free the frozen joints. This makes positioning and transfers easier than with frozen and rigid limbs.

Additionally, as a result of nonuse and being immobilized, the entire skeletal structure may develop osteoporosis. This condition weakens the bones, in part due to a loss of calcium. Certain types of bone spurs, which are essentially a build up of calcium deposits, may occur in various sites, particularly joints.

Osteoporosis increases the possibility of recurring fractures. This possibility poses a unique problem because the patient may be unaware that a bone has been injured. Have the orthopedic surgeon or neurosurgeon explain that bone can atrophy in a spinal cord injury patient just as the muscle tissue can. Have the health care provider review all of the skeletal and neurological problems facing the spinal cord injury patient, and explain why the patient will be susceptible to these problems for the remainder of the patient's expected life.

While some claim that a lack of sensation makes fractures irrelevant, in actuality a fracture can be a very serious injury to one who is paralyzed. SCI patients only have limited positions in which they can be placed anyway. Fractures and resulting surgeries can limit those positions and further harm the bones. It also restricts and limits the type and degree of therapies available to patients. In order to maintain muscle tone and strength in bones, the patient must be capable of therapy. In many cases those with fractures are not.

§ 10.5 Pulmonary Specialist and Respiratory Therapist

The pulmonologist is an important witness because this specialty will see the severe spinal cord patient—particularly quadriplegic—many times for respiratory infections and similar disorders. Patients who have a lesion at or above the C4 area will likely require respiratory assistance of some sort. Some high-level quadriplegics require suctioning and other respiratory assistance. Because of these types of problems, a pulmonologist may be required for management of the patient's care.

It is common for spinal cord injury patients to experience an inability or impaired ability to breathe properly. Activity such as coughing, blowing the nose, or even clearing the throat may be difficult or even impossible. Have the pulmonary or respiratory expert explain how the rate and depth of respiration is normally a process responsive to the needs of the body as a whole. Get an explanation of how an impaired breathing process affects the lungs, organs, and entire body. Are the muscles associated with the activity of breathing going to deteriorate over a period of time, and with what consequences? Does a sitting or lying position of a spinal cord injury patient affect the patient's lung capacity or ability to breath properly? The expert should also explain why the patient is now so susceptible to upper respiratory infections, with an emphasis on the fact that such infections can be devastating, even fatal, to a quadriplegic.

In patients with a large degree of paralysis, part of the daily regimen may be to be placed in various positions for purposes of drainage and helping overall respiration. For example, if the patient has to be placed in a head down position on a daily or periodic basis, ask if there is any affect on the blood supply to the lungs, or performance by the lungs during this time period. Obtain information on any type of equipment and medication that has to be used by the patient in association with any respiratory problems.

In short, this expert can explain various aspects of respiratory care, and the respiratory therapist can describe in detail the techniques for caring for these patients.

§ 10.6 Psychiatrist, Psychologist, and Counselor

With any serious injury, depression is a condition that patients inevitably face. In spinal cord injury cases, the role of a psychiatrist is enhanced as the patient must deal with complete and permanent lifestyle changes.

The psychiatrist is potentially one of the most critical medical witnesses the patient has. This physician can help a jury understand the long-term psychological effects of disability. Some subtle but important damages suffered by the client can be elicited without the information coming from the patient.

Often if the patient/plaintiff specifies a problem, it sounds like complaining. When it is enumerated by a psychiatrist or psychologist, it has a greater positive effect. This counters the natural inclination for plaintiffs to whine to a jury. Instead, the mental health professional presents the same complaints, but in a clinical manner that takes on the air of authority and definitiveness.

Psychiatrists are able to prescribe medications, so when that is not necessary often a psychologist or other certified counsel can best meet the needs of the SCI patient. Given the multitude of other medications the individual may be taking, many doctors feel it is often best to avoid psychotropic drugs in favor of counseling and other conservative methods.

There are batteries of tests and examinations the psychiatrist or psychologist can administer in order to assess and diagnose the patient. They range from the Minnesota Multiphasic personality Inventory (MMPI) to the Beck Depression Inventory. Many of these tests can quickly identify potential problems, both acute and chronic, so that the mental health professional can work with the patient. Interestingly, most SCI patients—both quadriplegic and paraplegic—do not feel that they would be better off dead. It is this focus on the here and now that psychologists and counselors can best utilize in helping the SCI patient cope with disabilities.

A strong psychological case may be made through the psychiatrist that the damages to the patient include a constant threat of suicide or psychological suicide, in which the patient allows deterioration. It is well accepted in the field that the suicide rate for SCI patients is higher than the general population. This can work for and against a plaintiff in litigation, as it might lead a jury to conclude that the SCI patient has a reduced life expectancy.

§ 10.7 Urologist

There are often significant bladder, kidney, and bowel problems that develop in any patient who has suffered in spinal cord injury. Urologic management is critical in controlling bladder and kidney infections, as well as preventing the formation of kidney stones (calculi).

A urologist may be involved early in the care and management of the spinal cord injury patient to determine what type of temporary or permanent care and instructions are to be followed by the individual affected. The urologist is usually one of the consulting physicians in a case when the spinal cord injury has a potential effect on bladder and kidney functions. After the patient is released for home care or outpatient care, a urologist may be consulted on a periodic basis, such as annually or semiannually, to insure that the correct regime is being followed, as well as to determine if there are any associated or developing problems.

Urine flows down the ureters to the bladder after it is formed by the filtration process in the kidneys. Emptying this urinary reservoir involves an arrangement of complex autonomic, sensory, and motor nerves. Bladder reflexes are controlled by a neuro pathway that enters the spinal cord above the conus medullaris. Injury to the spinal cord below the conus medullaris interrupts the normal spinal bladder reflexes; spinal cord injury above this level usually does not interfere with such reflexes.

It is important to find out from the health care provider whether all or part of the urinary system has been truly affected by the spinal cord injury. Depending upon the level of the spinal cord injury, the kidneys may still be functional in a paraplegic; however, the bladder and genital organ may be dysfunctional. Obtain a medical explanation in layperson's terms so that everyone involved in the case can easily understand to what extent the involvement is with the various components of the entire urinary tract system. Have the medical expert explain the treatment approach for the dysfunctional urinary tract system, particularly a dysfunctional bladder. This would involve a discussion of the use and placement of a catheter, along with any type of external urine container. A urologist can give a detailed explanation of the frequency of catheterization, as well as how the loss of spinal reflexes and muscle tone of the bladder contribute to an inability to void. Even with catheterization treatment, voiding may be incomplete. Urine remaining in the bladder is one of the biggest contributing factors leading to infections.

Have the expert explain whether the patient has any recognition of a full or partial bladder. How successful is the voiding (or emptying) of the bladder? Does the liquid ingested have to be monitored on a time and volume basis? How susceptible is the patient to urinary tract infections, making sure that the expert explains the short- and long-term effects of any such infection on the bladder, kidneys, or any other part of the urinary tract system.

Voluntary control of bowel function may be lost as a result of the connecting nerves being injured or severed between the brain and the bowel system. In addition to a catheterization program, a similar system of care would probably have to be established involving the use of enemas for bowel evacuation. Once again, one of the purposes of this regimen is to prevent infection, especially from contamination by bacteria in any residual bowel contents. The regular and constant use of enemas, however, may result in changes in blood pressure, as well as the development of involuntary spasms in the rectum, bowel system, and abdominal area. Needless to day, this aspect of the patient's lifestyle is also accompanied by embarrassment, inconvenience, discomfort, and feelings of helplessness. The emotional state of the patient can be more fully explained by the psychiatrist, psychologist, or counselor. Any expert giving opinions concerning the emotional condition should be fully informed of as much of the medical condition, treatment, and prognosis as possible.

The urologist should also be consulted concerning the interference with, or loss of, sexual function in the spinal cord patient. As can be expected, virtually every spinal cord injury patient will suffer from some degree of loss of sexual function. This area should be explored from a medical standpoint with the urologist, as well as from the emotional standpoint with a psychiatrist, psychologist, or counselor who is also involved in the care of the patient. The degree of detail concerning the physical, medical, or emotional aspect of sexual dysfunction will have to be tailored to each individual case, depending upon each patient's unique circumstances.

If a urologist is not directly involved with the care or treatment of the spinal cord injury patient, such an expert may nevertheless be very worthwhile to consult for purposes of obtaining opinions concerning the aforementioned aspects of this type of catastrophic injury.

§ 10.8 Plastic Surgeon and Wound Care Nurse

One of the consequences of being immobilized is the formation of decubitus sores and ulcers. As if suffering from partial or complete paralysis is not tragic enough, decubitus lesions present yet another horrible dimension to the condition of the patient, although this aspect can and should be preventable.

When SCI patients develop decubitus ulcers—pressure sores—and the wound is deep, they will generally receive treatment from a plastic surgeon. The surgeon's job is to facilitate healing with minimal disfigurement.

This is generally accomplished by debridement, cleaning, and repair of the wound, often through the use of a flap procedure and, in some cases, a skin graft. Experts can explain the causes and results of pressure sores and the nature and cost of treatment. Plastic surgeons are often not necessary when the ulcer is minor and superficial.

Continuous pressure presented by nonmovement of the limbs or torso leads to a deprivation of an adequate and necessary blood supply, and ultimately the death of the tissue due to a lack of oxygen. Since the patient has a loss of sensation, the patient is not able to detect if such an insidious problem is developing. If boils, ulcers, or sores do develop, they need immediate care by a plastic surgeon, with possible follow-up care being provided by a wound care nurse.

Of course, great care must be taken to prevent the situation from arising. The nurse or home care provider, as well as family members or friends who are with the patient on a daily basis, must take great care in making sure the patient is moved and turned on frequent and daily basis. If the patient is fortunate enough to have no lesions develop, a plastic surgeon or wound care nurse can still be consulted to give a detailed explanation of what type of care must be taken on a daily basis for the remainder of the patient's life to prevent such problems from occurring.

Once a decubitus ulcer or sore appears, it needs to be addressed as an immediate and major problem by someone who is experienced in the care of such wounds.

§ 10.9 Physical Therapist

Perhaps the most involved in the care of the patient, the physical therapist plays a major role in helping the SCI patient develop some measure of independence. The role also includes working with the patient to slow the effects of atrophy and bone loss through therapies designed to work the muscles and tissues.

Physical therapists can help avoid contractures and other disorders that tend to develop from disuse of limbs. Aggressive therapy makes a major difference in the tone of the patient's muscles and skin, and in warding off infection.

Many therapists videotape some therapy sessions in order to chart the progress of the patient. Sometimes these tapes are available, and can become valuable demonstrative evidence in the SCI patient's case. An effective use of this tool is using the tape with a voice-over of the therapist describing what is being done.

§ 10.10 Occupational Therapist

Occupational therapy is performed after or in conjunction with physical therapy. The therapist will play a significant role in conjunction with any vocational rehabilitation expert utilized by the patient.

Like many of the therapists, the occupational therapist can be coordinated through the social worker or rehabilitation nurse, depending on how the care is structured. Occupational therapy is particularly well-suited for patients who have lesions from T1 through T6 and have full use of their hands and arms.

§ 10.11 Rehabilitation Nurse

The rehabilitation nurse is a relatively new expert to the field. This expert may be a central figure in the care of the SCI patient in coordinating care. Especially in today's environment of managed care, health insurers and workers' compensation carriers often assign a rehabilitation nurse to the case to coordinate care and make assessments and recommendations to the carriers about the rehabilitation potential and other care needs.

Rehabilitation nurses play a wide range of roles in spinal cord injury care. They will often accompany the patient to a physician's office, making the nurse capable of testifying to much more than just care of the patient. They present another perspective about what the patient endures, and can often effectively paint a clear picture of the patient's overall treatment.

§ 10.12 Attendant Care Provider

Depending upon the degree of paralysis, a spinal cord injury patient may need care given on literally a daily basis. The type and degree of care may range from the requirement of a 24-hour-a-day nurse or attendant to someone who assists the patient for a few hours each day or every other day.

The patient may need assistance with movement in bed or wheelchair to prevent decubitus ulcers, sores, or lesions from forming. Various positioning of the patient may be necessary to maximize the patient's respiratory capacity. Assisting the patient with personal hygiene on a daily basis is often required. This may range from bathing the patient to the removal of fluid or solid waste products.

Someone who sees and helps to care for a spinal cord injury patient on such a frequent basis can often provide great insight into the daily living activities or restrictions that such a patient faces. This type of potential witness often presents more experience, and perhaps objectivity, than even a family may provide on this subject. In the final analysis, gaining an insight into the every day world of spinal cord injury victims is an objective that the nurse or home care health attendant may help with as much as any other person involved with the patient.

§ 10.13 Physiatrist

These rehabilitation physicians operate most rehabilitation programs. Most long-term care programs are handled by physiatrists. They often have therapy or rehabilitation backgrounds, which make them ideally suited for this type of care. The physiatrist is a multidisciplinary specialty.

§ 10.14 Social Worker

There are various types of social workers who play a role in SCI cases. Some serve in the capacity of mental health counselor. Others are administrative in their roles, often working in a hospital or institutional setting.

Those who do work institutionally assist in the coordination of care and help in ultimate placement of the patient in a permanent setting. Frequently an acute care facility will need to move the patient to a permanent or long-term care institution. The social worker acts as a conduit between the patient and family and the other facilities, and may assist in making recommendations.

Especially when the health care providers work in teams, the social worker serves an important role in the coordination of care, and should be consulted early. The social worker is an excellent avenue to the other care providers.

Social workers meet with the patient and family when the patient is nearing discharge from acute care in order to discuss and assess the financial aspects of long-term care. They assist in arranging for visiting nurses and aides and in securing necessary medical equipment.

CHAPTER 11

VOCATIONAL ANALYSIS OF SCI: FOUNDATION FOR LOST EARNING CAPACITY CALCULATION

Phillip B. Haber

§ 11.1 Introduction

The rehabilitation psychologist is an indispensable component in the task of understanding and evaluating the complicated nature of spinal cord injury (SCI) and documenting the degree to which SCI can be occupationally and financially devastating.

Rehabilitation psychologists play a unique role in the evaluation of the SCI client. They are essential in providing a thorough understanding of the disability's complicated vocational, psychological, and rehabilitative components. Through the use of rigorous and well-researched psychological and psychometric testing, the rehabilitation psychologist can present to the court and jury a comprehensive profile of the subject's physical, emotional, and intellectual functioning as it relates to the world of work. This information can then be used to project rehabilitation potential and evaluate the disability's effect on future earning capacity in a concrete manner.

It is the evaluation of the SCI client's rehabilitation potential that becomes the single most important contribution of the rehabilitate psychological evaluation. This information can lead to the development of specific annual dollar losses, which in turn will provide the proper foundation for the forensic economist's long-term loss of earning capacity projections.

The purpose of this chapter is to look closely at the extensive deficits and potentials of a SCI client from the perspective of a rehabilitation psychologist. Primary emphasis is on the predictive variables for success or failure in the rehabilitation process and the SCI client's ability to mitigate the extent of financial damages.

§ 11.2 Predictive Variables in Relation to Rehabilitation: A Literature Review

For a comprehensive discussion of the definitions of spinal cord injury (SCI) and the general classifications of paraplegia and quadriplegia see **Chapters 1** and **2.** To reiterate, the paraplegic has use only of the upper extremities and the quadriplegic (sometimes called a tetraplegic) has paralysis of all four. There is a fair amount of research on the ability of either to enter the would of work or, in cases of previously employed individuals, to return to work following SCI.

According to the National Spinal Cord Injury Data Research Center (NSCIDRC), only 20 percent of all SCI individuals are employed at Year Three Follow-up.[1] Based on another survey of prior research, DeVivo and Rutt found that the employment rate for SCI persons seldom exceeds 50 percent and is often much lower.[2]

More recent research confirms these findings. In 1990, evaluating 344 study participants, Krause found 45 percent gainfully employed, 14 percent engaged

[1] J. Young & N. Northrup, *Statistical Information Pertaining to Some of the Most Commonly Asked Questions about SCI,* 1 Spinal Cord Injury Dig. 23 (1979)

[2] M. DeVivo et al., *Employment after Spinal Cord Injury,* 68 Archives of Physical Med. & Rehabilitation 494 (1987); M. DeVivo & P. Fine, *Predicting VR Outcomes: Authors Reply,* 64 Archives of Physical Med. & Rehabilitation 233 (1983); M. DeVivo & P. Fine, *Employment Status of Spinal Cord Injured Patients 3 Years after Injury,* 63 Archives of Physical Med. & Rehabilitation 200 (1982); C. Weidman & A. Freehafer, *Vocational Outcome in Patients with Spinal Cord Injury,* 47 J. of Rehabilitation 63 (1981); A. El Ghatit & R. Hanson, *Educational and Training Levels and Employment of the Spinal Cord Injured Patient,* 60 Archives of Physical Med. & Rehabilitation 405 (1979); F. DeYoe, *Spinal Cord Injury: Long-term Follow-up of Veterans,* 53 Archives of Physical Medicine and Rehabilitation 523 (1972); W. Geisler et al., *Vocational Reestablishment of Patients with Spinal Cord Injury,* 22 Med. Serv. J., Can. (1966); P. Dvorch et al., *Vocational Findings in Post-disability Employment of Patients with Spinal Cord Dysfunction,* 46 Archives of Physical Med. & Rehabilitation 761 (1965).

in unpaid productive activities—school, volunteering, or homemaking—and the remaining 41 percent not engaged in any productive activities.[3]

The NSCIDRC has also reported that only 60 percent of the surveyed SCI patients were employed at the time of injury.[4] This would mean that 40 percent were either unemployed at the time of injury or had never held jobs, and this finding is consistent with the youthful age of SCI patients. Previous researchers failed to identify the fact that most of this 40 percent represents clients younger than normal employment age.

It is true that following discharge from a rehabilitation center, few SCI persons return to their former employment.[5] But this study is dated, and there is little new research on whether SCI persons have benefited from changes in the law or social attitudes. Weidman and Freehafer have observed that only one percent of midcareer-injured SCI persons return to the jobs held prior to injury, but the authors do not have data on an individual's success in finding alternative employment. Nor do they comment on the prospects for younger clients, who make up the bulk of the SCI population.[6]

Yet other research indicates that returning to work does not ensure continued employment, as many persons who work at some time after their injuries do not continue or sustain work experience.[7]

There are several major variables affecting independent functioning following a spinal cord injury and a client's ability to benefit from vocational rehabilitation such as would lead to employment.

Age

As might be expected, SCI occurs most frequently in younger age groups. Eighty percent are under 40 years old; the median age is 23 and the mean is 29. The most common age is 20. Fifty percent of SCI occurs between the ages of 15 to 25.[8]

---

[3] J. Krause & N. Crewe, *Long-term Prediction of Self-reported Problems Following Spinal Cord Injury,* 28 Paraplegia 200 (1990).

[4] J. Young & N. Northrup, *Statistical Information Pertaining to Some of the Most Commonly Asked Questions about SCI,* 1 Spinal Cord Injury Dig. 16 (1979).

[5] J. Felton & M. Litman, *Study of Employment of 222 Men with Spinal Cord Injury,* 46 Archives of Physical Med. & Rehabilitation 814 (1965).

[6] C. Weidman & A. Freehofer, *Vocational Outcome in Patients with Spinal Cord Injury,* 47 J. of Rehabilitation 64 (1981).

[7] M. DeViro et al., *Employment after Spinal Cord Injury,* 68 Archives of Physical Med. & Rehabilitation 496 (1987); A. El Ghatit & R. Hanson, *Variables Associated with Obtaining and Sustaining Employment among Spinal Cord Injured Males: a Follow-up of 760 Veterans,* 31 J. of Chronic Disease 363 (1978).

[8] J. Young & N. Northrup, *Statistical Information Pertaining to Some of the Most Commonly Asked Questions about SCI,* 1 Spinal Cord Injury Dig. 14 (1979).

From a vocational and rehabilitation perspective, the ideal age is between 25 and 40, when the client has both the vitality that comes from youth, and the experience that comes from age. This group has the best chances for rehabilitation success. One study calculated that SCI patients less than 24 years old at time of injury are 4.1 times more likely to return to work than their older counterparts.[9] Another study identified age as a significant predictor of occupational success.[10] They found the probability of a better outcome was almost 50 percent higher for every 10 years of younger age.

Conversely, James, DeVivo and Richards found that those injured between the ages of 46 and 61 are least likely to be reemployed.[11] These findings are consistent with many previous studies, all showing a correlation between younger age at a time of injury and eventual employment status.[12] In general, older age appears to be the most important predictor of negative occupational outcome independent of other factors.

Education

Nearly as important as the age variable in SCI, training and education are consistent predictors of favorable employment outcomes. As noted, few SCI individuals return to their former jobs following discharge from a rehabilitation center,[13] but El Ghatit and Hanson have found that educational level is more important than preinjury occupation in determining postinjury employment status.[14]

---

[9] M. DeVivo & P. Fine, *Employment Status of Spinal Cord Injured Patients 3 Years after Injury,* 63 Archives of Physical Med. and Rehabilitation 201 (1982).

[10] M. Taricco et al., *The Social and Vocational Outcome of Spinal Cord Injury Patients,* 30 Paraplegia 217 (1992).

[11] M. James et al., *Post-injury Employment Outcomes among African-American and White Persons with Spinal Cord Injury,* 38 Rehabilitation Psychol. 158 (1993).

[12] G. DeJong et al., *Independent Living Outcomes in Spinal Cord Injury: Multiple Analyses,* 65 Archives of Physical Med. & Rehabilitation 66 (1984); M. DeVivo & P. Fine, *Employment Status of Spinal Cord Injured Patients 3 Years after Injury,* 63 Archives of Physical Med. & Rehabilitation 201 (1982); A. El Ghatit & R. Hanson, *Variables Associated with Obtaining and Sustaining Employment among Spinal Cord Injured Males: a Follow-up of 760 Veterans,* 31 J. of Chronic Disease 363 (1978); W. Geisler et al., *Vocational Re-establishment of Patients with Spinal Cord Injury,* 22 Med. Serv. J., Can. 698 (1966); P. Dvonch et al., *Vocational Findings in Post-disability Employment of Patients with Spinal Cord Dysfunction,* 46 Archives of Physical Med. & Rehabilitation 765 (1965); B. Levenson & J. Green, *Return to Work after Severe Disability,* 18 J. of Chronic Disability 167 (1965).

[13] J. Felton & M. Litman, *Sltudy of Employment of 22 Men with Spinal Cord Injury,* 46 Archives of Physical Med. & Rehabilitation 809 (1965).

[14] A. El Ghatit & R. Hanson, *Marriage and Divorce after Spinal Cord Injury,* 57 Archives of Physical Med. & Rehabilitation 470 (1976).

The level of education completed prior to injury is an important factor, with those not completing high school at a severe vocational disadvantage.[15] El Ghatit and Hanson have found that the amount of postinjury education is more significant than absolute amount of education in predicting employment status.[16] They have shown that those earning a college degree after injury were more likely to obtain employment than those who already had one at the time of injury and did not further their education.

SCI individuals, by the very nature of their injuries, frequently must take jobs that focus on persuasion and intellectual skills. Persons with lower educational levels may find this transition considerably more difficult. Since SCI is unique in that it devastates the body but most often leaves the cognitive powers intact, persons with more years of education are, all other factors being equal, more likely to find employment. This has been documented in numerous studies and is a primary ingredient of post-injury adjustment and eventual employment success.[17]

Work Values

This variable indicates the meaning of work to the individual with disability. Continuing education is an essential component. Individuals without backgrounds or personalities that value work and education are often far less successful in postinjury vocational rehabilitation.

Obviously, the vocational rehabilitation approach to this type of person would be different from the approach to someone who had worked for 20 years or who had strong motivation to reenter the workplace. Goldberg and Freed found that clients with a healthy work ethic spend a greater percentage of their

---

[15] J. Krause, *Employment after Spinal Cord Injury,* 73 Archives of Physical Medicine & Rehabilitation 168 (1992).

[16] A. El Ghatit & R. Hanson, *Variables Associated with Obtaining and Sustaining Employment among Spinal Cord Injured Males: a Follow-up of 760 Veterans,* 31 J. of Chronic Disease 363 (1978).

[17] W. Alfred et al., *Vocational Development following Severe Spinal Cord Injury: a Longitudinal Study,* 68 Archives of Physical Med. & Rehabilitation 854 (1987); M. DeVivo et al., *Employment after Spinal Cord Injury,* 68 Archives of Med. & Rehabilitation 494 (1987); G. DeJong et al., *Independent Living Outcomes in Spinal Cord Injury: Multiple Analyses,* 65 Archives of Physical Med. & Rehabilitation 66 (1984) R. Goldberg et al., *Vocational Development of Spinal Cord Injury Patients: an 8-year Follow-up,* 63 Archives of Physical Med. & Rehabilitation 207 (1982); A. El Ghatit & R. Hanson, *Educational and Training Levels and Employment of the Spinal Cord Injured Patient,* 60 Archives of Physical Med. & Rehabilitation 405 (1979); A. El Ghatit & R. Hanson, *Variables Associated with Obtaining and Sustaining Employment among Spinal Cord Injured Males: a Follow-up of 760 Veterans,* 31 J. of Chronic Disease 363 (1978); W. Geisler et al., *Vocational Re-establishment of Patients with Spinal Cord Injury,* Med. Serv. J., Can. 689 (1966); *Vocational Findings in Post-disability Employment of Patients with Spinal Cord Dysfunction,* 46 Archives of Physical Med. & Rehabilitation 761 (1965).

time in gainful employment after hospital discharge.[18] Strong work values also correlated in their study with other measures of vocational development, such as educational plans and long-range work interests.

The person with a stable preinjury work history is likely to continue that pattern postinjury. And patients who maintain consistent work interests after injury are more likely to become reemployed. They not only tend to remain in school longer but also have fewer difficulties in obtaining and remaining at work postinjury.

Marital Status or Number of Dependent Children

As might be expected, with a predominately young SCI population, it is not surprising that most (52 percent) are single when injured.[19] Marital status is an important predictor of an individual's propensity to move into the competitive working world.[20] Number of children also correlates significantly with vocational adjustment. Those patients with children are more likely to return to work or school.[21]

Among those married at the time of injury, as well as those who marry after injury, the likelihood of the marriage remaining intact is slightly lower when compared to the uninjured population.[22] The likelihood of finding a marriage partner after injury is also reduced.

A stable support system must exist if the SCI patient is to focus energy on educational or vocational pursuits. A family can lend this support and incentive, which then serves as an impetus to further education and subsequent employment. El Ghatit warns, however, against inferring a causal relationship between postinjury marriage and vocational rehabilitation.[23] On the one hand, having a family may increase the individual's feelings of responsibility, but on the other, single persons interested in furthering their educational and employment prospects could be more likely to attract a potential mate.

---

[18] R. Goldberg & M. Freed, *Vocational Development of Spinal Cord Injury Patients: an 8-year Follow-up,* 63 Archives of Physical Med. & Rehabilitation 208 (1982).

[19] J. Young & N. Northrup, *Statistical Information Pertaining to Some of the Most Commonly Asked Questions about SCI,* 1 Spinal Cord Injury Dig. 16 (1979).

[20] A. El Ghatit & R. Hanson, *Variables Associated with Obtaining and Sustaining Employment among Spinal Cord Injured Males: a Follow-up of 760 Veterans,* 31 J. of Chronic Disease 363 (1978).

[21] R. Goldberg & M. Freed, *Vocational Development of Spinal Cord Injury Patients: an 8-year Follow-up,* 63 Archives of Physical Med. & Rehabilitation 209 (1982).

[22] A. El Ghatit & R. Hanson, *Marriage and Divorce after Spinal Cord Injury,* 57 Archives of Physical Med. & Rehabilitation 470 (1976).

[23] A. El Ghatit & R. Hanson, *Educational and Training Levels and Employment of the Spinal Cord Injured Patient,* 60 Archives of Physical Med. & Rehabilitation 405 (1979).

Severity of Injury

Approximately as many SCI persons are quadriplegic as are paraplegic, although paraplegics tend to have a higher percentage of complete lesions: 61 percent compared to 50 percent for quadriplegics.[24]

Common sense—and general public opinion—would dictate that the severity of the disability is the most important factor in vocational outcome among SCI persons; however, the scientific literature does not consistently support such a conclusion. In several studies, no differences in productivity or employment were found when participants were grouped according to quadriplegia versus paraplegia,[25] but a greater number of studies conclude that paraplegic persons are far more likely to return to work than quadriplegic individuals. [26]

In general, the higher the level of the spinal cord lesion, the more complex and frequent are the medical sequelae encountered. They can directly affect a SCI client's ability to engage in a program of vocational rehabilitation and subsequently obtain employment.

One study suggests that among quadriplegic persons with complete lesions, individuals with lower lesions (C6 and C7) are more likely to be working than those with very high injury levels (C5 and above).[27] Krause found no correlation between employment status and high-level or low-level lesions in quadriplegic individuals, or between persons with paraplegia and those with quadriplegia. He did, however, find that paraplegic persons worked more hours per week.[28]

In this regard, the complications, namely urinary tract infections, skin ulcers, pressure sores, and so forth will impact an individual's ability to work outside the home on a sustained basis.

Within this context of paraplegia versus quadriplegia, the independence factor in predicting a person's ability to return to the world of work must be taken

---

[24] J. Young & N. Northrup, *Statistical Information Pertaining to Some of the Most Commonly Asked Questions about SCI,* 1 Spinal Cord Injury Dig. 13 (1979).

[25] J. Krause & N. Crewe, *Long-term Prediction of Self-reported Problems Following Spinal Cord Injury,* 28 Paraplegia 186 (1990); A. El Ghatit & R. Hanson, *Variables Associated with Obtaining and Sustaining Employment among Spinal Cord Injured Males: a Follow-up of 760 Veterans,* 31 J. of Chronic Disease 363 (1979).

[26] M. DeVivo et al., *Employment after Spinal Cord Injury,* 68 Archives of Physical Med. & Rehabilitation 494 (1987); A. El Ghatit & R. Hanson, *Variables Associated with Obtaining and Sustaining Employment among Spinal Cord Injured Males: a Follow-up of 760 Veterans,* 31 J. of Chronic Disease 363 (1978); F. DeYoe, *Spinal Cord Injury: Long-term Follow-up of Veterans,* 53 Archives of Physical Med. & Rehabilitation 523 (1972); W. Geisler et al., *Vocational Re-establishment of Patients with Spinal Cord Injury,* 22 Med. Serv. J., Can. 698 (1966); J. Felton and M. Litman, *Study of Employment of 222 Men with Spinal Cord Injury,* 46 Archives of Physical Med. & Rehabilitation 810 (1965).

[27] W. Geisler et al., *Vocational Re-establishment of Patients with Spinal Cord Injury,* 22 Med. Serv. J., Can. 698 (1966).

[28] J. Krause, *Long-term Prediction of Self-reported Problems Following Spinal Cord Injury,* 28 Paraplegia 199 (1990).

into consideration. A recent study that grouped subjects according to degree of functional autonomy, rather than employability, found the breakdown highly discriminant between quadriplegic and paraplegic clients: 33 percent and 84 percent, respectively, were classified as independent.[29]

In psychosocial terms, it is extremely beneficial for an individual to be able to perform self care. Independence can enable the individual to feel less disabled. The ability to get up in the morning, dress, do a bowel program, fix leaky catheters or leg bags, travel to and from employment, and so forth can produce a more confident, motivated individual who wants to succeed regardless of disability.

The level of dependence that an individual has upon others also translates into significant lifetime costs of health care and everyday living expenses. The basic cost of survival for a SCI client is much more than for an able-bodied person. For example, the bare necessities of life include wheelchairs, leg bags, and so forth that the general public simply does not require.

Gender Considerations

SCI is predominantly a male disability. SCI males outnumber females 82 percent to 18 percent.[30] One study has shown that females are 1.9 times more likely to be employed after injury than males. But this sample includes homemakers, who are classed in other studies as unpaid productive labor.[31] Excluding homemakers, Young showed that men were twice as likely as women to find gainful employment.[32]

Women with paraplegia are also more likely to return to work than women with quadriplegia, and are also more likely to be younger rather than older, and relatively well educated.[33]

Race Considerations

A significant trend over time has been observed in the racial distribution of persons with SCI. Among persons injured between 1973 and 1977, 76.9 percent

---

[29] M. Taricco et al., *The Social and Vocational Outcome of Spinal Cord Injury Patients,* 30 Paraplegia 216 (1992).

[30] J. Young & N. Northrup, *Statistical Information Pertaining to Some of the Most Commonly Asked Questions about SCI,* 1 Spinal Cord Injury Dig. 13 (1979).

[31] M. DeVivo & P. Fine, *Employment Status of Spinal Cord Injured Patients 3 Years after Injury,* 63 Archives of Physical Med. & Rehabilitation 200 (1982).

[32] M. Young et al., *Vocational Status among Persons with Spinal Cord Injury Living in the Community,* 37 Rehabilitation Counseling Bull. 229 (1994).

[33] M. DeVivo et al., *Employment after Spinal Cord Injury,* 68 Archives of Physical Med. & Rehabilitation 494 (1987); M. DeVivo and P. Fine, *Employment Status of Spinal Cord Injured Patients 3 Years after Injury,* 63 Archives of Physical Med. & Rehabilitation 200 (1982).

were Caucasian, 14 percent were African-American and 6.2 percent were Hispanic. However, among those injured between 1990 and 1992 only 56.3 percent were Caucasian, 29.9 percent were African-American and 11.2 percent were Hispanic. As of late, the percentage of African-American SCI cases has risen higher than their statistical representation in the United States population (13 percent versus 11 percent).[34]

Racial minorities with disabilities often face double discrimination. Caucasian persons with SCI are three times more likely than nonwhites to be employed.[35] And postinjury, African-Americans with SCI are less likely to return to work than Caucasians with SCI.[36]

James, DeVivo & Richards have found that the variable most significantly related to postinjury employment for SCI African-Americans—but not Caucasians—was gender. African-American females are more likely to return to work postinjury than African-American males. The reverse is true among Caucasians with SCI. Specifically, African-American females were two times more likely to become employed (34.5 percent) than African-American males (16.2 percent). For Caucasians, the trend was the opposite, with 39.7 percent of males obtaining employment compared to 32.4 percent of females.[37] It has been hypothesized by James, DeVivo & Richards that these differences in employment outcome can be explained by inadequate skills, education, and employer discrimination. But they also found that education was a much stronger predictor of employment for African-Americans than Caucasians, serving as a deterrent against that discrimination. More research is needed in this area, but the current studies do demonstrate that these differences are significant enough that racial issues must be considered by the rehabilitation psychologist in evaluating the employment potential of the SCI client.

Financial Considerations

Previous studies have suggested an inverse relationship between annual disability income and return to employment.[38] Many individuals, by virtue of their need for frequent and costly medical care, personal assistants or care aides,

---

[34] National SCI Statistical Ctr., University of Ala. at Birmingham (1992).

[35] M. Young et al., *Employment Status of Spinal Cord Injured Patients 3 Years after Injury,* 63 Archives of Physical Med. & Rehabilitation 200 (1994).

[36] M. DeVivo et al., *Employment after Spinal Cord Injury,* 68 Archives of Physical Med. & Rehabilitation 494 (1987); M. DeVivo & P. Fine, *Employment Status of Spinal Cord Injured Patients 3 Years after Injury,* 63 Archives of Physical Med. & Rehabilitation 200 (1982).

[37] M. James et al., *Post-injury Employment Outcomes among African-American and White Persons with Spinal Cord Injury,* 38 Rehabilitation Psychol. 157 (1993).

[38] S. Better et al., *Disability Benefits as Disincentives to Rehabilitation,* 57 Milbank Memorial Fund Q. 412–27 (1979); R. Walls et al., *Negative Incentives to Vocational Rehabilitation,* 38 Rehabilitation Literature 143–50 (1977).

remain dependent upon government programs such as Medicare and Medicaid. Over the past two decades, numerous studies have documented the reluctance of many SCI clients to return to work for fear of loss of financial benefits.[39]

In a sense, unemployment for many SCI clients may very well be a financial and medical necessity. Many individuals cannot afford to take a job because of the economic losses and severe cuts in their health care benefits. If individuals acquire skills marketable within the economy, the limitations of private health insurance often present significant barriers to employment. It is not unusual for SCI clients to find that they simply cannot afford to forgo these benefits and must instead reluctantly give up jobs. Berkowitz, in his comprehensive review of work-related variables, indicated that fear of losing Social Security Disability Insurance and Medicare coverage was a primary reason for many not to return to gainful employment.[40]

At the time of this writing, health care benefits in the United States are in such disarray that an individual who desires employment may not be able to obtain it simply due to provisions in health insurance. These roadblocks could include a three- to six-month wait to become insured, limitations on home care, equipment, and transportation costs, and provisions that exclude preexisting conditions. These roadblocks to employment may account for the interesting findings that there is a lack of association between functional status and occupational outcome among SCI clients.[41] This suggests that the ability to work may not be correlated with the probability of employment.

§ 11.3 Rehabilitation and Psychological Assessment

The rehabilitation and psychological assessment is designed to afford the investigator an opportunity to examine the SCI client in a standardized, orderly, and systematic fashion. The goal is to provide scientifically reliable data relative to the SCI client's ability to benefit from vocational rehabilitation.

A suggested format for a vocational and psychological evaluation with the SCI client will be presented, but it is important to note that the specific measuring instruments used are not inclusive, nor are they presented as the only good tools in accomplishing a thorough evaluation.

---

[39] L. Shaw & B. McMahon, *Jobs Obtained by Spinal Cord Injured Rehabilitants: Implications for Job Placement Practices,* 16 J. of Applied Rehabilitation Counseling 50 (1985); G. DeJong et al., *Independent Living Outcomes in Spinal Cord Injury: Multiple Analyses,* 65 Archives of Physical Med. & Rehabilitation 66 (1984); M. Dew et al., *Reaction and Adjustment to Spinal Cord Injury: a Descriptive Study,* 14 J. of Applied Rehabilitation Counseling 32 (1983); C. Weidman & A. Freehafer, *Vocational Outcome in Patients with Spinal Cord Injury,* 47 J. of Rehabilitation 65 (1981).

[40] M. Berkowitz, *Work Disincentives,* 3 Rehabilitation Brief 1 (1980).

[41] M. Taricco et al., *The Social and Vocational Outcome of Spinal Cord Injury Patients,* 30 Paraplegia 218 (1992).

History

It is customary to begin the vocational and psychological evaluation with a comprehensive history. The history should cover such important items as the age of the client, the highest level of education completed, and particular areas of training or expertise developed by the client prior to the injury. In this regard, do not overlook hobbies, military experience or training, technical college, and so forth.

Work experience is part of the personal history and should be covered in detail. It is necessary to look at the depth and quality of the occupational background in light of its potential for revealing transferable skills in the rehabilitation process.

A comprehensive history is also important to determine what medications are currently being used by the client and for the examiner to be knowledgeable about the effects of these medications on the foregoing testing procedures. For example, certain medications used for muscle spasms or pain may also affect the client's ability to concentrate, recall, or remain on task to completion, and thus perform at an optimum level on testing.

A review of the medical data with the client reveals the appropriateness of certain forms of rehabilitation and psychological measurement. These include finger dexterity, eye and hand coordination, vision, and audiometric testing. All of these factors can be important in the selection of measurement instruments.

Psychometric Evaluation

The heart of the assessment process is the psychological testing that forms the foundation for evaluating the variables affecting educational and occupational functioning post-SCI.

Examination of a SCI client often presents the problem of psychometric evaluation with a more or less restricted test repertory. Almost all psychological tests have been constructed with physically-able persons in mind. When clients are handicapped, the examiner may have to find reasonable alternatives to the standard tests.

This is nowhere more evident than in the first measuring instrument used: the Wechsler Adult Intelligence Scale—Revised. The WAIS—R is an individually-administered and scored test of mental ability, consisting of two primary sections: Verbal Scales and Performance Scales. The Verbal Scales examine a person's ability to respond to questions relating to prior-learned information; that is, information that should have been learned from school, recreational reading, watching television, and daily living. The Performance Scales measure the examinee's ability to respond to new and different tasks. Ideally, these are tasks with which the client does not have previous knowledge or experience. The tasks are primarily visual in nature and allow the examiner the unique opportunity to observe the examinee's style of processing new and different information.

For the paraplegic client, the full-scale WAIS—R should present no problems in administration. Unfortunately, most quadriplegic clients often have difficulty accomplishing particular portions of the Performance Scales. Certain low-level quadriplegics may be able to complete some of the performance subtests, but their achievement with respect to speed of performance is necessarily compromised by the nature of the physical impairment. This section requires the use of hands to write and manipulate blocks, puzzles, and cards. Only the Picture Completion Scale of this test is within the conceivable physical ability of most quadriplegics.

The results of the WAIS—R yield information about the client's potential to benefit from academic programming postinjury, found to be an important criteria for a successful vocational rehabilitation outcome. There is no particular intelligence quotient (IQ) number thought to be an accurate predictor of success or failure. However, there is reason and research to believe that individuals with average or above-average intellects will fare much better in the world of post-SCI education than individuals of below-average intellectual functioning. In this IQ test, 100 represents a standard mid-average intellect, with 50 percent of the population falling below and 50 percent above this score.

Achievement Tests: Reading and Mathematics

The next group of measures provide the examiner with an estimate of the academic levels of the educationally and occupationally important components of reading and math ability. With respect to both vocabulary and comprehension, the Nelson Denny Reading Test or the Gates-MacGinitie Reading Test provide an excellent approach to assessing the reading grade level of the SCI client. The problem with this particular test, as with others, is that it is not always useful with quadriplegics. Some are unable to use the pencil to make answers on the scoring sheet and others, although they may be able to do so, may not be capable of completing the tests in an expeditious fashion. Both tests are timed measures, with speed of completion an important component of the final score. In these time-limited measures, where the statistical norms are calibrated for an uninjured population, the rehabilitation psychologist must use judgment and experience to assess the true significance of SCI clients' test scores.

A good alternative measure is the Wide Range Vocabulary Test by Wells, which provides a multiple choice approach to basic vocabulary and is administered in an untimed setting. This test gives the examiner good information regarding an individual's basic vocabulary recognition skills. Reading competency is a particularly important skill for both paraplegics and quadriplegics as the levels of educational programming prescribed by a rehabilitation psychologist will diminish as the client's ability to read and understand diminishes.

The mathematics section of the Wide Range Achievement Test—Revised is the preferred measuring instrument with regard to mathematical skills. This is also a timed test, but the timed aspect of the test is not customarily taken into consideration. Of more importance is determining whether or not an individual has mastered certain mathematical concepts. Thus, the client's ability to add, subtract, multiply, divide, work with fractions, measures, percentages, decimals, algebra, and so forth is vital to an individual's ability to engage in technical school and/or college level work. Speed at which a person is able to perform these calculations is not nearly as important in the real world. The actual outcome of the test or the score is not as critical to the evaluation as is the demonstration of the ability to master subject matter. In this regard, care should be taken in the interpretation of any timed test administered to the SCI client, since a low score does not necessarily mean a failure to comprehend the material or an inability to master subject matter.

Vocational Interests

Vocational interest testing is accomplished with a relatively sophisticated and well-researched set of assessment measures. The Strong Interest Inventory and the Career Assessment Interest Inventory, two highly regarded interest inventories, are representative of tools used for many years by rehabilitation psychologists. They have proven effective in helping a SCI client take a closer look at occupational interests. From a vocational standpoint, it is important to be able to isolate areas of interest within a SCI client's physical capacity. The professional literature has suggested that occupational interest does not usually change after SCI,[42] and the individual who is interested in being a plumber, carpenter, or electrician before the accident often retains that same interest. The interest inventories help the rehabilitation psychologist to direct a client into other areas of work satisfaction (perhaps related to the pretrauma pattern of interests). This is essential for successful vocational rehabilitation, especially when the subject's stated interests are clearly incompatible with the limitations imposed by their disability.

Personality Assessment

Typically, personality assessment will include an objective measure of psychopathology. The Minnesota Multiphasic Personality Inventory—1 and 2

---

[42] D. Rohe & G. Athelstan, *Change in Vocational Interests after Spinal Cord Injury*, 30 Rehabilitation Psychol. 140 (1985).

(MMPI—1 and 2) are felt to be extremely reliable tools. They are accepted throughout the United States and have been translated into many languages.

The MMPI is a 566-question true or false inventory designed to examine an individual's overall psychological functioning. Given the significant physical trauma associated with SCI and the psychosocial as well as medical sequelae of such an injury, a personality evaluation is clearly indicated. If an individual presents with significant adjustment problems, the ability to successfully manage a program of educational and vocational rehabilitation may certainly be compromised. In this case, some form of psychological or psychiatric care may be indicated prior to or contemporary with the individual's engaging in a program of educational and vocational rehabilitation.

Though the MMPI is considered an excellent objective measure of psychopathology, the individual personality evaluation can provide an enhanced picture of personal adjustment, administered by a trained clinical psychologist using additional psychological testing, that is, the Rorschach Inkblots, the Sentence Completion Test, and the Human Figure Drawing Test. Personality evaluation yielding an individual's psychological adjustment profile can provide valuable information relative to the potential to benefit from any program of rehabilitation.

Work Sample Testing

In a comprehensive rehabilitation center type evaluation, the work sample testing is of utmost importance. This testing, accomplished in a laboratory setting, seeks to compare the SCI client with either employed or entry-level employed individuals. A variety of scientifically simulated work activity is used to gauge performance of primarily light or sedentary work, such as clerical, laboratory, or administrative work. This testing is directly related to the real world of business and industry and offers the evaluated person an opportunity to discover individual aptitudes for a significant variety of work activity. Work sample testing is usually observed by work evaluators, who are individuals trained at the master's degree level in work evaluation and assessment.

In the laboratory, the paraplegic can be expected to be able to perform many of the simulated work tests. However, depending on the level of injury, a quadriplegic may find this testing quite challenging. In evaluating quadriplegics in a work sample setting, care must be taken to provide them with as many possible adaptive devices in order to ensure an adequate performance. Very often these individuals are limited to the clerical and administrative types of work sample testing. Of course, higher-level quadriplegics may have difficulty even with this level of simulated occupational evaluation.

Work evaluators are also charged with observing the SCI client progress through the testing procedure, and making behavioral observations based on training and past examination experience. They are looking for indications of fatigue, slow-down in response, weakness in performance, pain and discomfort, and so forth.

It is also, perhaps, important to note that multi-day evaluations conducted on consecutive days are highly preferable to single day assessments. This is a much better gauge of a SCI client's ability to sustain occupational activity. This type of testing not only assesses particular aptitude for specific job tasks, but also seeks to assess the SCI client's ability to engage in simulated work activity over time on a sustained basis.

The medical sequelae particularly provide a very useful predictor of whether an individual is capable of sustaining a vocational rehabilitation effort. One of these sequelae that may be obvious to the examiner and of primary concern to the SCI client is the issue of pain. Chronic physical pain is a very common and major cause of disability in a SCI client.

The experience of pain for the SCI client is often quite individual. The extent to which this recognized medical sequelae of SCI is a disability in and of itself is a phenomenon best evaluated by a doctor of physical medicine and rehabilitation.

Problems managing pain are an ongoing issue in SCI rehabilitation.[43] Pain and discomfort can increase disability to the extent that the individual is unable to participate for a full day or consecutive days of work in a simulated work environment. When chronic pain is identified, something very important has been learned about an individual's ability to cope to the extent of engaging in a program of educational and vocational rehabilitation.

§ 11.4 Barriers to Employment

The nature of a disability can often make ordinary jobs difficult or impossible to perform. But even when the limitations imposed by physical impairment are not insurmountable, other barriers can complicate and hinder a SCI client's access to employment.

Architectural Barriers to Employment

Little research specific to SCI has been found in professional literature concerning the impact of employment barriers on SCI clients. The most obvious barrier to SCI clients is frequent significant architectural obstructions in our society. These can limit the options of employment, increase the difficulty in going to and from a job, and sometimes pose dangers unrecognized by the unimpaired. These architectural barriers can be curbs on the street, bathroom

---

[43] T. Elliott & S. Wegener, *Chronic Pain and Spinal Cord Injury*, 8 Clinical J. of Pain 86–122 (1992).

doors not wide enough for a wheelchair, doors within office and work spaces not of sufficient width to accommodate a wheelchair, automobile controls and, in some severe SCI cases, even elevator buttons that the individual lacks an ability to depress.

Transportation Barriers

Clearly, transportation is a major problem for individuals with SCI. Though technological advances often allow SCI clients to drive their own vehicles, the higher the spinal cord lesion the more difficulty will be encountered, with the higher-level quadriplegic simply unable to drive. Public transportation for the handicapped exists in some communities, primarily urban rather than rural, but there are always problems of degree concerning access, range, and dependability.

A 1978 study pointed out that of those unable to drive, 16 percent obtained employment. But of those able to drive, 58 percent became employed.[44] The importance of independence in transportation thus becomes crystal clear. Though this reference is 15 years old at time of writing, nothing in this author's experience suggests that the situation is any different today.

Learning to drive as part of a rehabilitation program has ramifications beyond the client's ability to keep a job. It gives independence and freedom and restores to the client a sense of control. This sense of internal control is a prerequisite to goal setting and achievement in any area.

Many individuals who have the physical potential are licensed to drive and are able to do so with hand controls. However, most cannot afford a vehicle unless they work, and they cannot work unless they can get back and forth between the job and home.

Employer Resistance to Hiring SCI Clients

Overcoming the resistance of employers, supervisors, and coworkers in the employment setting represents the single most problematic and intractable barrier faced by the job-seeking SCI client. Disability raises doubts in the minds of individuals who are charged with making employment decisions relative to the ability of the SCI client to successfully meet the challenges of employment.

In this regard, the human resources professional is simply mirroring the stereotypes of society in general as they relate to SCI individuals. Recently, public and private efforts to alter these stereotypes by presenting the disabled more positively have increased. The promotion of wheelchair sports, advertisers' commitment to include wheelchairs in a variety of consumer advertising, and so forth, have been

---

[44] A. El Ghatit & R. Hanson, *Variables Associated with Obtaining and Sustaining Employment among Spinal Cord Injured Males; a Follow-up of 760 Veterans*, 31 J. of Chronic Disease 363 (1978).

part of a slow but evident move towards bringing the SCI client into the 20th century.

Cook, Dahl, and Gale note that societal expectations play a major role in restricting job opportunities for handicapped persons. Employers tend to minimize any interaction between the disabled and the public, even though many disabled persons are trained for exactly the types of clerical and professional positions that would bring them into contact with the public. Employers also tend to underestimate the abilities of the SCI client (by seeing them only as handicapped), and this becomes a self-fulfilling prophecy when the disabled do only what is expected of them.[45] Greenwood and Johnson concluded that employers, intent on profit, have doubts about the ability of disabled workers to be productive.[46] Crisp hypothesizes that prospective employers may also be discouraged by the same challenges that the disabled struggle to overcome—architectural barriers, lack of suitable transport, and medical and insurance problems—and that these contribute to a perception of the SCI job-seeker as a poor employment risk.[47]

In this regard, it is clear that employers often feel that SCI job applicants have prohibitive handicaps. They are seen by the gatekeepers of industry as potentially costly employees with regard to health, disability, and life insurance—benefits that are frequently funded in part or whole by an employer.

Seen as individuals who are difficult to promote, SCI persons are often overlooked (as they frequently feel from the perspective of a wheelchair) for advancement. Few corporations are willing to engage an employee whom they feel has little promotional potential. Trieschmann states that "Employers were very skeptical about any job in which the disabled person was expected to exercise authority over coworkers or function in a professional status."[48] Thus, there are significant psychosocial and perceptual barriers to an SCI client entering or reentering the world of work and finding within it opportunities for career growth.

§ 11.5 Positive Factors Facilitating Employment Opportunities

Not all social attitudes have worked against the disabled. The prevailing shortsightedness, indifference, and prejudice have been partially offset by several promising new developments.

---

[45] P. Cook et al., Vocational Opportunities: Vocational Training and Placement of the Severely Handicapped (1978).

[46] R. Greenwood & V. Johnson, *Employer Perspectives of Workers with Disabilities,* 53 J. of Rehabilitation 37 (1987).

[47] R. Crisp, *Return to Work after Spinal Cord Injury,* 56 J. of Rehabilitation 32 (1990).

[48] R. Trieschmann, Spinal Cord Injuries: Psychological, Social and Vocational Rehabilitation 207 (1988).

Innovative Technology

One of the most important of all technological developments of the last 20 years is speech recognition technology. Initially, these voice-activated computer systems were very simple mechanisms used by home and bed-bound quadriplegics to turn off lights, change television channels, and so forth. This may appear a minor advantage to the able-bodied, but to the bed-bound individual, this early speech recognition technology becomes a life-altering concept.

Within the last several years, speech recognition technology has evolved to provide quadriplegics with technological ability to engage in work activity. Many business-oriented computer programs are currently available for use with the more advanced speech recognition technology and are now being utilized in the world of work. Though this technology has not matured to the level that it is commercially viable nor has it dropped in price, it nevertheless has much to offer the quadriplegic client. Speech recognition technology is still prohibitively expensive for many potential users and, though widely publicized, few quadriplegics have yet enjoyed the benefit of this workplace aid.

Americans with Disabilities Act (ADA)

This federal legislation, enacted in 1990, is one of the most important new laws affecting SCI clients and handicapped persons in general.[49] It applies to all businesses with more than 15 employees and provides significant penalties to employers found to discriminate against the handicapped in the hiring, firing, and promotional process.

Though the legislation is comprehensive and the penalties for noncompliance substantial, this is a very complicated piece of law and is frequently not fully understood by either employers or employees. Discrimination in the world of work is often a subtle and insidious process and no amount of legislation, no matter how encompassing or well-meaning, can be expected to completely eliminate these social barriers. Considerable time can be expected to elapse before this law has the desired impact of providing full equal employment opportunity for individuals with disabilities. Nevertheless, it is a move in the right direction and provides a significant ray of hope for the future.

In this regard, it is important to note that similar legislation has existed in practically all the states under antidiscrimination or equal rights laws. But now, as federal law, the penalties for noncompliance are substantially increased. Those corporations that flout the ADA now run a much greater risk of litigation. However, it is important here to strike a realistic note. Although expectations for the ADA are high, attitudinal change is never instantaneous, and it

---

[49] 42 U.S.C. §§ 12101–12213 (1991).

will likely be some time before this piece of social engineering is an unqualified success.

§ 11.6 Earning Capacity Loss

The rehabilitation psychologist can provide important information to a jury about an SCI client's capacity to engage in work activity and realize income for efforts. Although it is not universally true that the SCI client will always sustain a loss in the capacity to earn, those exceptions where earning capacity is not affected are extremely rare, and no references have been found in the literature suggesting otherwise.

The actual calculation of long-term loss of earning capacity is necessarily the responsibility of a fully-trained forensic economist. But the rehabilitation psychologist's individualized evaluation of the SCI client and up-to-date knowledge of the labor market are essential in providing the database for the forensic economist's calculations.

The rehabilitation psychologist has a significant role to play in evaluating future earning capacity losses. Establishing pre and postinjury earning parameters is central to this responsibility. It is important to stress that the information supplied by the rehabilitation psychologist must be interpreted by a fully-trained forensic economist. Too often juries are experiencing the presentations of nonprofessionally trained (in economics) vocational counselors, rehabilitation counselors, or rehabilitation psychologists who are relying on prepackaged computer software programs of earning capacity loss. These programs are often inadequate for the rigorous demands of intense SCI litigation and the witness frequently lacks the educational foundation to present and defend this type of wage-loss testimony.

The investigation of pre and postinjury earning capacity typically begins with a comprehensive work history of the SCI client. This is taken during the initial portion of the rehabilitation and psychological evaluation. A common misconception about postinjury earning capacity calculation is that prior earnings are the sole standard on which it is based.

The calculation of pre and postinjury earning capacity is an extremely complex and sophisticated professional undertaking. It requires careful examination of educational records pre and post-trauma, earnings records pre and post-trauma, parental education and work history (assuming a younger individual) as well as the significant body of data impacting upon the rehabilitation potential of the SCI client. The latter is developed from the complete vocational and psychological evaluation, as discussed in § **11.30.**

The following paragraphs, will deal with the various strategies utilized by the rehabilitation psychologist in the development of a database to be used by the forensic economist.

As previously noted, most SCI occurs within the age range of 15 to 25, but this does not represent the sum total of SCI clients seen by the rehabilitation psychologist. Differences in age can sometimes necessitate different modes of evaluation. Certain testing procedures and protocols are often age-specific in regard to an individual's ability to perform the required tasks. This specificity can mean that a SCI client's true abilities or potentials are unrecognized or under-evaluated. On some measures, particularly with children, testing may need to be delayed until a later age.

This is also the case with work histories when a younger person may not have the benefit of gainful employment at the time of the injury. Compared with those who have completed high school, technical college, business school, or college-level work, young SCI clients without post-secondary education or work background can be at a disadvantage, not merely in regards to future employment, but also in terms of calculating a fair estimate of lost earning potential.

When evaluating a younger person, below the age of 5, psychological and psychometric testing (such as IQ and personality) are often not as valuable as they can be as the child matures. The rehabilitation psychologist then must examine the level of education or career achievement attained by the biological parents and, where appropriate, the siblings' education or work history. Using available longitudinal research regarding the relationship between parents' educational and occupational achievement and their offspring, rehabilitation psychologists can predict that the child would move forward educationally and exceed the parents by at least one grade level. The level of work this person could be expected to engage in (if any) postinjury can then be projected.

With clients old enough to respond to standardized psychological assessment procedures, it is possible to develop and present scientific frameworks for analyzing and understanding the individual's ability to successfully engage at different educational levels. For instance, if a 12-year-old C4–C5 quadriplegic possesses superior intellect, above average-level reading skills and baccalaureate level work is within the individual's capacity, then it is not unreasonable to argue that this particular client's potential has been severely jeopardized. This information may be developed through a combination of prior academic records as well as the aforementioned psychological assessment procedures. When using this approach and when there is scant education or meaningful work history, the rehabilitation psychologist will provide to the forensic economist appropriate and average wage expectations for the graduates of high school, college, technical school, and graduate school. Opinions will then be offered regarding this individual's ability to complete a level of education and to eventually engage in work activity post-trauma. If the individual is capable of working on a sustained and gainful basis following SCI, then comparisons can be made relative to what the client will earn on average in the postinjury career versus what the client had the capacity to earn absent SCI. This will be calculated for the first year following training or schooling, and projected by the forensic economist up until the time of retirement at age 65 or 70, depending on which ages are used for particular occupations.

Assessing clients younger than age 12 or older than age 50 represent exceptions to the rule. The majority of SCI clients are in the 15 to 25-year-old age range.

For this group, the standard rehabilitation and psychological evaluation, as described earlier in this chapter, is implemented. A number of possible occupational scenarios are developed preinjury based upon evaluation results. These scenarios are compared with the individual's earning capacity postinjury and ability to benefit from vocational rehabilitation. This difference, compiled by the rehabilitation psychologist and submitted for interpretation to the forensic economist, provides the basis for calculating a SCI client's projected loss of earning capacity throughout life.

Employment or reemployment of individuals who have sustained SCI is determined by a number of factors previously discussed. It is not unreasonable to assume that the SCI client will need retraining before being employed or reemployed. The length of time between injury and retraining varies depending on the type of injury, age of the client, outside support, motivation of the client, as well as other factors. The following are fairly typical SCI scenarios, although the possible range of injury, rehabilitation, and employment outcome is much wider. The seven hypothetical earning capacity scenarios illustrate the majority of cases and range of outcomes that are typically encountered in forensic rehabilitation psychology practice.

Scenario 1. Tom is a 24-year-old single male with no dependents. He is a high school graduate and joined the apprenticeship program for plumbers after graduation. He completed this five-year program and had been working as a journeyman plumber at the rate of $22 per hour or $45,760 per year (based on his W2 forms) at the time of injury. As a result of a car accident, he sustained an injury at the L5–S1 level and has paraplegia. Vocational and psychological testing found above-average intelligence and above-average clerical aptitude. Tom has a very positive attitude about himself and being reemployed. He will be able to find work as a city desk clerk at a heating and plumbing company at a rate of $7 per hour or $14,560 per year (based on a labor market analysis done of the area where he lives). However, because of the pain and fatigue noted in the work sample evaluation, he will be able to work only 20 hours per week. His loss of earnings the first year will be $31,200.

Scenario 2. Joe is a 27-year-old male who is newly married with no children. He is a college graduate and found employment right after graduation as an electrical engineer. At the time of injury he was earning $42,000 per year (based on his W2 forms). Because of a bicycle accident he is a quadriplegic at the C4–C5 level. His numerous and continuous physical problems render him physically incapable of work activity. His loss of earnings the first year will be $42,000.

Scenario 3. Terry is a 26-year-old single male. He lives with his parents who are very supportive. He is a high school graduate and completed two years of vocational and technical training and a five-year apprenticeship program for electricians. He was working as a journeyman electrician at the rate of $21.82 per hour or $45,386 annually (salary obtained by contacting the local Electricians' Union) at the time of his motorcycle accident. Injuries to his back resulted in paraplegia at a low level. Psychological and vocational testing indicates excellent math skills and spatial perception and good physical tolerance for full-time sedentary work. Terry will be retrained as an electrical draftsman. The training will take three years to complete (longer than normal because of the injury) at a cost of $5,000 per year. Beginning electrical draftsmen currently earn $9.50 an hour or $19,760 a year (based on information received from instructors and placement department of technical colleges). Terry's loss of earnings the first year will be $25,626.

Scenario 4. Jane is a 21-year-old who was involved in a car accident when she was a teenager. Her injuries resulted in T12–L1 paraplegia. She graduated from high school with an A average and has begun taking college courses. She would like to become a social worker. Testing indicates above average intelligence and excellent reading skills. Because of numerous urinary tract infections and pain in her neck and back, she has been able to only take a two-thirds academic load each quarter. These medical problems will continue throughout her life interfering with her education and ability to work on a full-time basis. She will be able to complete college, but it will take nine to ten years of study for the BA and Masters in Social Work and upon graduation, she will only be able to work part-time (20 hours per week). When she decides to have children (and that is in her plan), she will not have the physical ability to engage in work activity outside the home. When her children leave home, she will be able to return to the workplace on a part-time basis. Beginning salary for a full-time social worker is $27,500 per year (obtained by contacting companies and agencies employing social workers). Jane's loss of earnings begins after six years of college (normal length of time to complete work for social worker). She will not be earning a half-time salary ($13,750 per year—1994 figures for 20 hours per week) until ten years after beginning college.

Scenario 5. John is 17 years old, is single, and lives with his mother and four younger siblings. He quit school in 11th grade and was diagnosed as learning disabled while in school. Prior to a diving accident, he was working as a stock clerk in a supermarket earning $4.95 per hour. He had planned to work the next year as a construction laborer at his father's place of employment. The average salary for a construction laborer is $14.40 per hour or $29,952 annually (obtained from state-published salary survey 1992). As a result of the accident, John sustained a T7–T8 injury and has paraplegia. Results of the vocational psychological evaluation indicate a low average intelligence and confirm the learning disability diagnosis. Except for the accident, he had the capacity to perform the duties of a construction laborer. John is not involved in any outside groups and spends most of his day watching television. He has little aptitude and no desire to be retrained. His prognosis for reemployment is poor and given his multiple disabilities, he is considered permanently and totally disabled. John's loss of income the first year is $29,952.

Scenario 6. Peter is 47 years old, is married, and has two children (ages 13 and 15) living at home. He is a high school graduate and periodically has taken business courses at a local community college. He has been working as a real estate salesperson with his last salary at $50,000 per year (based on his financial records). His clientele had begun to grow and he was realizing a income rise each year. His wife works full-time as an executive secretary. As a result of an automobile accident, Peter has sustained a T2–T3 injury and has paraplegia. He is being treated for depression. Because of the pain and fatigue, he was not able to complete the evaluation. Peter is not a good candidate for retraining or for direct placement. Upon the evaluation of his physical tolerance, he does not have the capacity for full-time or part-time employment on a sustained and gainful basis. Peter's loss of earnings the first year is $50,000.

Scenario 7. Rob is 7 years old and lives with his parents and older siblings. His mother is a registered nurse with a four-year degree. His father completed a vocational technical program and works as an auto mechanic. A sledding accident resulted in Rob receiving injuries at the C5–T6 level and resulted in quadriplegia. Rob is in second grade and is a good student. He receives average and above average grades. He has expressed interest in being a truck driver like his older stepbrother. Except for the accident, Rob had the capacity to perform the duties of registered nurse, auto mechanic, and truck driver. Because of his injuries, he is now not capable of sustained employment. The average salary for a registered nurse is $15.60 per hour or $32,448 a year; for an auto mechanic, $12.50 an hour or $26,000 per year; and for a truck driver, $13.82 an hour or $28,746 per year. (These salaries are obtained from a state-published salary survey in 1992). Rob's loss of first year income would be $32,448, $26,000, or $28,746 (based on 1992 figures).

The loss of earning capacity scenarios presented above constitute examples of the approach that a rehabilitation psychologist may use in presenting the concept of loss of earning capacity to a jury. This information must be properly documented, utilizing available labor market literature, current salary data, and up-to-date statistics. This can provide the forensic economist (and ultimately the jury) with an accurate, comprehensive, and believable foundation for the subsequent projection of long-term loss of earning capacity.

CHAPTER 12

CROSS-EXAMINATION OF THE VOCATIONAL EXPERT WITNESS

David A. Stofferahn

§ 12.1 Introduction

Cross-examination of a vocational expert has much in common with cross-examination of other adverse expert witnesses. The focus here is on those aspects of cross-examination that are of primary significance in dealing with the issue of employability or earning capacity.

When reviewing a vocational expert's report, a key element can usually be identified that serves as the basis for the expert's opinion. The key element may be a labor market survey, assumptions of an injured person's functional capacity, or performance in testing. The key element serves as the foundation for the vocational expert's opinion. What is suggested is that the focus of the cross-examination should be on that key element. Although the vocational expert may never change opinion for the record, questioning the key element can serve as a basis to undermine the impact of that opinion. **Chapter 12** is aimed at identifying those parts of a vocational expert's opinion that may be the key element.

§ 12.2 Basic Sources

Cross-examination of a vocational expert requires more than a passing acquaintance with the sources of information used by the vocational expert in evaluating the claimant. Just as cross-examination of an orthopedist requires that the attorney become familiar with the anatomy of the injured part of the body and the diagnostic tests typically used by an orthopedist, the cross-examination of a vocational expert requires that the attorney become familiar with the material and background that the vocational expert brings to the evaluation. The failure of the vocational expert to follow the guidelines laid out in basic resource material could be the key element of the cross-examination.

In this regard, one of the most important sources to become familiar with is the *Dictionary of Occupational Titles* (hereinafter *DOT).*[1] Broadly speaking, the *DOT* is an attempt by the Department of Labor to identify all jobs that exist in the national economy, to distinguish among jobs by their significant requirements, and to categorize any job with other employment in the same area.

Assume the injured person's most recent job is that of working in an auto body repair shop. In the general index of the *DOT,* that person would be identified as an Auto—Body Repairer with a *DOT* code of 807.381-010. Turning to that code in the volume will provide a detailed description of the job as it is generally performed.

Reviewing the description of the injured person's past employment in the *DOT* should be the first step in preparing for the cross-examination of the vocational expert. There may be a question as to whether or not the injured person can return to previous employment or even a question about nature of that employment. The *DOT* description provides information regarding how the job is done, what tools are used, what physical activity is required, and what related jobs exist. The *DOT* is also detailed enough to provide information on jobs that most people do not know exist, such as cupola charger (*DOT* # 512.686-010) or sublimer (*DOT* # 542.685-014).

The *DOT* should be reviewed in combination with *Selected Characteristics of Occupations Defined in the Revised Dictionary of Occupational Titles* (hereinafter *Selected Characteristics*).[2] This volume takes the numbering system used by the *DOT* and identifies the physical requirements of that job and the training that may be required to perform the job accurately. In the previous example of the auto body repairer, the *DOT* code was 807.381-010. That *DOT* code is found in the index of *Selected Characteristics* and in reviewing that particular code, the job is identified as being medium in exertional level. *Selected Characteristics* defines *medium employment* as being work that involves

---

[1] United States Dep't of Labor, Dictionary of Occupational Titles (4th ed. 1991).

[2] United States Dep't of Labor, Selected Characteristics of Occupations Defined in the Revised Dictionary of Occupational Titles (1993).

exerting 20 to 50 pounds of force occasionally or 10 to 25 pounds of force frequently. It may also require standing or walking throughout the work day. The job of auto body repairer is also in a broader category, referred to as a GOE by the *DOT*, of metal fabrication and repair (GOE 05.05.03). It also has a specific vocational preparation level of 7, meaning that it takes from two to four years to learn to do the job competently.

These two volumes are important in several respects. An individual who has had a spinal cord injury may have had an extensive employment history in a particular occupation. Taken in combination, the *Dictionary of Occupational Titles* and *Selected Characteristics* will provide information as to the transferable skills and abilities that the individual will have acquired from employment. The vocational expert, who also identifies replacement employment of an injured person and identifies a particular job, is subject to challenge in those conclusions if the job identified is one that requires physical abilities or training that the injured person simply does not have. For example, if it is assumed that the injured person in the example has a reading deficiency, or has a limited educational background, the ability of that individual to move to employment that requires significant vocational preparation is doubtful at best. An example might be the adverse vocational expert who has testified that the injured person is capable of employment as a shipping clerk. Referring to the *Dictionary of Occupational Titles* will identify that the job title of shipping and receiving clerk has a *DOT* code of 222.387-050. *Selected Characteristics* considers shipping and receiving clerk to be medium employment. It may also require language and mathematic abilities, which the injured person does not have. If the testing performed by the adverse vocational expert has already identified that the injured person does have not have these attributes, then a conclusion that the individual may be able to return to a job as a shipping clerk is subject to challenge.

These two publications should be reviewed in conjunction with the regulations promulgated by the Social Security Administration. Individuals who are incapable of employment are entitled to Social Security disability benefits. The regulations, which provide the guidelines for the determination to be made by the Social Security Administration, are found in 20 C.F.R. § 404. The importance of the Social Security regulations for this discussion is that the Social Security Administration identifies certain assumptions with which most vocational experts, when pressed, would have to agree. The previous example involved an individual who had been employed as an auto body repairer. According to the *DOT* and *Selected Characteristics,* that employment is in the metal fabrication and repair category. According to Appendix 2 of 20 C.F.R. § 404, an injured person who is over 55-years old will be presumed incapable of performing employment in a different industry, even if still capable of sedentary employment. The auto body repairer over 55-years old should be assumed capable of employment in small engine repair since that occupation is in a different GOE, or category, that of mechanical work.

Although these presumptions do not necessarily establish the employability or lack of employability of an injured person, use of them during cross-examination provides the judge or jury with the knowledge that the vocational expert's opinion may be contrary to conclusions made by the United States Department of Labor and by the Social Security Administration.

In addition to these primary sources, there are secondary sources. Most states publish various types of employment outlooks and wage surveys. In Minnesota, for example, the Department of Economic Security provides a quarterly magazine that identifies the population of each county and identifies the number of jobs in each county. It also provides the unemployment rate in that particular county. This can be helpful when an injured person lives in a county in which there is a high unemployment rate. Most vocational experts will concede, on cross-examination, that a disabled individual is even less likely to be employed in an area in which the unemployment rate is quite high.

Do not overlook the fact that some of the vocational experts testifying may have been authors of magazine articles or textbooks that can serve as a basis for cross-examination. It is not unusual to find that in professional publications, the vocational expert may have been more candid than as an expert witness.

§ 12.3 Qualifications of the Vocational Expert

As in other cases involving the testimony of experts, the vocational expert may be vulnerable to cross-examination on the basis of qualifications. Qualifications can be questioned regarding education or experience and can be the key element in the cross-examination.

There is no single academic path to becoming a vocational expert in the same way in which there is for an orthopedist or physical therapist. Until fairly recently it was not even possible to get a graduate degree in vocational rehabilitation. The result is that some vocational expert witnesses have very little academic training in the area in which they are providing expert opinion testimony. The vocational expert witness may have had no education in psychological testing or kinesiology. Conversely, the vocational expert may have been trained as a physical therapist who has never had any academic training in the vocational tests that are being administered.

The professional experience of the vocational expert witness can be equally diverse. In Minnesota for example, the vocational expert might be a Qualified Rehabilitation Consultant (QRC), that is, someone licensed by the Department of Labor and Industry to provide vocational rehabilitation assistance to injured workers in the workers' compensation system. A person can be licensed as a QRC, and perhaps testify as an expert with only three years of so-called intern experience. Some vocational experts are notorious for never doing anything other than evaluations and should be questioned about familiarity with the real world process of helping a severely injured person find employment.

§ 12.4 Available History

The key element in cross-examination could be the vocational consequences that follow from the injured person's age, education, work experience, or medical history.

The age of the claimant has an important vocational consequence. According to the Social Security Administration, a younger worker is an individual under age 40. Most vocational experts, when pressed, will concede that an individual who is more than 40-years old has a vocational disability from age alone. Employers have a bias against older workers and, all other things being equal, an individual who is 45-years old will find it more difficult to secure employment than one who is 35. In addition, there is an assumption that the older worker will have more difficulty in adjusting to new situations, including new employment.

The education of the claimant is of major significance. Employers often seek employees who have diplomas or degrees even when the job does not require the skills of a high school graduate. It is simply a way of screening job applicants. The lack of a high school degree could serve to demonstrate that a claimant may not be capable of functioning in an environment that places importance on language or math skills. A construction worker with an eighth-grade education may not be capable of performing a job that requires extensive writing, even in the absence of a disability. Educational background should be viewed in light of the testing that has been done in the case. For example, the testing may show that despite being a high school graduate, the injured person is functioning with math skills at a third-grade level.

Previous work experience has a vocational significance. Most people develop skills from the work that they perform. However, some of these skills are not readily transferable from one occupation to another. For example, a commercial roofer has developed a skill in placing felt and hot asphalt on a flat roof, and is able to use those skills in a roofer's usual occupation so as to minimize usage of material and time. Those skills, however, are likely not transferable if the individual is no longer able to be employed as a commercial roofer. The work experience of the individual may also suggest that there are certain types of employment that would not be appropriate for that person.

The key element for cross-examining the vocational expert could be the medical information available concerning the claimant and what use was made of this information. Is there an accurate understanding of the diagnosis and of the treatment that has been provided to the claimant? One of the key questions in this regard might be whether or not the claimant's treating doctors have concluded that no further improvement or change in the claimant's condition is likely. Is the claimant still scheduled for additional physical therapy or other rehabilitation measures? An opinion that the injured is incapable of employment may be premature if surgery is still being considered. Medical history often changes during the pendency of the case and the vocational expert may not be aware of the additional treatment that has occurred since the vocational assessment.

Vocational experts approach the use of medical information in different ways. Some vocational experts have very few actual medical records available to them. They are not particularly interested in what the diagnosis might be because they are more interested in what restrictions are left as the result of the claimant's injury, rather than the label to be placed on that injury. Quite often, these vocational experts perform a functional assessment as part of their evaluation. Other vocational experts make little use of their own judgment and rely almost completely on the conclusions of the medical records in arriving at determinations as to the functional ability of the claimant.

In an adverse medical examination, an orthopedist may have concluded that the claimant is capable of sedentary employment. In a report, the adverse vocational examiner may simply repeat this conclusion and then provide a list of jobs that are sedentary in nature. In cross-examining the adverse vocational examiner, it is well to point out that the vocational examiner has made no independent study or testing of the claimant's actual physical abilities, but has relied completely upon a medical opinion and, in this instance, not the medical opinion of the treating doctor.

It is important to note that medical conclusions and vocational conclusions often become intertwined. A doctor may conclude that a particular individual is disabled. Unless the doctor means that this individual is incapable of any activity whatsoever, such as an individual who is confined to a nursing home, or an individual in a persistent vegetative state, the doctor is rendering not a medical opinion, but a vocational opinion. It is the doctor's province to state what specific physical activities the claimant may be capable of performing. It is then the vocational expert's job to translate those physical abilities or, as the Social Security Administration refers to it, the residual functional capacity into a question of whether or not employment activity exists which the claimant may be able to do. A vocational expert who disproportionately relies on the conclusions of the doctor is vulnerable to questioning. A vocational expert who has simply adopted the opinion of a medical doctor that the claimant is capable of sedentary employment can appropriately be questioned as to whether or not there is actually any independent purpose in the assessment done by the vocational expert and whether the assessment done could simply have been accomplished by reviewing appropriate employment data from various state agencies.

§ 12.5 Examination of Testing

The usual vocational evaluation consists of three types of testing: intellectual, psychological, and work sample or functional capacity. Each area of testing can be the key element for cross-examination.

An example of intellectual testing is the Wechsler Adult Intelligence Scale (WAIS), which gives a measure of the overall intellectual functioning of the individual tested. The WAIS may show a full scale intelligence quotient (IQ) of 92, placing the individual in the low average range of intelligence and indicating therefore that this person could not be satisfactorily retrained. Other testing could provide a measure of the individual's ability to read, write, and spell. These ratings are usually expressed either as a percentage of the population or by grade level. For example, in a reading test an individual might test at the 14th percentile, meaning that 86 percent of adults would read better than the tested individual. The person might test in arithmetic at the third-grade level, meaning that the individual is capable of performing arithmetic skills at the same level as would a third grader. These test results can be correlated with the employment that is allegedly available for the claimant. An individual who is capable of arithmetic only at a third-grade level, which typically involves basic addition and subtraction, would not be capable, for example, of being employed in a sales position if required to apply percentage discounts in computing prices, sales tax, and the like.

Psychological testing quite typically includes the Minnesota Multiphasic Inventory (MMPI). To some extent, for purposes of cross-examination, the MMPI could be called the malingering test. The individual taking the test is answering 500 questions relating to beliefs and other facts about themselves. A vocational expert who has administered the test will concede that the test results will reflect if the person has consciously overstated or exaggerated complaints in an attempt to present as being more disabled than they really are. Items in support of the injured person, such as depression, will show up in the test results as well. Reviewing the MMPI with the vocational expert is a good opportunity to discuss the claimant's sincerity or lack thereof.

Work sample testing is the final type usually done in a vocational evaluation. In its most basic form, work sample testing may be no more than handling a peg board or doing some assembly tasks to determine dexterity in the upper extremities. These tests can be combined with more extensive testing, such as a functional capacity evaluation done in a physical therapy setting. The results of the work sample testing or functional capacity evaluation should not be viewed in isolation. The functional capacity evaluation should make sense in the context of the claimant's actual ability to function as evidenced in daily activities and by medical records. The work sample testing may suggest that the individual is incapable of any significant use of the upper extremities. However, a prior deposition or information about the claimant's daily activities may provide the knowledge that, in fact, the employee has a hobby of knitting and does so frequently throughout a day. The functional capacity evaluation may suggest that the individual is capable of standing for six hours out of an eight-hour work day. The medical information may make it clear that, when the claimant has attempted this type of activity in the past, the claimant has been able to do this activity on a sustained basis.

§ 12.6 Challenging the Opinion

When combined, different elements of a vocational expert's evaluation constitute the opinion. That opinion should be subjected to a common sense analysis. A vocational expert may conclude that the claimant could be employed as an electronics inspector. It is true that such an occupation exists in the dictionary of occupational titles. What may be ignored is that if the claimant happens to live in a small town some miles away from any industrial area, the total number of jobs might be minimal. A claimant who has no driver's license or who is unable to ride in a car for a half hour may not be capable of commuting so as to find replacement employment.

The point is that sometimes there is no "smoking gun" in cross-examination—no obvious error made by the vocational expert in the evaluation of the injured person. In that case, the only available line of cross-examination is to emphasize whatever negative factors exist for the claimant and argue to the fact finder that the real world simply does not work the way the vocational expert has testified.

The vocational expert may have testified about hypothetical employment rather than real life jobs. The vocational expert may apply all the data and come to the conclusion that the individual is capable of sedentary activity and therefore that the individual is capable of employment in a number of jobs. An appropriate area of cross-examination is whether or not the vocational expert has done any type of labor market survey to see whether such jobs actually exist in the claimant's community. The labor market survey should also identify whether there are any actual job openings with real companies and the expectations that employers have in the real world of hiring individuals. It is in this area that some of the questions regarding the claimant's background, such as age, education, and work experience can affect whether or not an individual is actually capable of being hired. For example, if a claimant is 55-years old, the vocational expert should be willing to concede that, on the basis of age alone this individual has a limited likelihood of being employed despite the physical restrictions or other functional abilities that the individual might have. The injured person who is now seeking employment with a disability is doing so in an extremely competitive labor market and may be looking for work with other job seekers who are younger, more intelligent, more educated, and better trained in addition to having no disability.

CHAPTER 13

ECONOMIC DAMAGES

Donald R. House, Ph.D.

§ 13.1 Introduction

The attention of the court must ultimately turn to the issue of monetary damages associated with the injury. *Economic damages* are those damages that are shown to be related to increased medical expenses and lost income or earnings. There are typically other damages claimed in injury cases such as pain and suffering, but these are not measurable economic damages. This chapter deals only with economic damages consisting of increased medical expenses and lost income or earnings.

Among cases involving permanent injury, such as back injuries, the increased medical expenses ordinarily exceed the value of lost income or earnings. This is because medical treatment in these cases is very expensive and often life expectancy is quite long. To make the plaintiff whole financially, the plaintiff must seek an amount that will support all medical expenses and related expenses throughout the expected life of the plaintiff. When years of intensive care are required to keep the plaintiff alive and comfortable, the amount claimed by the plaintiff can be substantial.

Any judge or jury is aware of press reports describing the rising cost of medical care. Measurements of inflation in the health care sector consistently prove that the rise in the prices of medical care has far exceeded the rise in prices of most other goods and services purchased by the average household. More than once the press has announced the existence of a health care crisis, usually referring to the growth in health care expenses relative to the Gross Domestic

Product. Everyone in the courtroom, except perhaps the least informed, expects projections of rising future prices of health care. This expectation sets the stage for a sizeable damage claim.

§ 13.2 Sources of Damages

By the time of trial the injured plaintiff will have already suffered lost income and related medical expenses. These are the two major components of economic damages. However, there are minor components of damages in the form of additional costs that have been and will be incurred on behalf of the plaintiff. These minor components are sometimes excluded in the testimony, either due to a failure to recognize their existence or a determination that their introduction would not be helpful to the case. In some instances, these minor components of damages can become significant. The fact that some of these minor components were incurred sometimes broadens the portrayal of pain and suffering incurred by family members.

Medical Expenses

By the time of trial, records of past medical expenses must be compiled and totaled. Some of the types of care administered to the patient shortly after injury will not be repeated, such as expenses incurred in the trauma center, including medical procedures rendered that stabilized the patient. Drugs and pharmaceuticals will often be listed in the hospital bills and in records supplied to the family. Some once-and-for-all medical bills will come from special contractors, such as an ambulance service, medical specialists not employed by the hospital, and medical appliance dealers. The compilation of past medical expenses should be complete, but when lacking records are missing, a qualified expert can impute values for the missing records.

The determination of future medical expenses is a challenging task. This requires the determination of the bundle of medical procedures, supplies, and services to be purchased on behalf of the plaintiff until death. It also requires the determination of the expected future prices of the components of the bundle. There will usually be differences in expert testimony concerning the composition of the bundle, but if the plaintiff's expert has a solid foundation for projections, the projected prices of the components of the bundle can rarely be seriously challenged.

Transportation, Equipment, and Renovations

The immediate family often assumes early care-giving responsibilities and sometimes makes alterations in the home in order to better care for the patient.

For patient transportation, some families will purchase a van, modified to accommodate a wheelchair or a hospital bed. It is common for doorways in the house to be widened, ramps to be installed, and bathrooms to be renovated. Some major expenses planned for the future should be included in the damage calculations. Some families may not fully realize the extent of future renovations and should be so informed in order to obtain a more accurate assessment of future renovations.

Expenditure of Time

At the time of trial, family members are often assuming care-giving responsibilities for the patient. At least during the initial stages of disability (perhaps up to the time of trial), many would expect the family to provide care just as families take care of their own during times of illness. These are the responsibilities of family members. At some point, however, the demands upon the family extend beyond the routine. There is usually sufficient reason to argue that the family's long-term outlook of support to the permanently disabled victim is a source of damages for which compensation is due.

If family members have assumed care-giving responsibilities, it is important to establish a market value of these services. To be made whole from an economic standpoint, the family should be able to conduct lives in as normal a fashion as possible. This is possible only if outside services are employed to perform the supporting functions assumed by family members. For instance, if the mother currently spends time feeding the patient, it is important to obtain estimates of what it would cost for the future to replace the mother with professional staff. This does not suggest that the mother should not be performing these tasks, it simply means that she should, in the future, have the option of conducting full normal activities. For these time expenditures, estimates should include the cost of replacing family members in the care-giving role. This gives family members the valuable option of resuming their own lives full-time. This source of damages does not imply that family members should be paid for past time spent with the patient. It simply recognizes that the family should be free to return to normal routines.

Lost Wages

The injured person will have suffered some degree of disability that affects earning capacity and its related income stream. For those persons who were employed at the time of the accident, the measurement of past lost wages is straightforward. The expert must construct projections of lost earnings in the future. For partial disability, two sets of earnings projections are required—earnings in the disabled state and earnings in the uninjured state. The difference in these two earnings paths represent the net earnings loss. For persons in school, the impact of completed education and training on earnings must be evaluated in order to determine a reasonable *but for* earnings path. For preschool children, the task is less certain. The tenure of the future work life must be determined as well. Once future earnings are calculated, a proper discount rate must be applied in order to bring future wages back to a present value.

§ 13.3 Medical Testimony as a Foundation

Past medical expenses related to the injury are not subject to lengthy debate. The economist merely compiles these historical costs and presents sums in a meaningful manner. Future medical expenses is another matter. The economist must rely on the testimony of the medical experts in order to compute future medical expenses and the degree of disability in place until death. There must be an obvious consistency between the medical testimony and the assumptions underlying the calculations of damages. In the ideal case, the medical testimony is convincing and separates past medical expenses into appropriate categories. In the worst case, the medical testimony is confused, uncertain, and is void of sufficient foundation for the calculations of damages.

The defendants have the opportunity to introduce their own medical testimony. Any testimony that illustrates the absence of not-yet-seen medical treatment, a shorter life expectancy, or relatively inexpensive long-term care facilities can significantly question the level of future medical expenses. The economist can offer little in the way of selecting for the jury the best medical testimony. However, potential bias in the medical testimony (if present) can be detected by the economist through the application of statistics.

Any medical testimony that illustrates a case or cases in which treatment paths were less expensive than what the economist projects may be based on merely one or two observations in the complete distribution of possible outcomes. In contrast, what is being presented by the economist is a statistical expectation based on the complete distribution. The finding of one or more cases that yield significantly less expense is not necessarily meaningful. Both parties in the litigation could spend time reporting the expense extremes (maximum and minimum) that are contained in the distribution. However, this is similar to presenting only the shortest high school boy and claiming that the men's high school basketball team will not be successful because of the absence of a tall center.

The economist can also offer a reminder that, over time, the standard of care is improving. What was standard in the 1960s is not standard in the 1990s. Medical technology has continually advanced, and advancement is expected to continue. Few can offer convincing projections of future standards of care, but it is usually safe to claim that today's best care will be substandard in the future.

Consider the treatment for a cardiac arrest in the 1950s and the 1990s. Today's care is much more expensive (adjusted for inflation) than the care rendered in the 1950s. Clearly the outcome possibilities are vastly improved. Had the court convened in the 1950s, what evidence would have been relied on to project treatment costs in the 1990s? Any testimony that argues for the least extensive care today is arguing for substandard care in the future. This testimony can support the economist's position that any projections based upon past medical expenses are conservative since they freeze in motion any advances in medical technology that improves health outcomes. Unlike most industries, advances in medical technology commonly yield more expensive services—not less expensive services.

§ 13.4 Past Medical Expenses

The family of the injured plaintiff should have a compilation of past medical expenses. Copies of these records must be made available to the economist. In all instances, these medical expense records are not complete because care is ongoing and billings occur posttreatment. In some instances, the family will not be able to find complete expense records. These individuals were never trained for nor did they ever volunteer to be accurate record keepers. Only because of an unexpected accident are their record keeping methods found to be particularly important.

The sources of past medical expenses include physician fees, drugs, lab charges, x-rays, supplies, hospital billings, ambulance and other transportation costs, medical equipment suppliers, and fees of specialized personnel. The totals of each source must be combined, of course, but the details within each source and across the sources can assist in separating past expenses into the once-and-for-all category and the maintenance of health category.

The medical testimony ideally will assist in the separation of past treatment into two categories: once-and-for-all medical expenses related to emergency treatment and stabilization, and continuing medical expenses related to the maintenance of condition. The first category reflects expenses that form an important component of damages but cannot form a basis for future medical expenses. The emergency treatment performed shortly after the accident is not expected to be repeated. The past medical expenses incurred that form the beginning of maintenance of health are the basis for the projection of future medical expenses.

Records of attending physicians and hospitals include both categories of medical expenses. If medical testimony is not expected to offer any separation of expenses, the attending physician can usually assist the economist prior to trial in separating past medical expenses into these two categories.

Physician fees can be grouped by categories, such as the family physician, surgeons, neurological specialists, anesthesiologists, and others. Some physicians' fees will belong in the once-and-for-all category such as the orthopedic surgeon who set a fractured arm. Some surgery may have taken place to stabilize the patient, but be aware that future surgeries may be anticipated. Some conditions require series of surgeries.

Hospitalization will have taken place, at least during the initial time of stabilization. In severe cases, the injured plaintiff will have been placed in a temporary facility that offers round-the-clock nursing care. The treatment plan may later call for less intense nursing care, meaning that a less expensive long-term care facility will be utilized. In these instances, the historical costs of nursing homes cannot be used as the basis for future projections.

In most instances, past expenses have been partially reimbursed by third parties (insurance, government programs, or philanthropy). It is important to make projections of the total expenses, whether reimbursed or not. The task is to measure the costs of the resources expended on behalf of the patient—not the out-of-pocket costs of the family. Whether the family has the benefit of private insurance or a supporting community is irrelevant to the legal question of past resources expended and future resources to be expended. The defendant is rarely benefited by the good fortune of the injured party who enrolled in an expansive insurance plan or who has friends and neighbors who engage in fund drives to offset medical expenses.

§ 13.5 Future Medical Expenses

Future medical expenses associated with the plaintiff's injury will likely be the largest component of calculated damages. This component, however, is the most uncertain and most difficult to calculate. It requires convincing testimony from someone proficient in forecasting and knowledgeable of health care markets. The best outcome from this segment of the testimony is a calculation of a fund that will support future medical expenses throughout the remaining life of the injured plaintiff. The worst outcome is a ruling that all future projections are uncertain and speculative and unworthy of reasonable calculation.

The typical foundation for a forecast of future medical expenses begins with an assessment of life expectancy, an accumulation of past medical expenses, and a determination of the typical bundle of services that the plaintiff will purchase throughout the remaining lifetime. The life expectancy should be based upon statistical evidence such as data drawn from records of survivors of spinal cord injuries. Professor DeVivo, in **Chapter 14,** offers an abbreviated table of life expectancies among these victims. This type of evidence is preferred over most any other form of evidence available. The economist should be able to enlighten the court about methods by which life expectancies are determined and the typical mistakes made when projecting future costs without the benefit of a structured analysis.

The attending physician can list major episodes that typically occur in the future which introduces not-yet-seen medical treatment into the damage calculations.[1] These forms of medical treatment might include surgery, battles with infection, treatment of respiratory ailments, and others. In **Chapter 4,** Professor DeVivo suggests that patients are commonly rehospitalized due to respiratory complications, urinary tract complications, and decubitus ulcers. In the short time between initial stabilization and trial, few if any of these complications may have been experienced. The attending physician or a specialist can list the expected complications that require unusual concentrations of care to maintain health and to arrest downturns. This information would be specific to the conditions of the patient. The additional source of information concerning not-yet-seen medical treatments is the medical literature based on existing registries of spinal cord injuries. The published evidence from similar episodes introduces a higher degree of objectivity that can form a stronger foundation for the economist's projections of future medical expenses.

A year's medical expenses are the product of two factors: price and quantity. The medical experts are best positioned to determine the future quantity of care across broad classes of medical services, drugs, and hospital utilization. The medical experts are not usually qualified in projecting future prices of care. In this area, the economist should step forward with an analysis of historical inflation in the health care sector and a determination of future inflation. Too often the medical profession offers the costs of services if performed today. Many will not have a complete appreciation of past inflation rates for hospital services, physician services, drugs, and long-term care facilities. In almost every category of medical care, prices have increased significantly faster than the overall rate of inflation. Such a trend is expected in the future.

It is best to identify the types of medical care to be utilized in the future and group these types into categories that match existing price indexes. Currently there are several price indexes available in the health care markets:

Physician services

Prescription drugs

Nonprescription drugs and medical supplies

Nonprescription medical equipment and supplies

Internal and respiratory over-the-counter drugs

Hospital room

[1] *See* M. DeVivo et al., *A Cross-Sectional Study of the Relationship Between Age and Current Health Status for Persons with Spinal Cord Injuries,* 30 Paraplegia 820–27 (1992).

Inpatient services

Outpatient services

Dental services

Eye care

Services of other medical professionals

Some associations (such as the American Dental Association) provide more detailed calculations of historical changes in fees for selected procedures. Over the past twenty years or so, the annual increase in these and other related price indexes is remarkable. This history supports the projection on continuing high rates of increase in the future but recent developments in the health care industry provide some grounds for attack.

The mechanics of the calculations are relatively simple—price times quantity summed across all procedures. The not-yet-seen medical procedures pose a special problem in that the timing of these procedures are not known. It is always best to rely on a physician or the published literature to guide the timing of these expenses.

Since the 1970s, policymakers have been attempting to pass legislation that would introduce measures of cost containment. The Nixon Administration and the Carter Administration urged the concept of health planning and the capitation-based plan. More recently, the catchword is managed care. The selling principle in both capitation-based plans and managed care is to shift some risk to the provider so that overutilization of health care can be curtailed. This principle has been expanded to enable payors to negotiate reduced fees for health care providers and hospitals in order to reduce costs. The Clinton Health Care Plan that never left the launch pad was largely based on the managed care concept with added emphasis on reduced fees among providers and hospitals. Defendants can use this history to argue that historical rates of inflation in the health care sector will not be repeated in the future. The fact that no public policy has yet to curtail the rising costs of health care so far is little comfort to the defendants' arguments.

The important concept to remember is that private and public third-party payors have increased the demand for health care. With rapidly increasing demand and a slowly expanding supply, the price must increase. Additionally, the historical rates of inflation partly register the improvements in quality of care. This improvement in quality is expected to continue. With a continuing increase in the average age of the population, no sign of any downturn in health insurance coverage or Medicare programs, and a continuing increase in standards of living, there is little reason to believe that the demand for health care in the future will be restricted. No public program can offer a magic pill that will create a greater supply of health care and reduce the demand for health care. The portrait of continuing inflation in the health care sector should be secure.

§ 13.6 Discount Rates

An income or expense that is expected in the future must be expressed in terms of a present value to have any validity before a court. Economists, accountants, and appraisers all rely on discount rates to translate a future value into a present value. This process has become standard testimony. However, the selection of a proper discount rate has not become standard, and in many instances, the size of calculated damages is greatly affected by the value of the discount rate.

For spinal cord injury cases there are two discounting problems that must be solved by the expert: discounting future medical expenses, and discounting the loss of future wages. The values of these two calculations are of primary interest among all parties to the law suit, and if the damage calculations are of significant size, a great deal of attention will be paid to the methods of these calculations. Lower discount rates yield greater damages, all else being equal.

The Risk-free Case

For the future medical expenses, the damage expert in a world without risk seeks a discount rate that approximates the average rate of return that the plaintiff is expected to earn on a lump-sum award so that the future medical expenses can be paid out of the investment portfolio established with the damage award. At the end of the time horizon (the expected death of the injured plaintiff), the lump-sum award and its accrued interest are completely exhausted. In short, the court is being asked to award the minimum necessary sum so that future medical expenses can be satisfied.

The standard damage study for a business loss typically involves the loss of an income-producing property by an ongoing business. The standard approach looks at the business's internal cost of funds to determine the discount rate. The appraisal literature has a prescribed method of determining the proper discount rate for valuations of these income-producing properties when the plaintiff is a business. The American Institute of Real Estate Appraisers calls for the weighted average cost of debt and equity capital as the proscribed measure of the proper discount rate.[2] A particular business plaintiff would be assigned a discount rate commensurate to its own cost of funds. However, the plaintiff in a spinal injury case is most likely to be an individual whose assets are to be managed by the plaintiff's family. Although the family, just as a business, is

---

[2] American Institute of Real Estate Appraisers, *The Appraisal of Real Estate* 537–39 (9th Ed. 1987).

likely to maintain some level of debt, it is probably inappropriate to assume that the lump-sum award would be used to reduce the family's debts. Instead, it is more appropriate to assume that the family would invest the lump-sum award in a manner similar to other small investors. In this instance, the weighted average cost of debt and equity would be difficult to construct.

What is relevant is the expected return the family would receive on its investments, given the liquidity requirements of paying a flow of medical bills and of replacing a flow of lost wages. Up to this point, the expert is encouraged to find the expected rate of return on a reasonable investment portfolio and apply this rate of return as a discount rate for both future medical expenses and future lost wages.

For past medical expenses, the damage expert seeks a rate of interest (or capitalization) that will yield the interest the plaintiff would have earned had the funds spent toward past related medical bills were invested, earning interest. Since the past medical expenses and lost wages are known, there is no risk adjustment to be made, and the expert should seek a rate of return on a reasonable investment portfolio for the circumstances at hand.[3] If the family incurred significant consumer debts, the expert could argue that the interest rate charged on actual outstanding consumer loans during the time period is the appropriate rate of interest to apply to past medical expenses.

For past lost earnings, the damage study similarly seeks an interest rate that equals the rate of return to be earned on the lump-sum award. The minimum award would be that sum that reimburses the plaintiff for past lost earnings (and prejudgment interest if allowed) and for future lost earnings, taking into account interest that the plaintiff will earn on the lump-sum award. Again, if the family incurred significant consumer debt (especially if the injury caused an increase in consumer debt), the expert could effectively argue that the average rate charged on consumer debt is the appropriate interest rate.

Introducing Risk

Some experts are not comfortable or qualified to discuss the impact of risk on damage calculations. These experts determine the best estimate of future medical expenses and future lost wages, discounting each with a chosen discount rate without any adjustments for risk. The inability of the expert to effectively explain the proper inclusion of risk may convince the attorney to rely upon the risk-free case.

The purpose of introducing risk into the damage analysis is to justify a larger damage award that is commensurate with the risk to be borne by the plaintiff once the trial has concluded. In business transactions, those who are bearing

[3] In some instances there will be some uncertainty regarding past lost wages. If the plaintiff were unemployed at time of injury or if coworkers lost employment between time of the injury and trial date, determination of lost wages will be subject to some debate.

the risk of uncertain payments are reimbursed for this risk. The plaintiff, due to the circumstances of the case, must bear the risk of uncertain medical payments, and it is proper for the defendant to reimburse the plaintiff for this imposed risk.

The plaintiff always presents a larger damage calculation if risk is considered, all else being equal. The expert for the plaintiff must be sufficiently skilled to survive challenges from the defense, assuming that the expert for the defense is likewise skilled.[4] Risk adjustments are based on the notion that no one can be certain of the future and that the plaintiff is burdened with both the expectation of future losses and the uncertainty surrounding these future losses. For the spinal injured plaintiff, the defendant has allegedly caused the plaintiff to face future medical expenses that could vary widely. The simple expectation (the average) of the future expenses is not sufficient to compensate the plaintiff for the possibility that future expenses could be significantly greater than what is currently expected. The financial and economic literature offer methods of determining an award that would compensate the plaintiff for both the expectation of future medical expenses and the risk that these medical expenses could differ from the calculations presented at trial.

For purposes of trial testimony, two different approaches are possible: presentation of certainty equivalent values (discounted at the risk-free interest rate), and use of risk-adjusted discount rates applied to expected values. The literature contains debates regarding which approach is best under what conditions. Yet, virtually all of this literature applies to business problems—a business considering an investment project that faces uncertain future profits. The selection of an approach to future medical expenses caused by a spinal cord injury has not been addressed. The plaintiff's expert is expected to choose between the two approaches.

Certainty-equivalent Percentages

A certainty-equivalent approach to future medical expenses is, in theory, quite simple. Suppose an individual is facing a cash outlay of an unknown amount. Individuals who faced the same circumstance in the past had to pay, *on average,* \$1,000, but many paid over \$1,000 and many paid less than \$1,000. In fact, no has one actually paid exactly \$1,000. The certainty-equivalent value of the uncertain outlay is the amount the individual would pay to be rid of the uncertain obligation. Since the average individual seeks to avoid uncertain cash outlays, the certainty-equivalent will be an amount greater than \$1,000. The difference between the certainty-equivalent and the expected value (\$1,000) depends on the degree to which the amounts have varied from the average value. The greater the dispersion around the \$1,000, the greater the certainty-equivalent

[4] In some cases, the plaintiff's expert will find that the opposing expert and/or legal counsel are not sufficiently knowledgable and will fail to challenge risk adjustments.

will exceed the $1,000. If the individual agrees to pay (at most) $1,100, then the certainty-equivalent value is 10 percent greater than the expected value. Applying this result in the courtroom means that the certainty-equivalent of any single future medical expense must be represented by a figure 10 percent greater than its expected value. All future certainty equivalent values would then be discounted at the risk-free interest rate.

The application of the certainty-equivalent approach is difficult. In essence, the expert must determine what percentage above the expected value the plaintiff and family would be willing to pay in order to eliminate the risk. This certainty-equivalent percentage, once determined, is then applied to the expected values to reflect a risk-free value. The insurance marketplace offers measures of this percentage among pools of at-risk individuals. Medical insurance premiums always exceed the average insurance claim because insurance carriers must be reimbursed for administering claims and must earn a reasonable profit. The average insurance claim represents the expected value of the policy, and the insurance premium is the price purchasers pay to reduce risk. The fact that individuals are willing to pay more than the average insurance claim is a supporting fact for this approach. However, the percentage that the insurance premium exceeds the average claim is not the best measure of the certainty-equivalent percentage for an individual plaintiff. However, it provides a floor for the percentage. An appropriate certainty-equivalent percentage should exceed this floor since the floor is established as a market-determined percentage from pooling risks across large numbers of individuals. Almost everyone purchasing health insurance would be willing to pay slightly more in premiums than what market premiums require. For this purpose, it is what the average individual is willing to pay that is relevant—not what the marginal insurance purchaser is required to pay. The plaintiff does not benefit from pooling risks after the injury, so market-determined insurance premiums should not be a governing factor. The plaintiff stands as an individual known to have a spinal cord injury. The only remaining uncertainty is the flow of medical expenses associated with a known injury. The insurance industry does not offer a policy to insure this type of risk.

Risk-adjusted Discount Rates

The other approach applies a risk-adjusted discount rate to expected future medical expenses. Being future cash outflows for the plaintiff (for example, medical expenses), the proper method of adjusting the discount rate is to *subtract* the risk premium from the risk-free interest rate.[5] It is common for an expert to miss this fact since the problem of discounting cash outflows is unusual and, for cash inflows (for example, wages), the risk premium is added to the

[5] For supporting literature, *see, e.g.*, E. Brigham, and L. Gapensksi, *Financial Management, Theory and Practice* 414–16 (6th ed. 1991).

risk-free interest rate. It is imperative that the two approaches yield the same result, so it becomes obvious that the value of the risk-adjusted discount rate must be less than the risk-free discount rate for cash outflows.

For cash inflows, in the example of future lost wages, a risk premium would be added to the risk-free rate of interest (as in the conventional case of lost profits). However, the risk associated with future wages is probably less than the risk associated with future medical expenses. It would be unusual to correctly apply the same risk premium to the discounting of the receipt of future wages and to the payment of future medical expenses.

For the court, there are three major factors facing the plaintiff that affect future medical expenses:

1. Inflation among products and services consumed
2. Average annual quantity of products and services consumed
3. Longevity of products and services consumed.

Economists are quite capable of presenting forecasts of inflation among the products and services and measuring the historical risks of inflation. The second factor is difficult for any economist to quantify without assistance from a medical expert. Clearly, there are risks of an unexpectedly intensive treatment path. There may be sufficient case studies that would dictate the probabilities of each possible treatment path, but these would have been assembled over time and the costs are commingled with the effects of inflation. The third factor is governed by the plaintiff's life expectancy. Case studies would assist in this evaluation as well, but life expectancies tend to improve with advancements in technology. Older cases may tend to understate current life expectancies. In total, the economist is left with an uncertain future medical expenditure path with little quantification of risk.

Perhaps the best approach, in the absence of perfect information, is to identify existing discount rates in the financial markets that would be acceptable proxies for the risk-adjusted discount rate to be applied to future medical expenses.

Nominal versus Real

Projections of future prices, expenses, and wages can be presented in either nominal terms or real terms. Real terms do not contain any inflation projections; that is, they are adjusted for overall inflation. If the underlying rate of inflation is 4 percent and the prices of physician services is expected to increase at 6 percent, the real presentation would include an annual increase in the prices of physician services of only two percent. The presentation in real terms has two important advantages: 1) the testifying expert does not have to project an average rate of inflation because it is assumed to be zero, and 2) future values of medical expenses and wages appear smaller to the jury and thus appear reasonable.

The discount rate used in the real terms presentation must reflect the real rate of interest—the nominal rate adjusted for inflation. Historically (1970–1994), the real rate of interest has averaged about 2 percent, but there are periods of time, particularly during the 1970s, in which the real rate of interest was negative. With any significant risk adjustment, the real rate of interest would be negative, which can be difficult to explain to a jury.[6] The certainty-equivalent approach avoids this problem of appearance.

§ 13.7 Presentation

The presentation of direct testimony is challenging since the testifying economist must often present surprisingly large damage figures that dwarfs any historical expense yet recorded. The testimony typically comes late in the trial when the courtroom has already viewed the extensiveness of the injuries, perhaps photographs of the accident scene, and the personal pain suffered among family members. The economist must be prepared to explain the basis of price forecasts, discount rates, and life expectancies. The economist must be prepared to explain recent changes in the health care sector and possible legislative attempts to contain health care costs. These all must be comprehensible and convincing to a jury.

The presentation will include, as a minimum, past medical expenses, future medical expenses, past lost wages, and future lost wages. All future expenses and lost wages must be recalculated as present values back to the time of trial. In some states, prejudgment interest is allowed and the expert must calculate interest lost on past expenditures and past lost wages. In additional to these major components, the expert might include calculations of related expenses (transportation, renovations, and so forth) and the value of time to be expended in the future.

The expert selected to handle the damage portion of the plaintiff's case should have some knowledge of the history of the health care sector, especially the major changes that have occurred. It would be advisable to have an expert that can address the importance of first-dollar insurance coverage, government sponsored benefit plans (Medicare and Medicaid), and past attempts to contain costs. The expert will undoubtedly hear testimony about managed care and its solutions to the rising costs of health care. A diligent, thoughtful plaintiff's

---

[6] The literature includes several works that pose dangers with adjustments from risk to cash outflows. When risk premium adjustment exceeds risk-free market rate, results for calculations can be troublesome. *See, e.g.*, T. Gallagher and J. Zumwalt, *Risk-Adjusted Discount Rates Revisited,* 26 Fin. Rev. 105–114 (Feb. 1991) and B. Schwab, *Conceptual Problems in the Use of Risk-Adjusted Discount Rates with Disaggregated Cash Flows,* 5 J. of Bus. Fin. and Acct. 281–93 (1978).

expert should be able to demonstrate a sufficient understanding of the health care system and a proper foundation for his or her projections of future medical expenses.

The economist must be prepared for cross-examination that attempts to discredit credentials, to destroy the foundation of the damage calculations, and to make the results appear extreme. A testifying expert with past experience in forecasting health care prices is a plus, but not if the expert's past forecasts are at odds with the intended presentation. The economist should be able to argue that future health care prices are predictable and are not exclusively governed by unpredictable legislative efforts to contain health care costs. There are published economists that have argued that the health care sector is not responsive to traditional market forces.[7] For example, it has been argued that physicians merely create demand for their services, implying that a traditional market analysis approach is not appropriate.[8] An expert unaware of these debates could have trouble presenting reasonable price forecasts using tools of the trade instead of speculation without adequate foundation. The best economic analysis of the health care sector is based upon traditional analytic tools, and assertions that the health care sector is so unique that reliable economic forecasts cannot be attained are meritless.

It is common for cross-examination to include a display of an expense during the last year of life to attempt to show that the results are unreasonable. For example, a $40 drug prescription today would cost (at a 7 percent rate of inflation) $734 in 44 years (from age 21 to age 65). A $75 per day cost of care in a long-term care facility would cost (at a 10 percent rate of inflation) $4,518 per day in 44 years. Are these figures unreasonable? It can be instructive to place the jury back in time (in the year 1951 for the 44-year horizon) and attempt to project the cost of a loaf of bread, a gallon of milk, or a two-bedroom apartment monthly rental based upon the information available at that time. Projections of future expenses and wages in real terms largely eliminate the opportunities for these questions.

An expert with testimony experience and knowledge of the major debates over the health care sector should be able to withstand a vigorous cross-examination. Careful work will usually be persuasive to a jury if the foundation for the analysis is defensible. What the direct testimony should contain, how long should it last, and how is the evidence to be presented are all important decisions. The attorney should consider the strengths and weaknesses in both the analysis and the expert in making these decisions.

---

[7] V. R. Fuchs, Who Shall Live? 146 (1974). "One kind of limit is set by what economics can contribute *now;* that is, there are deficiencies in our theoretical framework and in our empirical knowledge that currently prevents us from answering particular questions about the health field. " This conclusion, however, is over 20 years old.

[8] *See, e.g.*, U.S. Dep't of Health, Educ., and Welfare, *The Target Income Hypothesis and Related Issues in Health Manpower Policy,* DHEW Publication No. (HRA) 80-27 (1980) for an early discussion of this theory.

CHAPTER 14

THE ECONOMIST

Gregory G. Jones

§ 14.1 Introduction

To get the most effective testimony from an economist in a case involving spinal cord injuries, it is necessary to have a full understanding of the injured plaintiff's physical, mental, and economic condition, in addition to a working knowledge of both macroeconomic and microeconomic concepts and vocabulary. A familiarity with the particular economist to be examined or cross-examined is a prerequisite as well. This information cannot be looked at in isolation. It must be viewed in the context of other aspects of the case. A thorough understanding of the case as a whole is necessary to properly prepare and conduct both direct and cross-examination of an expert in the area of economics. Thorough preparation, in direct consultation with the economic expert, will facilitate a coherent presentation that tracks the overall themes developed for presentation of the case.

A limited knowledge of economic principles and theory makes it difficult to conduct either direct or cross-examination of an economist. The expertise and knowledge of the economist should be utilized to educate the advocate. If an economist cannot communicate economic principles, theories, and opinions in a particular case to an attorney, that same expert probably cannot communicate essential principles in an understandable way to the jury. The economist must be a good communicator as well as a good economist. Find out whether or not an expert can be an effective communicator by having the economist educate the lawyer first.

In the process of being educated by the economist, the attorney has an opportunity to learn the strengths and weaknesses of the case that is being evaluated. This is crucial in preparing any examination. An attorney needs to understand both strengths and weaknesses of the economic analysis of a case so that the examination before the jury or in deposition emphasizes the strengths and explains, minimizes, or masks the weaknesses. In addition, when the attorney learns the strengths and weaknesses of the case with respect to the economic evaluation, the advocate can draw upon other aspects of the case to help bolster the economic inquiry.

There are certain topics that the advocate should understand before preparing the economic examination and testimony that will be presented regarding economic loss. These topics are not directly covered in this Chapter but are dealt with in other chapters. They include vocational rehabilitation, the life care plan, the testimony of medical and/or psychological experts, and an evaluation of the testimony that will be presented by a defense economist or annuitist. An intimate knowledge of each of these areas is required to effectively prepare a client's case for economic evaluation. The facts and figures that are deduced in these other areas of inquiry are employed by the economist to arrive at the opinions that will determine the economic value of the case. For example, the medical doctor will help to establish what type of physical limitations an individual has after a spinal cord injury, what type of medical care has been required in the past, and what will be required in the future. The doctor will need to testify as to the reasonableness and the necessity of the treatments, both past and future. That information can then be used by the economist to evaluate the cost of long-term medical care.

A psychiatrist may address the profound psychological implications of a severe spinal cord injury. Posttraumatic stress syndrome and clinical depression are conditions often associated with a traumatic spinal cord injury. These conditions can profoundly affect an individual's ability to engage in any type of activity, including work. In a spinal cord injury case in which the individual can perform certain physical tasks that would allow the individual to earn some type of income, the psychological factors may cause psychological dysfunction and effectively prevent any hope of economic gain through work or employment activity in the future. The economist will need this information to help evaluate potential future lost income or loss of wage earning capacity.

The vocational rehabilitation expert thoroughly examines an individual's medical, psychological, employment, and educational history to create a baseline from which to compare that individual's current condition with the past and/or with various population groups. The vocational rehabilitation expert and the economist ought to work in harmony unless the economist is going to merely take numbers from the vocational expert and determine a present value.

The testimony of an economist must be integrated with these other topics. Some discord is to be expected between various categories of knowledge and the advocate is well advised to determine where disagreement may lie early so that there can be communication, and hopefully accommodation, with respect to any conflict prior to naming experts or allowing each expert to review or rely upon the work of another.

Once the macrocosm of information and possibilities is fully explored, the advocate has a basic understanding of economic principles, and believes that the economist can communicate these principles effectively, preparation for examination and cross-examination begins. In preparing for examination of an economist it is helpful to create a summary, an index, lists or checklists, demonstrative evidence, and briefs. A summary and outline is used to become familiar with the case and to be prepared during examination, including redirect, to defense any attacks upon underlying assumptions and facts upon which the economist bases testimony. An index should be available so the advocate can turn immediately to other aspects of the case that relate to the testimony by the economist. An example of this would be the testimony of a doctor or a vocational expert. Lists and checklists are prepared to help ensure that baseline economic principles and facts that the expert needs to substantiate testimony are not left out. Demonstrative evidence helps the jury to understand the testimony of the expert and make it more interesting and memorable. Finally, briefs help meet objections anticipated from the defense. If each of these things is done, the advocate will not only be prepared for examination of the expert during trial but will also have learned the substance of that testimony.

Basic foundations of admissibility and relevance must be fully explored to prevent adverse rulings that could at best interrupt the flow of testimony and at worst actually exclude important testimony. The advocate should review the law applicable to the particular jurisdiction and court.

All avenues of potential impeachment ought to be carefully reviewed as if the advocate were preparing to cross-examine the advocate's own expert witness. Either the attorney who will be conducting the direct examination, or an associate or partner, can act the part of the cross-examining attorney in advance of trial so that the expert can be prepared to handle cross-examination and areas of impeachment can be explored and defused prior to trial.

There are many technical issues to be addressed in the actual subject matter of the testimony of the economist. There are controversies within the study of economics, both macro and micro. Assumptions that are made by the economist must be explored well in advance of trial. In cases that involve serious spinal cord injuries a greater number of these assumptions that an economist must use to arrive at a reasonable paradigm from which the economist can formulate opinions with respect to the case is more likely to be encountered. Each of these areas where assumptions are made or calculations are used should be carefully evaluated by the advocate, and perhaps by a consulting economist who can review the work of the testifying economist to determine whether or not there are errors or the assumptions are unfounded. Simple mathematical errors can seriously damage what may otherwise be good testimony from an economist.

§ 14.2 Understanding and Presenting Economic Principles

Economics as a subject is not easy. It is probably one of the most complicated subjects addressed in the courtroom. Economists work in a discipline that requires both science and art. The role of the economist, as an expert witness, can be as a damage witness who only translates the findings and evaluations of the rehabilitation and vocational expert into projected future dollar amounts and establishes the present value of those dollar amounts. Economics, however, is a much broader science than that. As a social science, economics is concerned with the use of resources for the production, distribution, and consumption of goods and services needed and desired by society. Most economists have had training in microeconomics as well as macroeconomics. Most economists, however, specialize in particular areas. Economists may specialize in medical economics, labor economics, or other areas. Unique areas of economics expertise include ranch or farm management, small versus large enterprises, start-up companies versus ongoing concerns, and determination of the intrinsic value of a business after a loss. It is important to know the background of the particular economics expert. A background in labor economics is helpful when dealing with individuals who have lost the ability to earn income. The economist should also have an understanding of inflation and overall economic trends on a macro basis. The expert will also need to have general knowledge of monetary institutions and financial markets in today's society. Since economists are combining both art and science it can be extremely difficult to explain to the jury the basic guiding principles of economics. Different schools of economic thought have their own set of basic guiding principles and disagreements abound.

The advocate must know and understand basic economic terminology. This is required so that the attorney can facilitate the economist in giving an opinion while interpreting that opinion for the jury. Review terms with the expert economist beforehand that will not be familiar to a layperson on the jury. Understandable and short definitions should be created for each term along with the use of synonyms and analogy that will help the jury to understand the basic principles involved.

Demonstrative evidence is critical in many aspects of a trial, but is certainly important in explaining economic loss. Prior to trial the attorney should meet with the economist, perhaps with a graphics designer, to devise demonstrative evidence that will help the jury to understand basic concepts. Charts and graphs can be very helpful. Sometimes the use of old newspapers or even an old merchandise catalog can be used to demonstrate the principles involved in inflation. The abstract principles and vocabulary used by economists do not translate well for the typical layperson. Therefore, demonstrative evidence is required to communicate these concepts and theories and to focus on the bottom line damage amounts.

It is a good basic rule not to try to educate the jury in difficult economic principles. Allow the expert to describe the basic principles that underlie the theories but only to the extent necessary to state the basic conclusions reached by the expert. If too much of an emphasis is placed on teaching the jury about abstract economic principles, the basic message of the amount of economic loss to the plaintiff may be lost in an overflow of information. Maintain focus by adhering to the basic trial themes developed in preparing the case.

Nevertheless, some of the more basic economic principles must be described to the jury. If this is done with demonstrative evidence, the jury is much more likely to recall what was said and understand it if it presented in a graphic form. A jury is much more likely to understand and appreciate a concept if it is presented in a way that is nontechnical. Juries appreciate it when experts and attorneys demonstrate a willingness to expend the effort to help them understand the concepts that are being used.

The use of any of these techniques must be covered thoroughly with the expert witness. The economist must feel comfortable with any demonstrative evidence, analogy, or other technique used to communicate the meaning of a term or concept. If the economist does not feel comfortable with the construct, the attempt could fail and damage both the credibility of the advocate and of the expert witness economist.

A clear understanding of the principles upon which an economist will base testimony begins with a full understanding of the vocabulary that is used by the economist. Review the report prepared by the economist to identify certain terms and concepts. Once these terms and concepts have been identified, reach a general understanding by reviewing basic economic texts and literature. Textbooks can be found by contacting the economics department at any major university or by going to a large public library. There are online services that have economic information that allow the attorney to study the basic concepts in economics. A review of continuing legal education materials and legal textbooks may explain some of these concepts. Concepts, terms, and theories that may be difficult for an attorney to grasp would, in all likelihood, also be very difficult for a jury to grasp. Once again, however, the tendency to become overly technical in making the presentation to the jury can be damaging to the goal of the testimony of the expert, which is to state the economic loss suffered by the plaintiff.

Learning the basic concepts and terminology of economics will also help the advocate cross-examine the economist hired by the defendant. It is very difficult to cross-examine an expert when the terms that are used are not understood or are understood differently. Seek to have the defendant's expert define the terms that are being used. Try to have the opposing expert recognize the basic economic treatises presented to come to an understanding of what these terms and concepts are. If there are differences in how these are explained, note the differences between those published in the texts and articles versus what the opposing expert states. If the opposing economist uses concepts that are difficult to grasp, it may be possible to portray the defense expert as aloof and impenetrable by the ordinary person. If an expert is not able to come down to the level of the trier of fact to help the trier of fact understand concepts, then that expert will probably lose the interest and respect of the jury.

Once the basic principles and terms are established and the economist can adequately explain and describe the economic concepts and definitions, the advocate should consult with a consulting expert (under Rule 26(b)(4)(B) of the Federal Rules of Civil Procedure). The consulting expert can provide the advocate with insight as to possible cross-examination techniques and weaknesses that may be inherent in some of the analogies or descriptions of concepts and definitions that have been created with the expert or by the opposing expert.

Establishing a strong foundation of understanding on the part of the advocate of the various economic concepts and terms will lead that advocate to understand both the strengths and the weaknesses of the case from an economic standpoint. The attorney is in position to emphasize the strengths of the case in direct examination and utilize those strengths to attack the weaknesses of the defense's case in the cross-examination of the defense expert. In like manner, the weaknesses of the plaintiff's case can be offset, explained, hidden, or balanced in both the direct and cross-examination of the plaintiff's economist as well as the cross-examination of the defendant's economist.

§ 14.3 Preparing to Cross-Examine the Adverse Economic Expert

Once an attorney has been fully prepared to handle the direct examination of the attorney's own economist, that same attorney is ready to begin preparation for the examination of the adverse witness on economic issues named by the opposition. Attorneys must first understand their own case before attacking the case presented by the other side. The case of the opposition is necessarily founded upon the case prepared by the plaintiff. From the defense point of view, the sole purpose in naming an economist as an expert is to attack the experts named by the plaintiff and the assumptions, calculations, and conclusions of the plaintiff's expert. If the plaintiff did not name an expert in the area of economics then, typically, neither would the defense.

When the advocate has a clear understanding of the case that will be presented by the opposing party at trial, including strengths and weaknesses of that case, the cross-examination of the opposing economist can be prepared. The knowledge that has been gained in evaluating an expert is utilized in preparing for cross-examination of the opposing expert. Any other approach to cross-examination of an economist would become generic and ineffective because it is not case specific.

Begin with a full review of the background of the adverse witness. First, a resume or curriculum vitae should be obtained and studied. Review the background of the economist. Learn what type of educational background this individual has. Establish whether or not the expert has received a doctorate degree in economics. There are a number of so-called economists who are not even trained specifically in the area of economics. Some may acquire a more generalized educational experience by obtaining business degrees. Ascertain whether or not the economist is associated with any study groups, think tanks, or other policymaking bodies. If so, determine whether or not these groups conduct public hearings or forums, and if so, their records can be searched for testimony of the expert. Determine whether or not this individual has testified before any legislative bodies on economic matters. Learn what interest group or groups may fund this expert's work individually or in conjunction with some type of policy group and determine what the group's agenda is. All of the credentials or background information that is verifiable in the resume should be checked. This is really relatively easy to do with typically no more than eight to twelve telephone calls. Explore inconsistencies relating to the individual's educational achievements, teaching experience, employment background, and awards given. If there are inconsistencies a follow-up should be made to determine the basis for the inconsistency. Any publications that are written by the adverse expert should be reviewed if the subject matter appears germane to the issues in the case. Determine whether or not this economist has a concentration in some particular subject area. Decide, in conjunction with your expert, whether or not the testimony that the expert is giving is within the sphere of the expert's expertise. Also, review the articles that are relevant to the anticipated testimony of the adverse expert to determine whether or not the expert has offered contradictory opinions in the past or opinions that contradict what the expert's current testimony is in the case. Investigate whether any article or monograph submitted by the expert has been refused for publication, and why. This may demonstrate careless work or work that is not accepted by the mainstream academic community in the particular subject.

Another source for information is the venerable *Readers' Guide to Periodic Literature* that can be found in every public library. The *Readers' Guide* can identify articles that this individual has written. Any article that has not been listed on the curriculum vitae should certainly be obtained since there may be some reason for leaving that article or monograph off of the curriculum vitae. More extensive research includes obtaining the names of coauthors for various articles and monographs, both listed on the curriculum vitae and those left off. Those names can then be researched to determine any other articles that these individuals have written. Coauthors may have written articles that are contrary to one or more opinions of the adverse witness. If that is the case it would be effective to cross-examine the adverse expert by pointing out that the expert's own coauthor (whom the expert will probably agree is authoritative) disagrees on one or more points of testimony.

When articles are published in scholarly journals, magazines, or reviews these articles may draw responsive letters or articles in a later edition. Such letters and articles can prove to be fruitful ground for attack of the expert's opinions. In addition, the author of the contradictory letter or article may prove to be a good source as a consulting expert, and perhaps even as a testifying expert witness.

On-line services are another source of information. A great deal of information can be identified relating to scholarly writings and research of an individual. Specifically, if the expert is associated with a university or college, this institution may have an Internet address that allows access to an internal bulletin board system or other databases through which further information on the particular faculty member and their activities and publications may be obtained. Other sources include various litigation groups sponsored and organized by attorneys. The Association of Trial Lawyers of America and national state and local trial lawyer organizations, both plaintiff and defense, also have databases that will allow an advocate to search for more information on the adverse witness. These same organizations may also maintain deposition banks from which previous depositions of this expert witness can be obtained and reviewed. In a similar manner, some trial lawyer organizations offer newsletters or other sources of communication that allow a request to be sent out for information relating to an expert witness. LEXIS® or Westlaw® can be used to locate any reported cases where the expert may have appeared. Specifically, the names, addresses, and telephone numbers of other attorneys who have inquired about or cross-examined this particular expert witness can be obtained and contacted to determine what type of testimony was offered. Old depositions and other documentation can be obtained from another attorney. Cross-check the curriculum vitae or résumé to determine if there have been any changes from previous versions, and if so, determine or ask why. Additionally, an attorney who has previously cross-examined the witness as an adverse witness, or has named the witness as an expert, may have insight into not only the expert's background but also the expert's style and mannerisms during cross-examination.

Through prior testimony of a witness, information both for impeachment and for obtaining admissions from the adverse expert can be found. If the adverse expert has previously offered a particular opinion on a subject in the past in a deposition, that opinion may be used to impeach the expert. Either way, this information is invaluable in carefully preparing the structure of a cross-examination.

In the process of discovery, the adverse witness' complete file should be obtained. Thoroughly review the file to learn what information the expert has relied upon. Identify all contacts between the expert and the opposing attorney, contacts between the expert and any other consulting expert, locate any financial agreements or arrangements between the expert witness and the defendant and/or the defendant's attorney. Determine when the expert was first brought into the case and formed an opinion on that case, and find out what information may *not* have been given to the expert by the opposing party.

Many of the steps outlined in preparing for the cross-examination of an adverse expert can apply equally to the preparation of an expert for direct examination. The background of the advocate's expert should be thoroughly investigated and reviewed to prevent any surprises or problems. The opposing counsel will certainly be conducting a full review in preparation for the cross-examination of the expert.

§ 14.4 Preparing for Direct Examination

Preparing for direct examination of an economist necessarily includes steps similar to those in preparing for the cross-examination of an adverse economist. The additional steps described in **§ 13.2** must also be followed. The advocate must be fully educated with respect to economic principles and thought that are relied upon in the expert's opinion. A full analysis of the background and experience of the expert witness is just as valuable in direct examination as when preparing for cross-examination. By anticipating the cross-examination of the opposing counsel, the direct examination can preemptively respond to the anticipated cross-examination, leaving the opposing counsel with fewer weapons with which to attack the expert witness.

The formulation of the direct examination takes place in the context of the universe of information that has been gathered from the expert and about the expert. The overall case strategy and case theme should be woven into the direct examination. The background information on the expert witness can be utilized to emphasize strengths and mitigate weaknesses in certain areas. For example, if the expert has an outstanding background, the attorney may not want to merely put a copy of the expert's curriculum vitae into evidence hoping that the jury may look at it later. They probably won't. If there are particular highlights that should be brought to the jury's attention, those items should be addressed in the direct examination. In addition, if there are particular aspects of the expert's background that would help to personalize the expert for the jury, that information should be provided during direct examination as well. For example, an expert who has appeared as an economic expert in an important, high-profile, and very complicated price fixing case that was recently covered by the news media may help to identify the witness as an authority. Other examples might include giving testimony before a committee of the United States

Congress or of a state committee. Even community involvement can help to personalize an expert.

Demonstrative evidence of all kinds should be created and reviewed by the advocate and the witness. Any demonstrative evidence that would help the jury to better understand the principles involved in the case and to remember the testimony of the expert ought to be utilized when it is fair and accurate. When possible the evidence should be put in a form that may, depending on the jurisdiction, allow the demonstrative evidence to find its way back into the jury room during jury deliberations as a piece of marked evidence. In some jurisdictions it is effective to create a separate jury notebook that contains a regular letter-size reproduction of the demonstrative exhibit so that the jury can follow along with the testimony during the course of the direct examination. The judge must be consulted to see if this technique will be allowed. However, it is low cost and highly effective.

Any demonstrative evidence should be carefully reviewed by the advocate and the expert to ensure that there are no mistakes, inconsistencies, prejudicial, or misleading aspects that may draw an objection that, if sustained, would destroy the usefulness of the evidence.

Rehearse each question and answer. There should not be any surprises in direct examination. The attorney should be completely aware of the full extent of each answer that the expert economist is expected to give.

§ 14.5 Foundations of Direct and Cross-Examination: Admissibility and Relevance

Federal and state courts are intervening more in the determination as to whether or not expert testimony is admissible. Admissibility and relevance of an expert testimony must therefore be directly addressed by the advocate. The assumption cannot be made that an expert's testimony will be accepted merely because the expert has the appropriate credentials and background to be recognized by the court as an expert in the area of economics. The basis for opinion testimony may be found in Federal Rules of Evidence 702 and 703. Under Federal Rule of Evidence 702, "If scientific, technical, or other specialized knowledge will assist the trier of fact to understand the evidence or to determine a fact in issue, a witness qualified as an expert by knowledge, skill, experience, training, or education, may testify thereto in the form of an opinion or otherwise."

In determining whether an economist is qualified, the advocate should carefully review the economist's background and qualifications for potential impeachment. If the economist is your expert, ensure that the expert cannot be impeached by record and background. On the other hand, if the economist is one called by the other side, carefully review the background and credentials of the economist to determine whether or not the individual can be impeached, and perhaps disqualified, based upon inaccurate or false information in the background.

Obviously a professor of economics or one who has been schooled in the theories of economics and has the appropriate degrees for this work will typically be permitted to testify as an economist. It is certainly preferable to locate an economist with an advanced degree, preferably a doctorate level of education in the area of economics. An individual who has been appropriately schooled in economic theory and is involved in economics statistics, labor, economics or economic appraisal work ought to be allowed to testify as an economist.[1] In one case an industrial psychologist was allowed to testify relating to loss of earning capacity in the future.[2]

A home economist was utilized to give testimony regarding the evaluation of the damages relating to the death of a housewife. This was allowed by the Iowa supreme court.[3] In yet another case an employment agency owner was allowed to testify as to the hourly rates of pay for various categories of jobs that have previously been held by the plaintiff and to which the plaintiff had testified. The employment agency owner had an agency that specialized in the placement of domestic help (such as dishwashers, housekeepers, handymen, and so forth); this was approved by the Third Circuit.[4]

Within the context of rule 703 of the Federal Rules of Evidence, testimony that is offered by nonexpert witnesses such as the plaintiffs, plaintiff's employer, teacher, or other lay witnesses, may be relied upon by the expert when such testimony is typically relied upon. More of the judiciaries are encouraged to carefully examine the bases for the experts' opinions. The court has to look closely at the reasoning or methodology that make up the underpinnings of the expert's opinion. The court must then determine whether or not that opinion is scientifically valid or acceptable.[5] An opinion under rule 702 must be based on some scientific method and must rise to a level of certainty greater than mere speculation or subjective belief. This was referred to as "evidentiary reliability."[6] Therefore, in direct examination the advocate should carefully set out for both the court and jury the reasoning and methodology used by the expert and the scientific basis for that methodology. It is not safe to assume that even the most generally accepted principles are known to the court.

In a like manner, cross-examination should be undertaken relating to the reasoning and methodology utilized by the defendant expert. This will take a lot

---

[1] Texas Steel Co. v. Recer, 508 S.W.2d 889 (Tex. Civ. App. 1974).

[2] *Id.*

[3] Schmitt v. Jenkins Truck Lines, Inc., 170 N.W.2d 632 (Iowa 1969).

[4] Haddigan v. Harkins, 441 F.2d 844, 852 (3d Cir. 1970).

[5] Daubert v. Merrell Dow Pharmaceuticals, Inc., 509 U.S. ____, 113 S. Ct. 2786 (1993).

[6] *Id.* at 481.

of homework on the part of the advocate if the cross-examination is to be effective. This type of cross-examination should only be undertaken after a clear understanding of the opposing expert's report and deposition. If not careful the advocate will merely emphasize the scientific validity of the expert's testimony to the jury unless the expert can be specifically impeached.

When relying on Federal Rule of Evidence 703, the facts and information relied upon by an expert to utilize as a basis for opinion do not have to be independently admissible. This is true if the information or facts are "of a type reasonably relied upon by experts in the particular field in forming opinion or inferences upon a subject."[7] When an expert's opinion is based on information that is not admissible into evidence independently, the court is required to determine whether the information is of a type that is "reasonably relied upon by experts in that particular field in reaching conclusions."[8] The facts that are used by the expert witnesses must be legally sufficient to form the basis for the expert's opinion.[9] The testimony of an expert relating to the amount of economic loss suffered by a plaintiff as a result of termination was allowed when objections were made to the bases of the expert's opinion. The objections went to "the weight, and not the admissibility" of the evidence.[10] If the court's evaluation of the underlying facts relied upon by the expert determines that the foundation of the expert is insufficient to reach accurate conclusions or that the expert's opinion is so misleading as to outweigh any probative value it might have for the jury, the opinion can be excluded.[11]

Generally a liberal interpretation of Rule 703 allows the economist to testify to evidence that supports the economist's opinion even though that evidence is not admissible in and of itself, without very much in the way of judicial restriction. Some jurisdictions carefully review information and documents reviewed by an expert in arriving at an opinion and allow the expert to testify as to opinion without allowing the inadmissible information, documents, or testimony to be introduced at trial. In addition, if an economist relies upon hearsay, the economist must be able to demonstrate some basis for conclusions based on another's opinions. If an expert is unfamiliar with methods and reasons underlying another expert's conclusions, the expert's testimony may not be allowed when there can be no effective cross-examination regarding the methods of the nontestifying expert.[12]

---

[7] Wilson v. Merrell Dow Pharmaceuticals, Inc., 893 F.2d 1149, 1153 (10th Cir. 1990); Head v. Lithonia Corp., 881 F.2d 941 (10th Cir. 1989); Greenwood Utilities Comm'n v. Mississippi Power Co., 751 F.2d 1484 (5th Cir. 1985).

[8] Head v. Lithonia Corp., 881 F.2d 941, 944 (10th Cir. 1989); Greenwood Utilities Comm'n v. Mississippi Power Co., 751 F.2d 1484 (5th Cir. 1985).

[9] Logsdon v. Baker, 366 F. Supp. 332 (D.D.C. 1973).

[10] Tyler v. Bethlehem Steel Corp., 958 F.2d 1176, 1188 (2d Cir. 1992).

[11] Logsdon v. Baker, 366 F. Supp. 332 (D.D.C. 1973).

[12] Tyler v. Bethlehem Steel Corp., 958 F.2d 1176 (2d Cir. 1992).

Federal Rules of Evidence 704(a) provides that "testimony in the form an opinion or inference otherwise inadmissible is not objectionable because it embraces an ultimate issue to be decided by the trier of fact." This rule is applied in federal court and in many state courts.[13] In federal court the expert's testimony must give the jury information that a layperson would otherwise not deduce from the evidence that is already on the record.[14] The Federal Rule of Evidence 704 did away with the per se rule against testimony on ultimate issues of fact to allow the introduction of evidence that may be helpful to the trier of fact.[15]

Finally, the expert's testimony must be determined to be relevant under Federal Rule 401. This is usually not difficult when the proper foundation has been laid by the plaintiff's testimony and the testimony of other witnesses relating to the injuries suffered by the plaintiff and the extent and duration of physical incapacity that the plaintiff will suffer as a result of a serious spinal cord injury. Particularly in spinal cord injury cases, which typically feature severe economic consequences in the long-term for the plaintiff, there should be little doubt as to the relevance of testimony by the economist. For purposes of cross-examination of a defense economist, expert issues of relevance ordinarily will not arise as the defense expert is typically responding to the plaintiff's expert and if the plaintiff's expert testimony in the area of economics is found to be relevant, certainly the testimony of the defense expert will be found to be relevant as well.

The particular subject matter or economic issues that may be addressed by the expert in testimony is more specifically covered in **Chapter 13.**

§ 14.6 Impeachment, Bias, and Admissions

In cross-examining the opposing economist, the credibility and the conclusions of that economist can be impeached through bias, prior inconsistent statements, a showing of a lack of knowledge on the part of the expert, or a lack of information given to the expert. Additionally, the opposing expert can actually help bolster your case by obtaining admissions that confirm aspects of expert's testimony or your client's situation.

Section 13.3 covers some of the potential areas for impeachment of an economic expert. The basic concept is to attack the credibility of the witness and the witness's testimony by way of various forms of impeachment. Impeachment can be accomplished by showing the bias of the witness. Impeachment can also be accomplished by using prior inconsistent statements made by the

---

[13] Birchfield v. Texarkana Memorial Hosp., 747 S.W.2d 361 (Tex. 1987).

[14] *In re* Aircrash Disaster, 795 F.2d 1230 (5th Cir. 1986).

[15] Owen v. Kerr-McGee Corp., 698 F.2d 236 (5th Cir. 1983).

witness, by a lack of knowledge on the part of the witness, by mistake, by a lack of information available to the witness, and by attacking the credentials of the witness.

Review prior reports or writings prepared by the economist for other litigation, for seminars, journals, books, as well as testimony before governmental hearings. In reviewing previous writings special attention should be paid to the expert's methodology. The methodology used in other instances may conflict with the methodology used in the report prepared for the litigation at hand. If the expert has actually used methodology that is similar or the same as that used by your expert, an admission from the opposing expert that your own expert's methodology is credible since the opposing expert has employed it in the past may be obtained.

Look for phraseology or stock language in the economist's report that can evidence a lack of attention to a specific set of facts in the case. Repetitive use of phraseology may evidence bias toward plaintiff's cases or defense cases.

Q. Doctor, you have previously prepared a report and testified in the case of *Smith v. Jones,* isn't that correct?
A. Yes, that is correct.
Q. I have a copy here of the report that you prepared in that particular case. Would you please look at what has been marked as Exhibit A and tell me whether or not you recognize that as being a true and correct copy of the report you previously prepared in the case of *Smith v. Jones?*
A. Yes, that appears to be a true and correct copy of my report in that case.
Q. If you would, Doctor, please read with me the portion of your report in the second paragraph that states: "It is clear, based upon a full analysis of the plaintiff's background, education, training, and past employment, and further based upon the medical evaluations performed that the plaintiff, in spite of this particular injury, could certainly return to some type of full-time gainful employment thereby minimizing any future economic loss which can be calculated." Am I reading that correctly, Doctor?
A. Yes, it would appear so.
Q. Do you recall using that same exact language in the report you prepared in this particular case?
A. I don't recall.
Q. Doctor, let me hand you what has previously been marked as plaintiff's Exhibit B and ask you to confirm with me whether or not this is a true and correct copy of the report you had prepared in this particular case.
A. Yes, it appears to be.
Q. Would you please look in the second paragraph and tell me if you utilized the same exact language in the report you prepared in this case as the report you prepared in the *Jones v. Smith* case?
A. Yes, it appears to be the same.
Q. Doctor, I further marked as Exhibits C, D, E, F, G, H, documents which purport to be reports prepared by you in cases involving litigation. Would

you please review each one of these and tell me whether or not they are true and correct copies of previous reports you have prepared for other cases that involve litigation?

A. Yes, I will. Yes, they each appear to be my reports as they are signed by me and I do recall at least some of these cases.

Q. Doctor, I have taken the liberty of highlighting with a yellow marker a phrase in each of those reports. Would you please review that for me?

A. Yes I will.

Q. Doctor, is the phrase that is highlighted in each of those reports the exact same phrase that we have been discussing that appears both in your report in the case of *Smith v. Jones* as well as in this particular case?

A. Yes, they do appear to be the same.

Q. Isn't it true, Doctor, that each of cases where you wrote a report using this language involved a case where you were hired by the defense in a personal injury case?

A. Yes, that would be true.

Q. In the small number of plaintiff's cases that you testified that you have handled, isn't it true that you have never used this particular phraseology or this language?

A. I believe that is true.

Q. Isn't it true that each of these cases involved a different plaintiff with his or her own unique background, a different defendant, different injuries, and physical limitations—none of which are in fact common to this case?

A. Yes, for the most part I suppose that would be true.

In similar manner, the use of a particular discount rate or method for determining present value may have been utilized by the expert in the past. The failure to use a similar approach in the case at hand can be used both to impeach the economist and obtain an admission, if appropriate.

Another way to attack an economist is to determine how many areas of expertise this economist claims to have. Is the economist willing to make judgments that fall into the expertise of a certified public accountant, a vocational expert, or even a physician? An economist who is overly broad in arriving at an analysis of the case may be impeached by showing just how little the economist knows in other areas where assumptions may have been made about the case.

Q. Doctor, you indicate that you believe this person is capable of obtaining and retaining employment in this job market?

A. Yes.

Q. While I've been referring to you as doctor that is only because you have a Ph.D. You are not a medical doctor are you?

A. That is correct. I'm not a medical doctor.

Q. In fact, you have not had any training in prognosis, diagnosis, or treatment of spinal cord injuries; isn't that right?

A. Yes, that's correct.

Q. In fact, you have not had any medical training whatsoever, have you?

A. That's correct—other than a first aid course.
Q. Would you agree with me that a first aid course does not qualify you to make any type of medical judgments relating to Mrs. Johnson, who has suffered a serious spinal cord injury in this particular case?
A. I suppose that would be correct.
Q. In fact, you have never seen Mrs. Johnson in person, have you?
A. No.
Q. You have never spoken to Mrs. Johnson, have you?
A. No, I have not.
Q. In fact, you have not identified any particular job that this person could actually, as you put it, obtain and retain, have you?
A. No, I haven't.
Q. You have also stated opinions relating to this particular person's ability to get and keep some type of employment; isn't that true?
A. That's correct.
Q. Yet you have no educational background in the area of testing and evaluating a person's abilities to get and keep employment, correct?
A. Yes, except perhaps in general terms of the overall workforce.
Q. You have never counseled individuals in respect to their ability to get and keep employment, have you?
A. No.
Q. You have never administered tests to any individual relating to his or her physical or psychological ability to obtain and retain employment, have you?
A. No.
Q. You have never actually placed any individual, much less a profoundly disabled person, in any type of employment, have you?
A. No.
Q. You have never authored any studies or papers specifically on the topic of vocational rehabilitation or placement, have you?
A. No.
Q. Have you ever administered the MMPI to anyone?
A. No.
Q. You are not qualified to do so, are you, Doctor?
A. No.
Q. Yet you have indicated that you are also a vocational expert, haven't you, sir?
A. Yes.

A very common bias is evidenced in identifying how the expert is being paid, by whom, and the amount of income that the expert generates from testifying in cases. The source of the expert's income should be closely examined since the expert may perform a majority, if not all, evaluations on behalf of plaintiffs or defendants in cases. Thoroughly explore the expert's relationship with the particular attorneys on the other side of the case. Also, investigate the expert's relationship to the particular law firm handling the case on the other side. Make the jury aware of any past relationships, contacts, or evaluations involving this particular economist and the law firm, the lawyer, or the particular defendant.

Impeach with errors and misinformation. If the economist has misstated medical evidence, for example, the expert should be impeached on this misstatement. Question whether or not the attorneys for the other side have provided the expert with all of the information necessary. Further, question the expert as to whether or not a change in the underlying data or assumptions would affect the final analysis. Omissions of information, such as medical information, can seriously damage an expert on cross-examination. By the same token, ensure that your expert has all the necessary information to make a full and complete judgment in the case. This includes giving your expert information that may not be as helpful to the case as you would like. Much greater damage will be done to the case by leaving information out or shielding the expert from negative information than to have the expert address negative information up front in the context of the overall analysis.

One of the most damaging ways to impeach an expert witness is to catch the expert witness in obvious errors. Carefully review projections and assumptions of an opposing economist with your own economist to find out whether or not mathematical errors have been made. Sometimes what is a seemingly small change in numbers can have a traumatic effect on the overall outcome of the analysis. A decimal point in the wrong place or a misreading of a work life expectancy table can allow successful impeachment of an expert. Even simple errors of addition and subtraction can be found.

Sometimes experts allow students or other employees to do some of the more mundane work for them. This can prove to be the greatest mistake of all since they can make errors that cause the expert to look bad. In addition, many experts utilize various types of computer programs in arriving at an analysis. Once again, human error in inputting data can cause grave errors that can destroy the credibility of an economist. While errors provide a great opportunity for the advocate in cross-examination, they can just as easily give the advocate a nightmare during direct examination or during a cross-examination of your own witness. Errors and omissions can bring in to question the very qualifications of the economist to evaluate the case.

Obtaining admissions from the opposing economist is a daunting task indeed. Any admissions should typically be obtained at the time of deposition since a good economist will rarely allow an attorney to box them in to a narrow response designed to admit or to confirm the opposing side's theory and interpretation of the facts. Sometimes broad agreements can be reached, such as an admission that the economist that you are using, who is known to the opposing economist, is an expert in the field and one that is respected by the opposing economist. Sometimes professional courtesy outweighs the battle of egos in the courtroom. Broad admissions as to general methodology and approach may also be used. In cases involving spinal cord injuries, admissions from the defendant's economist should be obtained with respect to the seriousness, and the life-altering effect of the injuries suffered by the plaintiff. There are very few people who would refuse to admit such a basic premise. Admissions can also be obtained that the economist would, for example, defer to the plaintiff's medical doctors with respect to the evaluation of the plaintiff's medical condition and the plaintiff's physical and mental abilities.

Impeachment of an economist by any of the methods described above is generally difficult. The economist's opinions and analysis are typically difficult for the jury to follow even when they are coherent. Impeachment of an expert is often more like work with a scalpel than with a bludgeoning instrument. Rarely do experts make horrendous mistakes. More typically errors, missteps, and bias are more understated and require careful and precise questioning. To effectively impeach, the objective must be communicated to the jury. Do not triumphantly sit down at the counsel table having thwarted the opposing expert only to look at the jury and realize that the jury has completely missed the advocate's moment of glory. Don't be afraid to challenge the expert when appropriate. A jury will expect an attorney to take on the opposing expert. It is essential to establish the bias of the economist in favor of the opposing party. When the expert is cross-examined on substantive aspects of testimony, disagreement and adversity is anticipated by the jury—don't disappoint them.

CHAPTER 15

DEFENSE'S ANNUITY EXPERT

Mark R. Kosieradzki

§ 15.1 Introduction

The proliferation of structured settlements in personal injury litigation has led to an increased use by defendants of annuity salespeople as witnesses to attest to the cost of an annuity and offer the evidence as a means of assessing an injured person's future damages.[1] Courts have reached different results on the admissibility of annuity cost testimony on the question of how the jury should award future damages.[2] The unifying characteristic of the disparate rulings is

[1] *See generally* Goldberg, *Barring the Defendant from Using Annuity Trial Testimony,* 10 Ill. Trial Law. No. 2 at 63 (June 1988); Holcomb, *Using an Annuitist at Trial,* 28 For the Defense 8 (Aug. 1986); Kolts, *Use of Structured Settlement Experts Prove Effective,* 3 For the Defense 4 (Oct. 1983); Middleton & Shaffer, *How to Counter the Biases of Annuity Witnesses,* 5 Trial 73 (June 1989); Moore, *The Use of Annuities in the Settlement of Personal Injury Cases,* 49 Ins. Counsel J. 50 (1982); Welcher, *Structured Settlement Expert as Defense Economist,* 4 For the Defense 27 (June 1983); J.J. Marticelli, Annotation, *Cost of Annuity as Factor for Consideration in Fixing Damages in Personal Injury or Death Action,* 53 A.L.R.2d 1454 (1975).

[2] Some courts have allowed such testimony as relevant under certain circumstances. *See, e.g.,* Vicksburg & Merican R.R. v. Putnam, 118 U.S. 545 (1886); Pruett v. Evertt Iowrance, Inc., 314 F. Supp. 282 (D. Tenn. 1970); Rooney v. New York, N. H. & H. Ry., 173 Mass. 222, 53 N.E. 435 (Mass. 1899) (instruction required that jury must first find facts that form a proper basis for the calculation of the annuity, and then it may be used as means of estimating present value); McNair

the degree to which the defense satisfied the essential elements of admissibility of the offered evidence: relevance, hearsay, and foundation.

Use of an annuity salesperson poses a threat to the fair assessment future damages. Economic assessment of the impact of inflation, taxation, rates of return, life expectancy, and other variables is best left to experts and not to salespeople, whose vested interest is in selling an annuity contract for the most profit at the least cost to an insurance company. That motive is so dissimilar from the function of a jury's formulation of fair compensation, that it should be excluded from the process of adjucating a claim, and not countenanced under the guise of a means of assessing present value.

This chapter addresses the grounds upon which proffered annuitants' testimony may be excluded, and suggests avenues of cross-examination open to the trial attorney confronted by an annuity witness whose testimony the court has not ruled in limine to exclude.

§ 15.2 Evidentiary Requirements for Admissibility

The offer of annuity-cost testimony through an annuity salesperson must meet the same criteria for admissibility as any other evidence. It must be relevant to the matter in controversy, its relevance must not outweigh the prejudicial effect of its admission, it must not contain inadmissible hearsay, and it must be introduced through a witness whose expertise and foundation make for competent testimony. Each of these factors should be considered in the practitioner's development of a motion in limine to exclude annuity-cost testimony.

§ 15.3 Relevance

Federal Rule of Evidence 402 makes it clear that "[e]vidence which is not relevant is not admissible."[3] Relevant evidence is that which has a "tendency to make the

---

v. Berger, 92 Mont. 441, 15 P.2d 834 (1932) (requiring instruction that jury consider the defendant might profit by comparison); Spence v. Commercial Motor Freight, 99 Ohio App. 143, 127 N.E.2d 427 (Preble County 1954) (straight annuity allowed); Guinn v. Kansas City S. R.R., 547 P.2d 1310, 1314 (Okla. Ct. App. 1975); Gulf, Colo. & D.F. v. Hampton, 358 S.W.2d 690, 691 (Tex. Ct. App. 1962). Other courts have declined to so rule. *See, e.g.,* Taylor v. Burlington N.R.R., 787 F.2d 1309, 115 (8th Cir. 1986); Diede v. Burlington N.R.R., 772 F.2d 593, 596 (9th Cir. 1985); Farmers Union Federated Coop. Shipping Ass'n v. McChesney, 251 F.2d 441, 444 (8th Cir. 1958); Caldwell v. Southern Pac. Ry., 71 F. Supp. 955, 958 (S.D. Cal. 1947); State v. Guinn, 555 P.2d 530, 547 (Alaska 1976); Hinsdale v. New York, N. H. & H. R.R., 81 A.D. 617, 81 N.Y.S. 546 (N.Y. 1903); Bartlebaugh v. Pennsylvania Ry., 150 Ohio 387, 82 N.E.2d 853 (Ohio 1948) (refund annuity that gave survivors the benefit of payments if victim predeceased annuity benefit schedule was admissible); Kerrigan v. Pennsylvania Ry., 194 Pa. 98, 44 A. 1069 (Pa. 1899); Herman v. Milwaukee Children's Hosp., 361 N.W.2d 297 (Wis. Ct. App. 1984).

[3] Fed. R. Evid. 402.

existence of any fact that is of consequence to the determination of the action more probable or less probable than it would be without the evidence."[4]

While hypothetically offered as a means by which to assist the trier of fact in assessing the present value of the stream of lost future earnings, the cost of periodic future medical costs, or the per diem impact of pain and suffering, annuity-cost testimony has a markedly ulterior motive. It suggests that if only the plaintiff had been willing to accept a reasonable out-of-court settlement represented by an annuity that the defendant could have purchased, the jury's time in resolving damages issues would have been spared. Rule 408 makes evidence of "furnishing or offering or promising to furnish . . . a valuable consideration in compromising or attempting to compromise a claim . . . is not admissible to prove . . . invalidity of the claim or its amount."[5] The subtle message that a structure had been offered and rejected by the plaintiff is inherent in any discussion of annuities by the defense.

Even assuming that a curative instruction could avert the inference without itself drawing undue attention to the implication, annuity-cost testimony lacks relevance. There is never a requirement that the plaintiff accept an annuity, nor is there ever evidence that the plaintiff will in fact invest the proceeds of a verdict into an annuity. The issue of the cost of an annuity is therefore irrelevant to the means by which the jury should resolve the question of damages.

Its only genuine relevance would be to purportedly assist the jurors in ascertaining what the present value of a future damages award would be. While the premise may meet the minimal requirements of Rule 402 for relevance at first glance, upon any reasoned scrutiny, the probative value of an annuity fades.

There is a material difference between the proper estimation of diminished future earning capacity, for example, and the cost of an annuity on a purely commercial basis. Indirect evidence of present value of lost future earning capacity by comparing annuity costs, should thus be rejected wherever the plaintiff sufficiently demonstrates in limine the differences between the issue to be proved (for example, lost earning capacity) and the evidence offered (that is, what one insurance company will charge for certain periodic payments). A discussion of significant differences follows.

Taxability versus Nontaxability

Under a Revenue Ruling of the Internal Revenue Service, the nontaxability of a personal injury settlement is preserved.[6] This is true of structured settlements as well,[7] with the exception of interest earned on the funds after receipt. Once

---

[4] *Id.*

[5] *Id.*

[6] Rev. Rul. 74–75, 1975-1 C.B. 47.

[7] *Id.* 79-220, 1979-02 C.B. 74; 26 C.F.R. 1-104-1.

either an installment of a structured or nonstructured settlement or verdict is paid to the plaintiff, however, the amount of interest earned by the recipient when investing the funds paid to the recipient, is subject to tax. Herein lies the substantial advantage of a structured settlement, and the material fallacy of the offer of annuity-cost evidence.

A structured settlement has the advantage of tax-free treatment of the interest earned by the insurance company's investment of the settlement money until that money is paid to the plaintiff. Once the plaintiff receives the funds, constructively or actually, any earnings on the funds received are subject to tax.[8] Since the jury cannot award a stream of income or the periodic payments that constitute an annuity, but rather only the present value of the annuity's cost, and since the plaintiff will be subject to tax on the earning power of the verdict, but would not have been had a settlement for the annuity been agreed to, the plaintiff is denied the principle advantage of the annuity tax-free generation of interest income until receipt of a periodic payment.

Even if this disparity is pointed out to the jury through cross-examination or with the benefit of a jury instruction, the cumbersome recalculation of what the true cost of an annuity would be to yield the same tax-free investment vehicle to the plaintiff may be both beyond the expertise of the annuity witness[9] and unduly confusing to the jury.[10]

Inflationary Impact on Annuity's Value

Since annuities often include no adjustment for the impact of inflation on an award, and since such a factor has a direct bearing upon the value of a future income stream,[11] the annuity is further distinguishable from the actual function the jury is to perform: making a rational assessment of the present value of a future damages award.

---

[8] *See, generally,* J. Staller, *Structured Settlements,* The Art of Advocacy, *Settlements* § 10.50, at 10-5-7 (1983).

[9] It would be inadmissible for want of adequate foundation for expression of an expert opinion. Fed. R. Evid. 702.

[10] It would be inadmissible as prejudicially irrelevant. Fed. R. Evid. 403.

[11] Evidence of the impact of inflation on an award is permissible in many jurisdictions. *See, e.g.,* Sauers v. Alaska Barge, 600 F.2d 238 (9th Cir. 1979); Bach v. Pennsylvania Cen. Transp. Co., 502 F.2d 1117, 1122 (6th Cir. 1974); Beanland v. Chicago, Rock Island & Pac. R.R., 437 F.2d 109, 116–17, 117 n.1 (8th Cir. 1973) (Bright, J. concurring); Willmore v. Hertz Corp., 437 F.2d 357, 359–60 (6th Cir. 1971); Burke v. City & County of SF., 111 Cal. App. 2d 314, 244 P.2d 708, 713 (Cal. 1952); Burlington Transp. Co. v. Stoltz, 191 F.2d 915, 918 (10th Cir. 1951). Other courts have refused to allow evidence of inflationary impact on damage awards. *See, e.g.,* Markham v. Cross Transp., Inc., 119 R.I. 213, 222–23, 376 A.2d 1359, 1364 (R.I. 1977); Williams v. United States, 435 F.2d 804, 807 (1st Cir. 1970); Sleeman v. Chesapeake & Ohio Ry., 414 F.2d 305, 307–08 (6th Cir. 1969); McWeeney v. New York, N. H. & H. R.R., 282 F.2d 34 (2d Cir. 1960); Sleeman v. Chesapeake & Ohio Ry., 414 F.2d at 308 (6th Cir. 1969); *see also In re* United Steel, 436 F.2d 1256, 1280 (6th Cir. 1970).

Even when an annuity salesperson builds certain assumptions into an annuity to factor in an estimate for inflation, such an estimate must be based on admissible testimony from someone with sufficient expertise to actually assess the economy and to project what the inflationary impact will be: an economist. It is otherwise inadmissible.[12]

Actual Availability or Unavailability of Annuity

Since all annuity salespeople will concede[13] the highly transitory nature of the costs of annuities in the volatile market of structured settlements,[14] the annuity about which the witness testifies may in fact not be available by the time the trial concludes. The offer of evidence for comparison to the present value of damages, which itself is obsolete by the time the jury considers it, is a meaningless exercise in which the court should not engage.

Not all Future Damages are Subject to Discount

While each state's substantive law must be considered, some states do not permit the discount to present value of pain and suffering.[15] Annuity testimony offered as a vehicle of assessing pain and suffering on a per diem basis in those states would thus be improper.

Preinjury versus Postinjury Life Expectancy

The common-law rule relative to loss of future earning capacity is that:

> [i]f the injury and decreased earning capacity are permanent, recovery for the decreased earnings capacity will be granted for the plaintiff's life expectancy prior

---

[12] *See* Fed. R. Evid. 702.

[13] It is strongly recommended that before proceeding with a motion in limine to exclude an annuity salesperson's testimony as irrelevant, that the practitioner first obtain a deposition of the witness to establish this type of admission and others useful to the motion. If a deposition is unavailable, plaintiff's economist or another annuitant may be the source of a necessary affidavit to establish the basis for the information that would otherwise be established through admissions. Another possible vehicle would be Requests for Admissions under Fed. R. Civ. P. 36.

[14] Offers of a structured settlement are often available for very limited periods of time, subject to changeable rates of return in the investment industry, ten days of availability is common.

[15] Many jurisdictions do not allow discounting awards for future pain and suffering. *See, e.g.*, Busch v. Busch Constr., Inc., 262 N.W.2d 377 (Minn. 1977); Friedman v. C&S Car Serv., 108 N.J. 75, 527 A.2d 871 (N.J. 1987); Drews v. Gobel Freight Lines, Inc., 144 Ill. 2d 84, 578 N.E.2d 970 (Ill. 1991); Beaulieu v. Elliott, 434 P.2d 665 (Alaska 1967); Braddock v. Seaboard Air Line R., 80 So. 2d 662 (Fla. 1995). Some other jurisdictions allow discounting if the amount is reasonable. *See, e.g.*, Debus v. Grand Union Stores, 159 Vt. 537, 621 A.2d 1288 (Vt. 1993); Johnson v. Pearson Agri-Sys., Inc., 119 Wis. 2d 766, 350 N.W.2d 127 (1984).

> to the injury. If, as a result of the injury, the plaintiff's life expectancy is shortened, he is not limited to a recovery based upon that shortened life expectancy.[16]

Since an annuity would be paid to the plaintiff during the plaintiff's life—and has little value after death—the annuity's failure to take into account the entitlement to compensation at the preinjury life expectancy makes it irrelevant to the actual issues in controversy.

Use of an annuity salesperson poses a threat to the fair assessment of future damages. Economic assessment of the impact of inflation, taxation, rates of return, life expectancy, and other variables is best left to experts and not to salespeople, whose vested interest is in selling an annuity contract for the most profit at the least cost to an insurance company. That motive is so dissimilar from the function of a jury's formulation of fair compensation, that it should be excluded from the process of adjudicating a claim, and not countenanced under the guise of a means of assessing present value.

Instability of Insurance Industry

Highly-rated annuity insurance companies have filed for bankruptcy in past years. An annuity represents a *single* investment vehicle, not a balanced portfolio. Present case value analysis must reflect the variability of the marketplace over the long term. Such variability is recognized by economists and investors through the use of a balanced portfolio.

The risk of loss associated with the use of a single investment vehicle raises the question as to whether the plaintiff will ever receive all of the proceeds of the proposed annuity. Such risks must be considered by the court in weighing the prejudicial relevance of the proposed testimonies.

Given the serious and substantial differences between the facts that are "of consequence to the determination of the action,"[17] and the facts presented by the cost of a commercially available annuity, a just basis exists to exclude the offer of an annuity salesperson's testimony on the grounds of relevance alone.

§ 15.4 Prejudicial Irrelevance

Rule 403 of the Federal Rules of Evidence makes it clear that the inquiry into the admissibility of proffered evidence does not end with the threshold question of relevance. It acknowledges that, "[a]lthough relevant, evidence maybe excluded if its probative value is substantially outweighed by the danger of unfair prejudice, confusion of the issues, or misleading the jury, or by considerations

---

[16] 22 Am. Jur.2d *Damages* § 92 at 134–35.

[17] Fed. R. Evid. 401.

of undue delay, waste of time, or needless presentation of cumulative evidence."[18] The relevance factors considered have equal applicability in weighing whether cumulatively the discrepancies between the annuity and its avowed purpose—assessing present value—justify exclusion of the testimony as confusing or unfair:

> [T]o allow an actuary to place before the jury an abstract figure of what it would cost to secure an annuity—which is what was offered and refused—is not as counsel contended . . . to be fair . . . but to mislead the jury into accepting a hypothetical figure of another instead of an actual figure [of present value] to be arrived at by them under the instructions . . . .[19]

Since the cost of an annuity is not the same thing as the present value of the damages in issue, given the discrepancies enumerated above, the prejudicial effect of the annuity witness, testimony is unmistakably inherent in every discussion of an annuity, and forms the basis for exclusion of the evidence on that ground.

§ 15.5 Foundation

A witness must be competent to give the testimony offered.[20] A witness may not testify to a matter unless evidence is introduced sufficient to support a finding that the witness has personal knowledge of the matter.[21] The requirement of personal knowledge exists even as to opinion testimony by a lay witness. To be admissible, the opinion testimony must both be "(a) rationally based on the perception of the witness and (b) helpful to a clear understanding of the witness, testimony or a fact in issue."[22]

Unless foundation has been laid by the defense that the annuity salesperson is indeed an expert in the essential elements of calculating present value—life expectancy, proper rate of discount, inflationary adjustment, and so forth—the witness is not an "expert under the rules."[23] While experts can rely on evidence—including hearsay—that is not otherwise admissible, if it is "of a type

---

[18] Fed. R. Evid. 403 advisory committee's note. " 'Unfair prejudice' within its context means an undue tendency to suggest decision on an improper basis, commonly, though not necessarily, an emotional one."

[19] Caldwell v. Southern Pac. Ry., 71 F. Supp. 955, 958 (S.D. Cal. 1947) (emphasis added).

[20] Fed. R. Evid. 601.

[21] *Id.*

[22] *Id.* 701.

[23] Fed. R. Evid. 702 indicates the foundation necessary for satisfying the designation of a witness as an *expert:* "If scientific, technical or other specialized knowledge will assist the trier of fact to understand the evidence or to determine a fact in issue, a witness qualified as an expert by knowledge, skill, experience, training, or education, may testify thereto in the form of an opinion or otherwise."

reasonably relied upon by experts in the particular field,"[24] lay witnesses cannot base opinions on hearsay or other inadmissible evidence and must rely on actual knowledge.

Failure of the defense to qualify the annuitant as an expert in anything other than sales of annuities will thus justify the exclusion of the salesperson's testimony.

§ 15.6 Hearsay

Typically an annuity salesperson relies almost exclusively on hearsay in the presentation of testimony regarding the cost of an annuity. The salesperson has spoken with one or more other salespeople for insurers or brokerages and has obtained a quoted price for an annuity from them, which the individual seeks to relay to jurors.

As noted in **§ 15.5,** only experts may rely on hearsay in the formulation of their opinions,[25] and then only to the extent hearsay is "reasonably" relied on . . . in forming opinions or inferences upon the subject . . . .[26] Since the subject in controversy is the present value of future damages, and a bid from one or more companies on what they would charge for an annuity or how they calculated their bid is a materially different inquiry, the most basic element of the annuitant's testimony—the cost of the annuity—is itself inadmissible hearsay that cannot be the subject of the annuitant's testimony. Moreover, even assuming that the annuitant can be qualified as an expert, it is most likely beyond the scope of the expert's knowledge to supply the hearsay basis for how suppliers reached a specific bid. That issue is the subject of inquiry on cross-examination, even if it is not disclosed in direct testimony.[27] The annuitant's inability to explain such essential features as how the annuitant's suppliers assessed life expectancy, considered inflationary impact, and so forth, deprives the opinion of any substance. The opinion is therefore rendered meaningless and subject to rejection as prejudicially irrelevant.

§ 15.7 Cross-examination Techniques

Should the court decline an in limine motion to exclude the testimony of an annuity witness, counsel should prepare for cross-examination bearing in mind the following likely admissions.

---

[24] Fed. R. Evid. 703.

[25] Fed. R. Evid. 703.

[26] *Id.*

[27] "The expert may in an event be required to disclose the underlying facts or data on cross-examination." Fed. R. Evid. 705.

Market Volatility

Annuity costs are highly volatile and will shift as the relevant interest rates change, making them appear as a far less reliable method of calculating future value than the plaintiff's expert economist.

Outcome Variability

The actual present value formula used by economists takes into account certain set variables including the applicable interest rates for discount and investment, the rate of return in contrast to the impact of inflation, the victim's life expectancy, whether the price quotation is for a so-called rated life of the victim, the length of the annuity and whether it is guaranteed or left to an estate, and the tax implications of each alternative. The annuitant must admit that if any of these variables changes, the cost of the annuity will shift if the variables adopted are the same as those considered by the plaintiff's expert economist. The result of the annuitant's calculation and the economists will be equivalent.

Lack of Expertise

As a salesperson, the annuitant must admit lack of expertise in life expectancy estimation,[28] calculation of rates of return on investment, and tax and inflationary factors. The annuitant's function is extremely limited, that is, taking other's assumptions and bidding in the investment market for a contract that will supply an income stream. Since annuitants typically work in close association with insurers, they often decline to place annuities privately for plaintiffs. Not only does this establish bias, but it also may mean that the annuitant could not or would not place the annuity for the plaintiff even if the plaintiff were inclined to ask for one.

---

[28] The annuitant would typically either rely on an actuary or upon actuarial tables to assess life expectancy—the same source the jury must use—or upon the hearsay "rated life expectancy" evaluation of the underwriting department of an annuity company that has reviewed the plaintiff's medical records.

CHAPTER 16

THE USE OF NONEXPERT DAMAGES WITNESSES

William D. Harper

§ 16.1 Theory

Logic is pretty. We're taught to live with it, trained to use it, and though we may not worship it, the process becomes part of the life of a lawyer. What they never teach in law school is that logic is simply the medium that allows a jury to get to wherever it wants to go, and that the trial counsel has to present a jury with a logic jury members can use to justify their destination. Logic, however, is only a small part of the art of trial lawyering. Passion, individual elegance (however clumsily that may be at times), dedication, and commitment to the case in a major part define the nonverbal goal—and the lay witness can provide beautiful logic to justify a jury's affirmative conclusion on the case.

In a catastrophic spinal cord injury case the client, like the ancient Greek figure Tantalus, is caught in a quagmire and will forever be reaching for the unattainable golden apples. The lay witness can express what the golden apples are that the client will never be able to enjoy. Each client has individual dreams and aspirations; each reaches to become more fully himself by different means, each person in a catastrophic spinal cord injury case will be forever limited in the ability to reach individual aspirations—golden apples. The lay witness is crucial to communicating the core of who the client is and shedding light on that client's limitations.

§ 16.2 Practice

Before law school I was a garbageman, banker, prize fighter, teacher, commercial fisherman, insurance man, father, hunter, husband, son, forklift operator, truck driver, artist, and student; all life experiences are much more important to an attorney with a lay witness on the stand than being a lawyer. The lay witness is a part of the medium of artistry that can't be purchased. Juries understand and are more forgiving of the innate bias of a friend, relative, workmate, or spouse than they are a paid expert. They can appreciate even through cynical blinders the colors that the lay witness can contribute to the picture counsel is painting as an advocate. Though a visual metaphor (painting) is used to define the context of the lay witness, an attorney must be mindful that not all jurors see the world in visual terms, and not all lay witnesses prefer visual information. It is every bit as important that that jury feel and hear the testimony as it is that jurors see it. If a lay witness can create sounds, create feelings, and create images, those will stay with a juror much longer and much clearer than a paid professional witness. Listen to the lay witness. Does the witness use visual words (observed, saw, glimpsed, viewed, pictured, watched, perspective, imaged, light at the end of the tunnel, and so forth); does the witness use auditory words (heard, listened, smacked, crashed, banged, noise, called, said, questioned, rings true to me, and so forth); does the witness use kinesthetic words (felt, sensed, smelled, pained, saddened, heated, cold, grasped, run, angered, feel good about, and so forth). The lay witness will not be aware of a preferred choice of the three equally valid ways of communicating (visual, auditory, or kinesthetic) but an advocate will find jurors that will resonate with each preference; modify questions to establish rapport not only with the lay witness, but also with those jurors who identify with the preference of the witness. Vignettes by whatever preference of language that are contributed by lay witnesses don't even have to be logical to be effective. They simply need to reflect the golden apples.

Years ago I tried a case and called the sister of a severely impaired teenager to testify about how she and her other siblings dressed their male and female dogs in a dress and tie and had an imaginary marriage ceremony and threw rice on them as the dogs paraded down the hallway (a very visual image). I know the jury wondered why that lay witness was called to testify about that particular event, and were only able to understand its context when I was able to talk to them in closing argument about the comfort and society siblings can share, in even the minutia of their lives and imaginations. The feelings in that case came through the visual image created by words.

The logic is secondary to the communication by the lay witness and the communication is secondary to how the lay witness says it. How the lay witness says it is a function of who the witness is. It is incumbent upon every trial lawyer to spend some time with the lay witnesses to find out who they are and what's important to them, and to have the fortitude to reject a witness who wants to testify. One of the most difficult lessons to learn is to rely on instincts when they indicate that in that eagerness the potential lay witness will taint communication by becoming an advocate.

In the same way that power does not come from logic, neither does it come from education. The most powerful witness I ever experienced was a Hispanic woman with an eighth grade education who had raised her children and at the age of 50 was learning how to drive. My client had sustained a catastrophic spinal cord injury and subtle but significant brain damage in a grinding automobile collision. The witness had met my client in a swimming class at the YWCA and knew her before her injuries and after injuries. She was the most powerful witness I have ever seen on the stand because she shared her observations with the jury in her own way and with her own words and intimation. Her testimony carried with it a genuine concern for my client that was unimpeachable. She looked that jury square in the face when she told them she loved my client like a sister, and the defense attempted impeachment by pointing out that she lied to the hospital staff when she told them she was my client's sister so she could see her in the hospital—which only strengthened her testimony and did not impeach at all. She said it her way and though it wasn't grammatically precise, it was from the heart; it was genuine; it was said with integrity and it was powerful.

Not any lay witness will do. Juries come with their own agenda and expectations, and I believe that one of those expectations is that you as advocate for your client will only put on clients that are beneficial to your case, so woe be it to you and your case if your lay witness says something damaging, because that will remain foremost in the juror's mind given a presumption that your witness comes to the proceeding with a bias in your favor. Jurors aren't simple. They know experts are paid by both sides, and unless there are exceptional circumstances that cause loss of credibility of an expert witness, they often cancel themselves out, and the weight on the scales of justice can many times fall to the lay witness. Doctors can note reports of pain and discomfort in the records, but it doesn't carry the power of a lay witness testifying to observations.

Never call a witness unless you (not a law clerk, paralegal, or investigator) have met with that witness and have come to know the witness. In the artistry of advocacy, what is not asked is every bit as huge as what is asked. In trying a catastrophic spinal cord case I once needed to talk with the highway patrol officer on the scene of the collision where the driver had been killed and my client had been a passenger. I met with him and drove to the scene of the crash in his squad car. In the course of asking him about his report and the events of the evening, I came to find out that the very evening of the crash he had been to the local hospital to interview my seriously injured client (a fact not evidenced in his report). He told me that my client's only response to him was "all I remember is waking up in the front passenger seat, seeing the oncoming headlights, and *grabbing the steering wheel.*" He told me he hadn't told the insurance company investigator those facts because the investigator had not asked that question and anyway he thought my client was delirious and didn't know what he was saying. Before calling him to the stand I confirmed that the insurer still didn't know of his visit to the hospital and brought him through his testimony to that point in time when he left the scene. The jury returned a significant verdict with no comparative fault on my client. If I hadn't spent the time with the witness, my case could have been destroyed.

We all hunger to be loved and understood. It is the role of an advocate to make sure that the jury understands who clients are, why they are lovable, and how they have been changed. There is nothing more destructive in a catastrophic spinal cord injury case than calling your own witness to whine about injuries. An attorney should have the client talk about what the client *can* do and should have the lay witnesses clarify what the client *cannot* do. There is nothing more valuable an asset in a catastrophic spinal cord injury case than a lay witness to assist in allowing the jury to see, feel, and hear the client and learn about the client's injuries through the witness.

TABLE OF CASES

Case	*Book §*
Logsdon v. Baker, 366 F. Supp. 332 (D.D.C. 1973)	§ 14.5
Markham v. Cross Transp., Inc., 376 A.2d 1359 (R.I. 1977)	§ 15.3
McNair v. Berger, 92 Mont. 441, 15 P.2d 834 (1932)	§ 15.1
McWeeney v. New York, N. H. & H. R.R., 282 F.2d 34 (2d Cir. 1960)	§ 15.3
Owen v. Kerr-McGee Corp., 698 F.2d 236 (5th Cir. 1983)	§ 14.5
Pruett v. Evertt Iowrance, Inc., 314 F. Supp. 282 (E.D. Tenn. 1970)	§ 15.1
Rooney v. New York, N. H. & H. R.R., 53 N.E. 435 (Mass. 1899)	§ 15.1
Sauers v. Alaska Barge, 600 F.2d 238 (9th Cir. 1979)	§ 15.1
Schmitt v. Jenkins Truck Lines, Inc., 170 N.W.2d 632 (Iowa 1969)	§ 14.5
Sleeman v. Chesapeake & Ohio Ry., 414 F.2d 305 (6th Cir. 1969)	§ 15.3
Spence v. Commercial Motor Freight, 127 N.E.2d 427 (Preble County 1954)	§ 15.1
State v. Guinn, 555 P.2d 530 (Alaska 1976)	§ 15.1
Taylor v. Burlington N.R.R., 787 F.2d 1309 (8th Cir. 1986)	§ 15.1
Texas Steel Co. v. Recer, 508 S.W.2d 889 (Tex. Civ. App. 1974)	§ 14.5
Tyler v. Bethlehem Steel Corp., 958 F.2d 1176 (2d Cir. 1992)	§ 14.5
United Steel, *In re*, 436 F.2d 1256 (6th Cir. 1970)	§ 15.3
Vicksburg & Merican R.R. v. Putnam, 118 U.S. 545 (1886)	§ 15.1
Williams v. United States, 435 F.2d 804 (1st Cir. 1970)	§ 15.3
Willmore v. Hertz Corp., 437 F.2d 357 (6th Cir. 1971)	§ 15.3
Wilson v. Merrell Dow Pharmaceuticals, Inc., 893 F.2d 1149 (10th Cir. 1990)	§ 14.5

INDEX